The Toynbee Factor in British Grand Strategy

An Executive Intelligence Review
Strategic Study

by Lyndon Hermyle LaRouche, Jr.

New York City, July 10,1982

The Toynbee Factor in British Grand Strategy

An Executive Intelligence Review Strategic Study

by Lyndon Hermyle LaRouche, Jr.

New York City, July 10,1982

www.larouchepub.com

Amazon Print on Demand Edition 2018

ISBN: 9781980595922

The Toynbee Factor in British Grand Strategy

An Executive Intelligence Review Strategic Study

by Lyndon Hermyle LaRouche, Jr.

New York City, July 10,1982

Contents

Author's Foreword:

"Advise and Consent"

Lord Carrington's close collaborators will not disagree so much with what is reported in this report, as the fact that the matter has been brought into public light. Turnabout is fair play. Lord Carrington; your lads have been peddling U.S. secrets eastward in spurts over the post-war period, it was only proper some of your secrets should fly westward for a change.

If this report, composed for the occasion to assist the U.S. Senate's function of advice, is an unusual sort of production to appear in those precincts, perhaps it is because such a report has been long overdue. It was composed for submission in the form of an appendix to testimony on the nomination of Secretary-designate George Shultz, the beginning, one may hope, of some startling improvements in the conduct of our foreign policy.

Implicitly, this report establishes that the writer is of the persuasion that not all of our nation's notably less-than-empyreal achievements in foreign policy are to be blamed on Mr. Haig's curious innovations in diplomatic prose. The catastrophe which now envelopes that function of our government has been a long while a-building. Rehashing old issues in the old way has, in point of fact, tended to divert our attention and our passions away from those subtler issues which have been chiefly responsible for the wide discrepancy between avowed self-interest and executed result in that Department.

In brief, since Henry A. Kissinger claimed putative fatherhood to psychological warfare in our strategic and foreign-policy posture, following his indoctrination at the London Tavistock Institute--the "mutually assured destruction" nonsense--things, for us, have been going, predominantly, from bad to worse, now verging giddily proximate to worst. It was past time some one took up the question, "How come?" So, this report has found its way to the Senate and the public domain.

Lyndon H. LaRouche, Jr.

New York City

July 10, 1982

1.

The Pivot of Our Foreign-Policy Crisis

This report introduces many readers (but not all) to a new, and perhaps frightening dimensionality of our nation's strategic and foreign-policy problems. The suitable name for this might be *The Manipulation of Culture As A Method of Warfare.* That could have been an alternative title. We have judged that our adopted title draws attention to the more urgent implications.

It is perhaps tiresome, but unavoidable, that every treatment of our foreign policy must concentrate on subtleties of actual or hypothetical Soviet implications, almost to the exclusion of attention to other quarters of our policy-making. It may be pleasing therefore, that the present treatment of that question probes aspects of the Soviet issue which, to our knowledge, have never been treated publicly, although, as we demonstrate here, they are points of more or less fundamental importance in any long-term approach to this area of policy-making.

So, we begin.

No analyst nor government could possibly have a competent strategic assessment today unless it understood the significance of historian Arnold Toynbee's rather long tenure at the head of the British foreign-intelligence service. To bring an American strategic analyst's mind into focus upon the implied questions, a series of preliminary observations are required now.

On May 10, 1982, an astonishing public event occurred at London's Chatham House; for once in his life, Henry A. Kissinger told the truth. It was not precisely the whole truth and nothing but the truth, but fairly accurate as far as Henry went in the matter. Perhaps it was because the very idea of Kissinger's telling the truth was so unbelievable, that almost no one in Washington, D.C. paid any attention to what Henry said. They should have, but they clearly had other things on their minds at that moment.

This was the period official Washington was down on all fours in front of the British Embassy, kowtowing to the Queen each like some Mandarin flunky before the Manchu Emperor. From Robert S. McNamara's moon-struck shores of the Potomac, to the Capitol Hill men's rooms, thousands of doleful throats rumbled out the constantly repeated chant: "Om, mani, padme, hm: Britain is our oldest and dearest ally." Francis Scott Key would not have dedicated a new stanza to "The Star Spangled Banner" in memory of such an occasion.

Meanwhile, back at Chatham House in London, Henry Kissinger was showing better sense than to attempt to persuade the British that they had ever been exactly the allies of the United States. Kissinger didn't go through the history of the matter. He did not refer to the fact that Britain was determined to crush the American colonies beginning 1763, and was committed continuously to the military reconquest of the United States from 1776 to 1863, or that we were on the edge of clobbering the British during the early 1920s. Henry focused his audience on the nub of the post-war Anglo-American relations.

It must be remembered, to understand the manner in which Kissinger presented his point to a Chatham House audience, that Kissinger had been an "American colonial" agent of the Chatham House branch of British intelligence since the time the man who "invented Kissinger", Fritz Kraemer sent Henry up to the British intelligence training-center under Elliot at Harvard University. On May 10, Henry was speaking to his spiritual mother, jogging her memory on certain details of Kissinger's own work against the United States in her interests. Henry was saying, in effect: "Mother, please remember what a good son I have been to you." That was Henry's immediate motive in presenting that particular public address, and the address must be appreciated in light of that motivation and associated circumstances.

Henry reported, implicitly, that Jimmy Byrnes, Dean Acheson, John Foster Dulles, Henry Kissinger, Cyrus Vance, and relevant gentlemen in between had sold the United States down the river by aid of secret, often unwritten agreements with Britain. Henry called his spiritual mother's loving attention to evidence that he, Henry, had been the most treasonous scoundrel ever to occupy the post of U.S. Secretary of State. Mother gave Henry the acknowledgement of a sphinx-like version of a faint loving smile; perhaps she was thinking of Cyrus Vance at the moment. As for ourselves: the behavior of our Secretaries of State does not fit exactly our legal definition of "treason," but something closer to "adultery," "prostitution" or "sodomy."

Kissinger said, in effect, that Britain has successfully dictated U.S. foreign-policy, with a few interruptions, since London breathed a sigh of relief at President Franklin Roosevelt's death, down to the present moment. If countries of Ibero-America, Africa, the Middle Fast, Asia, or Moscow itself should ever find themselves ferociously offended by aspects of U.S. foreign policy, from Byrnes through Haig, the emotionally appropriate behavior would be to bomb London.

This is not accomplished entirely through wicked State Department officials or the political heirs of Aaron Burr in and around the New York Council of Foreign Relations. We, fools that we are, are induced to believe usually that we developed our foreign policies through thorough assessment of a massive ingathering of intelligence.

Broadly speaking, and most emphatically since Henry Kissinger, James Schlesinger, the *New York Times*, and Walter F. Mondale accomplished demolition of most of U.S. intelligence capabilities, the United States has depended increasingly upon second-hand intelligence. The British give us such intelligence without charge; the Israelis, who desperately need the funding for their foreign-intelligence activities, prefer to sell it to us. Additionally, there is a large chunk of what passes for foreign intelligence received from Central European sources reflecting the old Venetian Central European black oligarchy based in Venice, Switzerland, Austria, Bavaria, and so forth. Most of our East bloc foreign intelligence comes second-hand through such channels.

What is usually emitted from the mouths of Washington officials enriched by secret-intelligence briefings reflects information we have earlier observed marching in the direction of Washington, D.C. from the varieties of sources we have indicated. Something must be said of the quality of this intelligence supplied by such putatively friendly sources. To speak with utmost diplomacy, these ostensible friends do not bore us with any of the details in excess of what they decide that we "need to know." To speak frankly, a greater mass of horse-manure and garbage was never dumped by one nation upon the shores of another.

In our introductory observations to this point of our report, we have identified the two principal foreign sources for those post-war foreign policies by means of which we have been sold down the river. To complete our introductory remarks bearing upon the Toynbee syndrome, we must adduce a summary of that feature of our post-war ideology which prompts our government to that state of pathetic credulousness, the which our susceptibility to foreign manipulation reflects. We summarize this problem of ideology on two levels of approximation.

Broadly, our prevailing ideology today reflects a long process of fundamental shift in our national character. This shift is dominant over a span of approximately a hundred years to date, and has accelerated with devastating effects since such signal and relevant developments of the turn of this century as the founding of the Socialist Party of America and the British-intelligence-assisted assassination of President William McKinley. During the post-war period, this process of shift underwent principally two, successive phase-changes, including the post-1962 phase-shift into an anti-technology, anti-rationalist mode.

This shift in our national character is most simply demonstrated as fact by comparing the intellectual quality of our political life around the time of our Federal Constitution and the same categories of our national life and culture today.

It is not generally known today, for example, that at the time of the 1790 U.S. Census, when we were more than 90 percent rural, we enjoyed a literacy-rate of more than 90 percent, a literacy in terms of classical literature which caused typical American farmers to be described in Europe as "Latin farmers." Contrary to the myth of Fredrick Jackson Turner and others, we were not a nation of semi-literate, unwashed frontiersmen, but constituted the most literate and civilized people of any nation of the world. The point is illustrated by reference to the Federalist Papers, the political documents widely circulated at that time, which won a majority of the electorate of this nation to adoption of the 1787 Constitution. At that time, the literacy-rate in Britain was in the range of 40 percent, and the productivity of the British manufacturing operative or farmer was approximately half that of the American, a difference reflecting entirely the superior cultural level of the average American.

It was the conscious emphasis upon enriching our cultural potentials with the technology of French science and French industry, then the most advanced in the world--e.g., the case of the DuPont chemical firm--which, during the period of 1766 to about 1828, set into motion what became the greatest economic power in the world. The revival of West Point under Commandant Sylvanus Thayer--until President Jackson began wrecking the improvements--illustrates the point. It was our assimilation of the military and technological policies of Lazare Carnot and Carnot's Ecole Polytechnique which caused the British during the 1820s and 1830s to include the United States among the nations dangerously more scientifically advanced than Britain at that time. West Point was a center of reasserting Franklin's science policies for the nation as a whole.

The shift in our national character is not to be explained simplistically in terms of waves of immigrants. The republican, anti-monarchy party of England which established the United States drew not only from the most literate parishes of Britain, but also Germans and others fleeing the horror and aftermath of the 1618-1648 Thirty Years War in Central Europe. True, we suffered the consequences of a post-1876 policy of recruiting immigrants to serve as merely cheap, uneducated labor, but the cause of the cultural erosion was not those immigrants, but rather the fact that our standards in educational and other policies had been subverted by the forces such as British agents Morgan and Belmont, which had reflected their financier and political power in forcing the enactment of the 1876-1879 Specie Resumption Act. In the aftermath of 1876 we shifted, most emphatically, our immigration policy from that of a true "melting pot," toward the policy reflected in the horror of urban planning in New York City, the disunification of our people into ghettos. We began transforming our people from the rank of citizens into the status of ghettoized collections of subjects. We fostered the myth of the White Anglo-Saxon Protestant (WASP). The degeneration of our cultural standards of public and university education, a degeneration which accelerated after 1876, combined with WASP-centered chauvinism, was key to the transformation of our national character. True, all these elements of policy-shift had been insurgent during the preceding decades; after approximately 1876-1879, these became the dominant trends in our national policy of internal practice.

Today, the average citizen of our nation has descended into a relative illiteracy and intellectual banality, that he or she could not understand conceptions of the variety featured in those Federalist Papers which won a majority of the 1787-1789 electorate of this nation to adoption of our Federal Constitution.

There is another, happier aspect to our national character. Despite the rise of anti-rationalist ideologies from approximately the same time as the assassination of President John F. Kennedy, it's a fair estimate that about three-quarters of our adult population adheres to those notions of morality, rationality and reliance upon technological progress which brought our nation to its former greatness. Unfortunately, this persisting morality and rationality among the majority of our citizens locally has tended to vanish from the process of composition of our national policies and deliberations of policy among leading circles of our major political parties and other prominent policy-influencing institutions.

The reasons for this discrepancy between the private morality of a majority of our citizens and the public morality of our national policy-shaping are quite lawful reasons. St. Augustine wrote extensively on this matter; the entirety of the great *Commedia* of Dante Alighieri is devoted to this problem of statecraft. The ordinary moral citizen is so beset by the immediate problems of securing some semblance of "earthly paradise" for the individual, the family, and local community, that the great, broader issues of national life and foreign policy are usually beyond the citizen's comprehension, except as those policy-matters are seen to impinge directly upon his or her more immediate and day-to-day individual, family and community self-interests. Hence, the citizen does not apply to larger matters of national policy-making the same morality and rationality he or she esteems most highly in personal and community relations. The citizen is mystified by most matters of national policy, and substitutes adoption of prejudices in these matters for an attempt to comprehend them rationally. If corrupt influences operate among the leaders of institutions to which the citizen affords allegiance, the citizen will tend to share the opinions imposed upon those institutions up to the point, as at the present time, that economic depression and other calamities of national self-humiliation prompt the citizen to break off his or her allegiance to the responsible institutions.

In a properly ordered republic, as the forces around Benjamin Franklin and George Washington understood this point correctly, the greatest single source of potential danger to the republic is the very sort of estrangement of the citizen from rational comprehension of national policy-issues which prevails in the United States today. This, as we shall shortly demonstrate, impinges directly upon the Toynbee syndrome. The most essential thing for a republic is to develop the citizen into an adult with the qualities of a true citizen. These qualities subsume the ability of the citizen to focus upon and to comprehend in a rational way the great issues of national policy.

The entire history of modern civilization demonstrates that such qualities of citizenship can be cultivated in a people in only one manner. That manner is a teaching of classical literary culture, classical musical culture, classical principles of plastic arts' composition, and classical principles of scientific thinking, all situated within the frame of reference of a comprehension of national and world history as a process of universal history. In the Judeo-Christian tradition of republicanism, we devote public primary and secondary education to these subjects, and present history from the standpoint of reference of St. Augustine's *City of God*. We present universal history as a comprehensible process of those developments of knowledge and of social institutions which represent the republicans' struggle to perfect the individual and society, a struggle against the evil forces of oligarchism typified during our early history by the British monarchy and the forces behind the 1815-1848 Holy Alliance.

The new citizens emerging from our secondary institutions then become persons armed with the kind of knowledge required to judge both the immediate and medium-term future historical impact of policies upon the well-being of our nation and advancement of civilization generally. That was the adopted purpose of the principal framers of our Constitution. That is the policy-outlook and educational policy which has become chiefly mislaid and neglected under the impact of the indicated shift in our national character.

It is sometimes said that the cause of our undoing has been that we have become too materialistic. That is true in a large sense, but is a dangerously inadequate representation of our moral decadence. This commonplace observation has been commonly too easily twisted by wicked tricks of rhetoric. Wicked rhetoric deduces from that casual truism the argument that we are undone by too much of the fruit of technological progress--in other words, that we have adhered too faithfully to the injunction of the Book of Genesis: To be “fruitful and multiply, and fill the earth and subdue it.” Are we to swallow that ancient, heathen bucolic rhetoric, that it has been Judeo-Christian principles which have been the undoing of Judeo-Christian republican society?

We have not become too “materialistic” in the sense the “environmentalists” insist. On the contrary, we have become too much like them; we have become a hedonistic counterculture, rejecting all higher purposes and morality for sake of an anarchistic philosophy which argues that the function of society is to gratify irrationally defined individual "inner psychological needs." We have become degraded into such a Hobbesian morality, into the immoral, irrationalist radical hedonism of such 19th-century British philosophical radicalism as that of Jeremy Bentham, and such followers of Bentham as John Stuart Mill, William Jevons, Alfred Marshall, Aleister Crowley and our own existentialist pragmatists such as William James, John Dewey, and the intellectual elite orbited around the Socialist Party of America. The burgeoning of that "Age of Aquarius" proposed at the beginning of this century by such arch-fascists as Friedrich Nietzsche and theosophist Dionysus-worshipper Aleister Crowley, is presently reflected by the growing degradation of our youth into the hedonistic rock-drug-sex counterculture of that modern court of the Emperor Nero known as our "jet set."

In other words, we are destroyed by a Hobbesian every-man-for-his-own-pleasure degeneracy, steeped with that same reek of dionysiac cultural pessimism which earlier produced such phenomena as Benito Mussolini and Adolf Hitler, a culture whose Nietzschean principle is that "everything is permitted" according to the individual's "inner psychological needs."

Driven deeper into cultural decay in that direction, over the past hundred years our national institutions have undergone a succession of phase-changes, an ordered succession of descent into hedonistic philistinism reminding us properly of the descent into the Pit in Dante's "Inferno." So, beyond the banal philistinism of our own turn-of-the-century "Edwardian" period, we plunged into the dionysiac "Roaring Twenties." At the end of the war, most veterans quickly lost that firm moral resolve never again to allow the world to degenerate so, and too many among them occupied themselves with seducing their neighbor's wives in the new real-estate developers' "earthly paradise" called corporate suburbia. The pretty children stuffed with toys by adulterous parents of the 1950s became infantilism rampant in the emergence of the "New Left counterculture" of the 1960s and 1970s. So, step by step, we have marched toward the Pit.

Our people have lost their moral moorings. They have lost a sense of their individual connection to an historical process, lost all sense of the connection between one's own individual practice and the consequent good or evil bequeathed to subsequent generations. They stir in narrow mental circles, in a society whose benefits were bequeathed to them by the work of our Founding Fathers, but they echo Cambridge University's Charles Beard in spitting upon the memory of our Constitution and our Founding Fathers. Of the good they enjoy, that chiefly because of our Constitution and its ordering of our affairs, they speak as if they, individually, or their little family, had accomplished everything for themselves, as if to argue that the world had been created with the founding of the family fortune by a grandfather, or simply the day they were born into the undeveloped primeval forest they improved entirely by their own efforts. They may not assert such things in those exact words, but what they do say and believe implies nothing but such an ungrateful, arrogant assumption.

If one such person leaves a faulty stove neglected, and the neighbors die in holocaust as a result, "only in theory" would many consider themselves morally responsible for the consequences of their own actions. They are "practical people," with a healthy contempt for "mere theory."

They have lost the distinguishing moral and intellectual qualities of true citizens of a republic; they have renounced our constitutional commitment to shape the consequences of all of our present policies of national practice as those consequences impinge upon our posterity. Me, mine, and now become in the main part, the outer limits of their "practicality," and immediate, tangible relations to family, neighbors and local community become, in the main part, the outer limits of application of their morality. We as a people have neither an historical sense of the existence of either the nation or ourselves, nor a sense that there are higher, universal principles of lawfulness which determine whether entire nations rise or destroy themselves.

This defect in our transformed national character defines the prevailing political ideology of our nation. It is that ideology which governs our national credulity in such matters as the delusion that Britain is our dearest ally, or the delusion that second-hand horse-manure delivered as foreign intelligence by putatively friendly sources is the ingathering of actually competent policy-shaping intelligence.

It is against this background, and upon this foundation of ideology that our nation's post-war foreign policy has been shaped. The potentially fatal flaw of oversight in our shaping of our policy toward the Soviet Union, the principal subject of policy-making reference for our treatment of the Toynbee syndrome, can be efficiently adduced only in the terms of reference of our national ideology, as we have outlined the root of the matter so far.

U.S. Post-War Soviet Policy

It is possibly apocryphal, but psychologically truthful nonetheless, that the Secretary of State, General George Marshall, at one point despaired of getting through the Congress what became known as the Marshall Plan. A senior figure of the Senate offered him the encouraging suggestion, that if Marshall were to present his Plan to the Congress as a blow against the Soviet Union's influence, the Congress would pass it easily.

By 1947-1948, Washington was pretty well whipped up into committing the United States to preparing a "preventive nuclear war" against the Soviet Union, as proposed by Winston Churchill and as proposed publicly by the anti-nuclear-energy pacifist figure and generally degraded scoundrel, Bertrand Russell. The same forces which backed Robert Oppenheimer's fight against Dr. Edward Teller's development of the H-bomb were behind this project for preventive nuclear war. They assured the United States that Moscow would require a decade merely to duplicate the development of a design for a deployable fission-weapon, by which time the Anglo-American fission-weapon arsenal would be adequate for eliminating the existence of the Soviet Union as a nation-state.

Such advice had not sooner embedded itself into policy-outlooks than, contrary to the advice, the Soviets first developed an operational fission-weapon and next overtook Teller's group in the race to develop a deployable H-bomb. With Soviet development of both fission and fusion weapons, Bertrand Russell's anti-nuclear, pacifist fantasy of imminent "preventive nuclear war" was rapidly discarded. However, just as Bertrand Russell's standing as an anti-nuclear pacifist world leader seemed to blossom rather than fade on account of this episode, so the remnants of the "nuclear preventive war" delusion continued to be embossed upon the minds of strategic policy-thinkers.

The story of Marshall, actual or apocryphal, defines the central, almost exclusive principle of U.S. strategic and foreign policies down to the present time. It is almost the axiom of all such policy-making; and, broadly speaking, every domestic and foreign policy tends to be judged earlier or later in the degree it meritoriously contributes to the anti-Soviet cause, or diverts our efforts into some direction which suspiciously lacks some appropriate direct or indirect source of injury to what are plausibly Soviet or pro-Soviet interests.

Granted, there are currents in the Soviet leadership which would rejoice at our destruction, and the only serious war we might face within the foreseeable span of the future decades, would be the nastiest war of all history, fought against the forces of the Soviet Union. This circumstance does imply certain rules of conduct, and must be taken prominently into account in our military and other thinking. We shall turn our attention to that particular point at the appropriate location here later in this account.

The point to be brought forward immediately, is that by making a pure and simple sort of anti-Soviet doctrine implicitly the entirety of our strategic and foreign-policy doctrine, we have made a farce of our strategic and foreign policies overall. How, and to what effect that is the case is the principle subject of this report, the core of our subject which we are now approaching with aid of these situating observations.

The general shape of our argument begins to emerge as we look back a step to the time before the death of President Franklin Roosevelt. We examine briefly Roosevelt's proposed post-war U.S. policy, and then examine the way in which Churchill's policies of the post-war period savagely undermined the most vital strategic interests of the United States.

The manner in which the cited problem of American ideology intersects and reenforces the undermining of our most vital strategic interests will become clearer, step by step, as we proceed.

At various points, from the onset to close of the Second World War, Roosevelt and other sources, including an issue of *Time* magazine, alluded to an "American Century" doctrine for the post-war world. The implications of this doctrine are shown most clearly by reference to Elliot Roosevelt's published eyewitness account of two of the conferences between his father, the President, and Prime Minister Winston Churchill. Three points of Roosevelt's observation to Churchill adequately capture the kernel of the matter.

Roosevelt warned Churchill that the United States was not going to fight a second World War to repeat the post-war folly of the first such enterprise; the United States would not fight a World War to the end-result effect of preserving the British Empire. Secondly, Roosevelt stipulated that the world's economic affairs had already been subjected too long to "British 18th century methods," signifying the doctrines associated with Adam Smith's *Wealth of Nations*. Thirdly, the post war world was going to be transformed by American methods, which the President illustrated by outlining a project for transforming the semi-arid African Sahel into the breadbasket of Africa.

What such a strategy subsumed in practice, necessarily included the ordering of monetary and economic relations among nations according to the gist of three policy-papers submitted to the U.S. Congress during 1790 and 1791 by George Washington's Secretary of the Treasury, Alexander Hamilton: *Report on Public Credit* (1790), *Report on a National Bank* (1790), and *Report on the Subject of Manufactures* (1791). These are the three works which define what has been known since the last of these three reports as the "American System of political-economy."

This American System was directly based upon the founding of economic science by the work of Gottfried Leibniz, as the success of the development of the colonies and the United States up into 1791 richly corroborated Leibniz, as well as completely refuting the false doctrine of Smith. In principle, the institutional developments effected in France under the direction of Lazare Carnot were the same American System, complementing Hamilton's accomplishments in the matter of development of technology as such. The effects of Carnot's work were significantly incorporated in the revival of the American System--following the devastating effects of Jefferson's and Madison's following of Smith--from 1818 through to the inauguration of Andrew Jackson (who ruined the U.S. currency and economy once more by reintroducing the same Adam Smith whose conceptions had ruined the United States under Jefferson and Madison.)

In every instance of the successful development of a modern economy during the 18th and 19th century, except Britain, it was the application of the policies of the American System which guided the nation to this accomplishment. Britain's development was based, as the *Wealth of Nations* outlines this, on the looting of a vast colonial empire and augmenting this source of foreign income through London's skimming of international finance and commerce through the dominant position of the London market in world finance and trade, especially from 1815 onwards. The American System is the only political-economic policy through which capitalist economic development has occurred in modern times without looting one's neighbors.

To bring the American Century into being required that the United States convert its war-economy mobilization into large-scale export of capital goods (chiefly). This would be fostered only by relying upon issues of gold-reserve-denominated U.S. Treasury currency-notes as the dominant credit-mechanism for bank-lending in both U.S. domestic commerce and in export of capital goods for economic development. Such large volumes of exports would have a more important indirect benefit to the U.S. economy than the profits from sales of such exports. The accelerated turnover of capital invested in exporting industries (and their vendors) would mean high rates of injection of more advanced production technologies inside the U.S. economy, and consequently a very high rate of growth of productivity.

This meant a head-on collision with the crowd which Roosevelt sometimes named "the economic royalists." The establishment of such policies of credit, banking and commerce, meant a suppression of the relative strength of two categories of income, ground-rent and usurer, limiting profit chiefly to the profits developed through production and circulation of, chiefly, newly-produced agricultural and industrial goods. In short-hand terms of reference, this meant a life-and-death struggle of the American Century against those "economic royalists" typified by the British and their colonial allies among the Manhattan anglophile rentier-financier crowd.

The effect of an American Century policy of practice

upon both our domestic and foreign-strategic interests is properly more or less self-evident. The United States would not be exploiting anyone (at least in no sensible usage of the term "exploit"), would be contributing a great benefit to many nations (although on an equitable financial and economic basis for the United States), but the good the United States contributes to its partner-nations in this enterprise vastly augments the power of the United States at home and provides it great strategic power internationally.

Without considering at this point the non-economic correlatives of such an American Century policy, it is evident that such a policy defines in the clearest way one might desire what constitutes a well-defined notion of the vital foreign-policy interests of the United States. Furthermore, it should be clear enough, that if any nation or other powerful force is truly an adversary of the United States, it will define itself as such an adversary in terms of reference of the American Century policy.

The introduction of Churchill's version of an anti-Soviet strategic policy-commitment turned everything on its head. For the sake of some, often dubious, anti-Soviet scheme or other, vital U.S. interests--as the American Century implicitly defines such interests--were scrapped. If such a paradox were noted and raised with sufficient vigor as an objection to the scheme in question, the delphic rhetoricians of the anglophile news media would raise a hue and cry concerning the need to "sacrifice" this or that vital national interests "for the sake of the overriding need" to combat the Soviet menace.

The case of U.S. support for Britain in the war against Argentina is a most recent illustration of this point we have just stated.

Our relations with Ibero-America are, on several levels, among the most vital foreign-policy interests of the United States, as reflected in a mass of treaty-obligations premised on the Monroe Doctrine. Moreover, as to the issue of the islands themselves, Ibero-America has always recognized Argentina's rightful claim to the islands--which were Argentine territory at the time the Monroe Doctrine was enacted. As to the gag about "self-determination," the rightful inhabitants of the islands were forcibly expelled by the British when the islands were stolen and occupied by force. All this was known in relevant Washington circles. Our self-interest and our law dictated that British military forces be kept out of the area.

Despite some self-deluding chatter around the Washington bars, to the effect that all will return to sweetness and light in U.S.A. relations with Ibero-America, precisely the opposite is true. Under present policies in Washington, the damage to Ibero-American relations is profound and virtually irreparable. No matter what lies some tell, for the sake of appearing to avoid criticizing the current policy, every relevant expert on Ibero-America knows this fact. This was known at the time the decision to support Britain was adopted.

The argument for supporting Britain was not really the

hyperventilated mumbling about "oldest and dearest ally." The convincing argument was that we had to "sacrifice" our vital interests in Ibero-American relations, for the sake of our British *anti-Soviet ally.* Virtually the entirety of our post-war foreign policy (with brief exceptions) has been shaped by the erosive, repeated application of that same variety of argument.

The history of Vietnam from World War II on to the present is a model illustration of the same perverted practice of "sacrificing" vital foreign-policy interests for the sake of a policy-dictate of our British *anti-Soviet ally.*

During the war, we dropped an OSS team into Indochina to work closely with Ho Chi Minh. In close collaboration with his American allies, Ho Chi Minh modeled his design of the post-war nation on the constitutional lines of the young United States. With General Douglas MacArthur's friends in the Philippines, and other available arrangements, most of the region associated with the ASEAN group of nations today would be close American partners during the post-war period.

Churchill insisted, "No!" We "sacrificed" our partners in Indochina for the sake of our British *anti-Soviet ally.* We used Japanese armed forces in Indochina, after the armistice, to keep Ho Chi Minh's nationalist American allies suppressed until the British could deliver French colonial troops to take possession. This was not for the sake of France, but for certain Franco-Swiss rentier-financier interests who were determined to ensure that Americans had indeed fought and died in the war to preserve the old colonialist order of things. The French Fourth Republic was, to all intents in practice, a British errand-boy. In 1954, and so on and on, in Indochina we always toed the British line, "sacrificing," as we did in the ten-year war in Vietnam and Cambodia, for the sake of the policies of our British *anti-Soviet ally*.

To the present date, at least under Haig, we opposed all of our friends in the ASEAN nations on this same point of Southeast Asia policy.

Non-Economic Considerations

What kind of government do we rightly prefer in various parts of the world? What foreign policies of such governments do we prefer? Do we overthrow governments, as Henry Kissinger and his British friends overthrew the Bandaranaike government of Sri Lanka and Mrs. Gandhi in India, because Kissinger and the British objected to the August 1976 Colombo resolution favoring (in fact) an American Century ordering of North-South relations? Or, do we overthrow and kill them, as Kissinger threatened he would do (and did) to Pakistan's President Bhutto, over the same issues, the issues of the August 1976 Colombo resolution?

What we should desire in a government of another nation, is that it should reflect in some efficient way a commitment to and a process of becoming a state ordered by the principles we identify with the Judeo-Christian republican tradition. Our prefatory discussion of the decay in our national character referred to some of the crucial implications of this policy. It is not our business to superimpose our design upon nations, but we are fools if this cited desire does not guide us in the way our actions influence the choices of various nations of the world.

The case of the Pol Pot regime in Kampuchea is an illustration of this. Policy toward Khomeini's Iran is another good illustration.

Henry Kissinger, aided by Alexander Haig, who was aided by Thomas Enders, brought the Lon Nol government to power in Kampuchea, and at the same time aided the overthrow and mass-murder of the members of that government by the forces of Peking's asset, the Khmer Rouge. The Khmer Rouge, under Pol Pot, conducted the most monstrous genocide in modern history--three out of seven millions Kampucheans were murdered, with general details well known to our State Department. This Pol Pot government undertook military operations against Vietnam, to the point that Vietnam allied with the group around Heng Samrin and assumed the military burden of freeing Kampuchea from Pol Pot's genocide.

What is our policy in this matter? Since Vietnam is ostensibly a Soviet asset, rather than Peking's, we support the seating of the Pol Pot government at the United Nations, and pressure our allies and other nations to support us in that noble enterprise. None of the ASEAN nations (we ignore the special case of Singapore) wishes this monstrous policy, but we do it nonetheless.

The "Islamic Fundamentalism" of the "Ayatollah" Ruhollah Khomeini is, next to the Pol Pot forces, the most evil political force of any notable size in existence today. We connived with London (and, also Moscow) to destroy a long-standing and firm ally, the Shah of Iran, to bring this beast Khomeini to power--who repays us by funding terrorist groups in the United States and among nations of our allies.

What is called "Islamic Fundamentalism" is a resurrection of the Asharism which destroyed the Islamic renaissance's culture from within. The modern revival of Asharite pestilences was begun in Calcutta under the British East India Company, and was an ongoing project of the India Office until St. John Philby, the father of KGB General H. "Kim" Philby, persuaded the British government to spin off an entity called the Arab Bureau from the India Office during the 1920s. The Asharite cults run from the India Office side of the British Secret Intelligence Service are supplemented by the Muslim Brotherhood cults--there are the proverbial "57 varieties" of them--run out of the British SIS Arab Bureau centers at Aden, Cairo, and Beirut, or, after President Nasser shut down the Cairo office, from the British SIS Arab Bureau offices in Switzerland and London, with cooperation via Munich and Vienna. Ayatollah Khomeini, much like George Papandreou of Greece, is a second-generation British India Office/Arab Bureau agent.

Under the auspices of Henry Kissinger, a leading official of British SIS's Arab Bureau, Bernard Lewis, was brought to the Princeton center for advanced studies and to Georgetown University's CSIS, to conduct what was represented as an original Middle East policy-research study under the auspices of the Aspen Institute (an institution whose British pedigree runs from British Petroleum to Robert O. Anderson to Aspen). This "study," actually a product of British SIS, was conduited into U.S. policy by Kissinger as the "Bernard Lewis Plan." Brzezinski, who is slightly mad, retitled the Bernard Lewis Plan "The Arc of Crisis," but was otherwise faithful to the design handed over to him by Kissinger. It is a scheme for destroying every nation-state (excepting Israel) in an arc starting with India, sweeping up through into Turkey, and down through all Middle East Arab nations into the Horn of Africa. This scheme, which Brzezinski and Carter sometimes mouthed under the title of "Islamic Fundamentalism Card," was set into full-scale operation approximately January 1978, destroying Iran, to bring Khomeini to power, and to unleash similar varieties of murderous lunatics upon the nations of the Middle East generally.

These operations are directed from Britain, typically as concoctions of Sussex or Leicester, and are aided significantly by Swiss and Central-European black-oligarchical circles, but usually the United States and its State Department carries the ball visibly in such matters.

For example, the current intent is to divide India into five distinct separatist entities. One of these proposed entities is named "Khalistan." This particular project, affecting the predominantly Sikh Punjab region. This separatist movement is developed among the Sikh residents of Britain, under Sussex (Tavistock) direction. It is aided by a most-curious British non-stop aircraft flight from Birmingham in England to Amritsar in the Punjab. However, the movement has excellent connections in Munich and into the Non-Governmental Organizations office of the United Nations, and also connections to the neo-Nazi international based in Switzerland, according to a leading spokesman for the separatist movement.

All of these separatist movements, and the international terrorist groups associated with them are interfaced with networks of anthropologists and church figures which are, in turn, interfaced with the Nazi international's present form of organization. Bretons, Basques, Alsatians, Corsicans, Sardinians, Sicilians, Tyroleans, Armenians, Turkish Grey Wolves, the Khalistanis, indian-tribal separatist projects in the Western Hemisphere, and so forth and so on, are all part of this configuration. In the Middle East, these interface the personalities and organizations associated during the 1930s and 1940s with Admiral Canaris's Second Division of the Abwehr, as do key elements of both the Falange and the Arab terrorist groups.

The U.S. policy toward the Khomeini entity has been shaped by several intersecting policy-influences. First, it is a Kissinger-conduited project of our British *anti-Soviet ally*, although promoted with significant assistance from General H. "Kim" Philby's section of the Soviet KGB. Second, the Arc of Crisis scheme as a whole has been presented as a means for spilling "Islamic Fundamentalism" into the populations of Soviet South Central Asia. It is also argued that by not supporting Khomeini, in part through our Israeli surrogate, we would push Iran into Soviet arms--notwithstanding the fact that we already could do nothing effectively were the Soviets to decide simply to walk in and take it over in any case, whether we support Khomeini or not.

Not only do we support regimes as adopted "surrogates" contrary to not only our morals but also our practical strategic interests. Not only do we overthrow governments which are valuable partners (e.g., Bhutto of Pakistan) and in agreement with our proper moral criteria for preference. We often engage in such practices of folly not because we judge the government itself to be either usefully anti-Soviet or Soviet-leaning, but because we credulously define as *anti-Soviet* some evil scheme such as the Bernard Lewis Plan.

These moral criteria are not merely a rightful business of moral preferences. They are a vital strategic interest. Our desire must be not only to develop a community of trading-partners, each committed to using technological progress to increase the productive powers of labor in agriculture and industry. We must desire that this economic progress should foster the emergence and maintenance of certain qualities of nations and governments, nations and governments which share with us the indicated principles. That twofold aspect of development defines for us a *community of principle* which we must intend should become the overwhelming power in the world.

Yet, whenever we credulously embrace some cockeyed policy contrary to our own vital strategic interests, we define as an adversary, and hence potentially if not actually pro-Soviet, any ally or merely partner who objects to that current policy. The Percy-Glenn stipulation on non-proliferation policy is symptomatic of such folly. So, our vital moral-strategic interests in the world at large are destroyed by our practice of foreign policy just as our vital strategic economic interests are similarly eroded by our own folly.

2.

Our Ideology's Role in Policy-Making

The wicked Henry Kissinger's boastful confessions of May 10, 1982 imply that neither the President nor the Senate of the United States actually makes our nation's foreign-policy. He argues that the kernel of our foreign policies is designed in Britain, and that such British concoctions are then either forced upon the U.S. government by British pressure-tactics, or planted upon unsuspecting Presidents and Congresses. Kissinger's argument, supported by much important evidence bearing directly on this point, is that the foreign-policy function the British assign to our President and Congress is not the making, but *the process of adoption* of such policy.

There is nothing malignant per se in the fact that our government may adopt a foreign-policy, or any other category of policy, which may have been *designed* outside the deliberative processes of our government. Nor is the mere fact that the British government or its Secret Intelligence Service may have designed a policy, in and of itself be cause for pointing a finger of shame against a President or the Senate. An industrial firm would be silly to refuse to buy a useful patent simply on grounds that invention had been produced by an "outsider"; government should not hesitate to accept proposed designs which are the best available from any source, and government may otherwise plagiarize whenever that practice is truly to our nation's advantage. Kissinger did not imply anything resembling such a healthy practice; he insisted that Presidents and the Senate have been persistently hoodwinked into adopting foreign policies which are in fact contrary to the vital interests of our nation.

Put to one side, for a moment, the matter of scoundrels in both our government and electorate generally. Restrict our analysis for the moment to what we have indicated earlier as the healthy majority of our citizenry, and also those members and hired servants of government who attempt to honestly reflect the interests of our nation, and to regard that healthier portion of our citizenry as their electoral constituency. Address our criticism entirely to that variety of member of government and citizen we rightly love and prefer as friend and neighbor. Let us define such people as the people to whom we hold ourselves implicitly accountable for everything we do bearing upon the policies and practice of government.

As we address even scathing criticism against such people, let us never use any pronoun but "we." It is we who are being hoodwinked, and it is we who suffer those flaws of judgment which render us easy prey of the hoodwinkers. We shall cease to be sorrily hoodwinked people and a woefully hoodwinked nation, only on condition that we permit no passion of misguided pride to prevent us from discovering and remedying such a flaw in ourselves.

It has been, and continues to be the style of this present report, to see the workings of our own minds, and to gauge the connection between certain characteristic ways in which we so think, against the demonstrable consequences of a practice informed by such thinking. We must see such matters as the unfolding of a process. We must see that process as if it were a drama unfolding to our observation on a stage, and we for a moment here, reading this report, are directing our consciousness to see our own consciousness elaborated on that stage.

As the tragedy of the drama manifests itself to us, we must sense the wish that the self we see on stage might avoid the tragedy by the obvious means. "No," we in the audience wish to cry out to our self on that stage, "don't you see to what you are leading yourself." At first, it is our impulse to shout out to the character on stage. "Don't do it--Please, don't do that!" Then, we become more anguished, and without one color of sacriligious oath-making, we wish to cry out: "For God's sake, stop doing that before it is too late!" Then, our frenzy sinks into a moment of depression; we cannot stop the drama from unfolding so. The script has been written; Fate can not be altered in this matter.

Can this not be altered? Can the tragedy be turned? Why could we not change the consciousness of that character, our selves, on that stage? Of course it could be changed. Whence our depression, then? We reached a moment in which we passionately desired to change the ordering of our own processes of conscious judgment. At that precise moment, we lost the power to act. We lacked precisely, in that moment, the quality of strategic command which Clausewitz's *On War* attempts to circumscribe with the German term *Entschlossenheit.* Even seeing our own consciousness as a character apart from our selves, we could not bring ourselves to change what we recognized as *our own consciousness.* That is the tragedy of the characters on the stage; that is our own tragedy in real life.

What we have stated so far in this report has established the fact that we are presenting a tragedy. The climactic point, at which we cry out, "For God's sake, let us change our consciousness in this matter!" has not yet been reached. Until we present Mr. Toynbee and what he exemplifies as if in the living flesh, we shall not grasp the full dimensions of this tragic enactment through which our nation has been living in real life so far to date. Yet, the point in this report has been reached at which we must proceed to look beyond the clash of battles and into the processes of decision by which such battles and their outcome are ordered. To accomplish this service, we must interpolate these present observations, as if the writer were the actor playing the part of reciting Prologue at the opening of Shakespeare's *King Henry VIII,* or the character Hamlet soliloquizing to the audience at the close of Act II.

We do this interpolation in the manner we present it here that we may draw from within you, the reader, the advantage of multiplicity of most valuable resources otherwise at your disposal for the undertaking in which we are here engaged. There is a device most famous in our culture, exemplified by a certain principle of composition of dramas. This device, drama composed in the manner of Christopher Marlowe, Marlowe's protégé Shakespeare, and the dramas of Friedrich Schiller, in which the tragic principle of human history is presented to audiences in a manner of entertainment by which they are inspired to improve themselves, to accomplish that moral, intellectual act of *Entschlossenheit* which is the essential quality of great military commanders such as, we suspect, the late General Douglas MacArthur, and statesmen of the quality of a Benjamin Franklin, a George Washington, a Freiherr vom Stein, or a Charles de Gaulle. It is that quality of willful self-improvement, situated in a great military commander or statesman, which accomplishes what we rightly regard as astonishing and beneficial changes in history. If you, the reader, can gain at once a better insight into the essential features of tragedies such as those of Shakespeare and Schiller, and can bring that improved perception of such drama to bear upon the stage of life reflected into the pages of this report, it will not be this writer who causes you to alter your opinion in the matter before us, but rather that will be accomplished by the summoning of the power of your own conscience.

The method we employ here, which we have learned from Aeschylus, Socrates, Shakespeare and Schiller, among others employing that principle of tragic composition, is a method which the ghost of Arnold Toynbee will never forgive this writer for presenting to you in this setting. It is the Socratic method, the method of Cardinal Nicholas of Cusa, and the method of Socratic dialogue directly applied by Shakespeare and Schiller, among others, to the design of composition of dramatic tragedy. It is a method designed, and demonstrated to accomplish the higher political purpose which Friedrich Schiller prescribed as the intent impelling his accomplishments as a Jena University Professor of Universal History and as the composer of the most powerful dramas ever staged, to move an audience to bring the principles of the American constitutional republic to the shores of the Rhine. It is, as Schiller stated, a method for transforming "little people" into big people, for prompting citizens to uplift themselves, out of "littleness" of outlook and passions, to become true patriots and world-citizens without any contradiction between the two.

We have in each of us the power not only to view our own conscious processes as an object to willful consciousness. We have the power to change our consciousness in such ways as are most celebrated as fundamental scientific discoveries. We do this more or less unwittingly in the transformation of our first bawling hour as a hedonistic, irrational infant through childhood, adolescence into that state some of us finally attain, called maturity. This is a reflection of that aspect of our nature which we associate with the divine potentiality of every individual person, on which grounds we are obliged to regard each life as sacred. It is sacred not because it is living, not because of that which it shares with a cow, but because that quality, that power so reflected is a reflection of the divine. So, we must appreciate the grandeur of Dante Alighieri's *Commedia*, perhaps the greatest exposition of the fundamental principles of statecraft ever composed.

This is the power to free ourselves from the tragic grip of any ideology, it is the power to free our nation from the tragic grip of credulity, to free ourselves from that condition for which so mean a scoundrel as Henry Kissinger may publicly mock us for the amusement of his masters at Chatham House. It is the power to free ourselves from that destruction of our republic which now looms immediately before us, a consequence which is the fruit of that our national credulity, over which the despicable Henry Kissinger, who has abused us, now mocks us.

The function of this report, so composed, is to provide the appropriate object for those conscious powers of the readers. To know itself, consciousness must have an object. So, that special function of consciousness associated with the creative potentialities of mind can not function willfully, as a consciously directed creative power, unless it is made conscious of itself and its powers by means of focusing such variety of object, some variety of empirical object, that by acting willfully upon that object, the creative aspect of consciousness sees itself reflected in altering that object willfully. So, one finds for statecraft that power which Clausewitz attempted to circumscribe by the term *Entschlossenheit*. The most efficient means presently known for rendering the appropriate variety of object to consciousness, is the principle of composition of tragic drama exemplified by the work of Shakespeare and Schiller.

When the proper acquaintance with Shakespeare was ripped out of our schools' curricula, what our nation lost was persons adequately developed to become future citizens of this republic. Without Shakespeare, Milton and Shelley in our secondary schools, those schools will produce chiefly eternally adolescent functional illiterates or worse. This importance is not because of the fame of those authors as such, but because these works represent a distillation of those aspects of our English-speaking culture by means of which true citizens are produced.

It is from this vantage-point that we discover the root of our proper quarrel with Communism. We shall unfold by steps, as this matter intersects the successive sub-topics of this report, on what premises we are obliged to say that the Communist doctrine represents a danger to civilization, a danger which is most exactly located in dialectical materialism's denial of the existence of that quality in the individual person we rightly associate with the divine.

The Soviet state has a twofold, paradoxical character. In one aspect it is a sovereign nation-state, dedicated to improvement of the well-being of its citizens through aid of technological progress. Insofar as this aspect of the Soviet state is reflected in a corresponding Soviet nationalism, we could have no proper cause for seeking anything but normal relations of state to state with that superpower. At the same time, and now we shudder in horror, what kind of a world would come into being if it were ordered by Communist ideology?

This matter of Communist ideology is a double problem for us, if we see the matter rightly. Not only is a world dominated by such an ideology abhorrent. This ideology renders the Soviet mind more or less incapable of grasping certain classes of conceptions.

Even the highest quality of personality among Soviet representatives reflects this pervasive impairment of conceptual powers among Soviet leaders generally. Their exaggerated esteem for "objectivity," the side of statecraft on which their performance is approximately as expert or sometimes better than our own recent decades' performance, reflects also an obsessive quality of apparent incapacity to comprehend things of crucial importance bearing upon the "subjective" aspects of social and political processes. Confronted with empirical demonstration of such latter processes, they characteristically brush the key point of evidence aside, often by one or another of those standard-liturgical, delphic "objective explanations" of the matter produced by the putative dialectical materialists, or borrowed from the pages of the British empiricists.

If the implications of this impairment of Soviet leaderships' judgment is not grasped adequately, our policy-makers have failed to understand the crucial strategic implications of this problem, and are most poorly equipped for effective diplomacy in those quarters.

There is a strong case for the assessment, that President Franklin Roosevelt grasped the practical implications of this paradox. It is certain that General Douglas MacArthur did, and that these two influences had a beneficial impact on the policy-outlook of President Dwight Eisenhower, and perhaps also aspects of the thinking of President Richard Nixon. Except for the continued impact of Roosevelt's and MacArthur's outlook within our policy-influencing establishment, the making and conduct of our nation's Soviet foreign policy has been either wickedly wrong, as the Kissinger and Willy Brandt approaches illustrate, or pathetically amateurish work of intellectual lilliputans.

This summary observation on the illustrative case of our Soviet problem should be taken both at face value, and also as illustration of the point that the point of view, correlative with that of classical tragedy, which we are elaborating here, is the minimal level of thinking adequate for conduct of our foreign policy.

The credulity of our honest policy-shapers in government is essentially a product and constituency-influenced reflection of the corresponding tragic flaw in the pervasive ideology of our citizenry. In all the worst aspects of our best ordinary citizens, those citizens have been often most efficiently represented in government most of the time during the recent decade and a half or so.

Even to the most-widely traveled strata of our citizenry, the world outside our borders is a Walt Disney life-size reproduction of pictures and descriptions in a collection of travel-folders. Those among us who are not evil in the sense Henry Kissinger is, and who have reasons to travel to meet friends in governments and so forth of other countries, shudder with horror whenever we spy a fellow-citizen in a foreign nation. We may be lovable, good people in our home-setting, but once abroad, we are walking through a Walt Disney reproduction of a travel-folder. Our observations, as tourists, are as false and degrading to that country, and also degrading of ourselves, as we might expect from any of most among our leading New York City or Washington, D.C. journalists. At each turn, manifesting utter blindness of the spectacle we make, we perpetrate another monstrous solecism. Yet, at home, in our neighborhoods, we are lovable, moral and rational people.

The phenomena we have encapsulated at this point is, without exaggeration, a kind of mental behavior not unrelated to clinical schizophrenia. *The real life of nations and peoples abroad is not real for us*. They are merely objects of our fantasy-lives, in the same sense a soldier in combat describes in lusty fine detail, at the latrine or in the Saigon bar, the character and family life of each and every combatant and his grandmother on the other side of the barbed wire. The foreign nation is something from a movie, or something whose essence was neatly packaged in two adjectives transmitted as gossip by a neighbor "who reads the *New York Times* a lot."

Travel through this land of ours, outside New York City, Boston, Washington, and a few other such cosmopolitan centers. Pick up the morning newspaper in any fair-sized city of this country. Think as you glance at that newspaper of those policy-issues of national domestic and foreign-policy whose practical outcome will rather immediately affect changes in even the immediate circumstances of life of many families and so forth in that city. With that knowledge for comparison, examine the leading local newspaper on two levels. First, measure approximately the number of total column inches of editorial content in that publication, and divide the treatment of topics as a corresponding part of those total column-inches. Now, compare the relative importance the newspaper thus apportions to each topic with what you know to be the actual ranking of importance of those issues in terms of effects upon the lives of large portions of that community.

Now, continue the investigation to other media. Watch the coverage of local and national news on the TV channels in that locality. Next, survey the local radio news-broadcasts. Pass by a newsstand, and pick up copies of *Time, Newsweek* and the *U.S. News & World Report*. Examine these national newsweeklies both by the same criteria applied to local media, and also examine the quality of content of what those weeklies purport to cover in usually a glib, slick and highly distorted fashion. Even our allegedly sophisticated news publications are not news media, but consist chiefly of current political propaganda-operations of the crudest character as to content against something or someone, or boosting something or someone.

Next, study the kinds of publications and visual entertainment in general circulation, and compare patterns and quantities of circulation of each type--with the legalized pornography heading the list. Examine the content of motion-picture and television entertainment, and compare this with the "Radio Research Project" developed as an Anglo-American intelligence inquiry against the minds of the American people out of the last world war.

This wretched pattern has two interdependent aspects. On the one side, we are often quick to judge that our citizens are being foully brainwashed by the inundation of such combined journalism and entertainment. Yet, as most among the more honest and patriotically concerned editors will quickly instruct us, this miserable state of journalism and entertainment appears to be what the public desires. Both sides are each correct as far as they examine the matter.

One of the more effective ways of tracing the process of change in our moral and political outlook during the post-war period is accomplished by referencing the publishing history of the legalized pornography of *Playboy* magazine, together with the phenomena of the Playboy clubs and related impedimenta of what might be aptly described as a "Playboy cult-phenomenon." The correlations to be made should emphasize the treatment of naked girls as thing-like sex-objects, the promotion of the use of "recreational substances," and a "philosophy" of hedonism parodying the distinctions of Nero's court.

Think back. One of the hosts of Nero's court-circles observed a guest's eye lingering a moment over a half-clad serving-girl--she couldn't be much more than fourteen. The host signaled to the girl. She recognized the instruction. The guest was duly served in whatever ordinary or exotic manner his sexual preferences inclined him at that moment. (Tomorrow night, it will be a boy.)

With that statement, we have just entered into the area of intelligence-gathering which defines the critical importance of Arnold Toynbee's selection to head British foreign intelligence.

During the period of Lord Shelburne, the ruling faction of the British oligarchy retained the services of the one-time fiancé of the Madame de Staël, Gibbon, to conduct a study of the Roman Empire. This study was employed as the added model of reference for developing the British Empire on the general model of law, morality, and so forth of the Roman Empire, but with the added feature of hoping to avoid certain of the calamities which befell Rome. This sort of activity continued through the 19th century, with the Acton family prominent in the projects, leading into Toynbee's attempt to extend the research into the broadest terms of reference of human history and pre-history as a whole.

It is the conceptions associated with study of developmental and decay features of many nations and cultures viewed in this way which inform the mind's eye of the top-most British intelligence policy-planner.

The "practical American," who despises such considerations as "impractical," "not down to earth," as "mere theory," should be informed that for every battle such a "practical fellow" wins with aid of his narrow-minded objectivity during the short-run elaboration of a local situation, blokes like Toynbee will always defeat the practical fellow over the longer run.

With that observation, we have placed our finger precisely on the essential point of formal incompetence in the strategic and foreign-policy incompetence of the government of the United States, on the reasons for failure of our intelligence institutions. Correspondingly, we have indicated why the writer and his associates, with a relatively infinitesimal scope of material means, have emerged in the forward rank of strategic analysts today. We have developed the capacity to play the same game as Toynbee et al., but from the opposite side of the table, so to speak.

We Americans simply do not think nowadays in the terms of reference required to understand "how things happen." We overlook the historical significance of such projects as publishing *Playboy* magazine (and correlated actions). We do not understand that it is through small wedges introduced to the cultural life of a people that the wicked minds who have really studied history can, over the span of successive decades, ruin any targeted nation which is not alert to the implications of such things. "Oh. you're talking about conspiracies, again," our typical fellow-American protests; "I think conspiracy-theories are a lot of crap!" Our practical fellow probably could not believe that Kissinger said what he said on May 10, 1982, and if our practical fellow once acknowledged the fact of what was said (and later mimeographed for general edification of all comers in Washington, D C.), our practical fellow would insist, "Things don't work that way." History, like foreign nations, is simply another Walt Disney reproduction of a tourist-guide for our practical fellow.

Trace the circulation, and emulation of *Playboy*. Trace the gradual transformation in popular values in respect to the three features of *Playboy* policy-thrusts cited. Note, the approximate phase-changes in that gradual process, such as those of approximately the 1962-1964 period, and, again, of the 1967-1971 period. Observe how the emergence of the rock-drugs-sex counterculture was passed down from the Neronic "jet set," through the adulterous business-professional strata of *Playboy* readers, and into the emergence of the dionysiac cultism of the "Age of Aquarius" transformation of values, which erupted in the wake of the 1968 Chicago riots led by Tom Hayden et al. Note that today Hayden is being pushed as a "respectable" exemplification of a major factional force within the Democratic Party.

Then, examine the interconnections of *Playboy* to this rock-drug-sex youth-counterculture. Guided by Robert Gutwillig, now a putatively respectable official with a division of the Times-Mirror publishing empire, the Playboy Foundation was created to fund the drug-lobby organization, NORML. This was formally a Yippie project, interlocking the Yippies, *High Times* drug weekly, NORML, NORML endorser and publicist William F. Buckley, Jr., the Playboy Foundation, *Playboy*, the *Chicago Sun Times*, the Field family, the Field Foundation's funding of radical projects, and so forth and so on, all in the same multiply interconnected package.

Then, examine the social-psychological role of the radio-TV "soap opera." Innocent, if banal stuff? If we think so, we miss the political point.

The characteristic effect of the soap opera on the mind is the romanticization of smallness of intellectual outlook, the romanticization of banality and pathetically neurotic behavior. The effect on the mind is, speaking metaphorically, the same result accomplished by soaking one's brain in alum-solution. The Tourist-Syndrome pathology we cited earlier was a relatively galactic reach of human comprehension of world affairs by comparison with the results implicit in a heavy diet of soap-opera "culture." We shall be more specific on this point.

To focus only upon those among the features common to soap operas which have the relatively greatest impact on the political-ideological corruption of our population, these few features are to be identified. The physical setting is either the interior of family homes or a non-home setting, such as a hospital, in which all the social-spatial rules bounding the behavior and interaction of the characters duplicate the soap opera's standard treatment of social interrelations within the interior of homes. The definition and relations of the characters are those of what is called "small-group theory," and the plot elaborated in a seemingly random way corresponding to the Tavistock doctrine of brainwashing by means of the "leaderless group," as this latter approach is associated with the 1930s work of Bion.

The most general of the principal effects of the use of addictive viewing of soap opera is this.

In a healthily functioning society, the home is the most significant social institution in respect to the immediate development of the child's capabilities for achievement in the real world outside the home. For all members of the family, it is a place in which to renew moral and physical strength for one's assault on the problems of the real world the following day.

It used to be acknowledged, and rightly so, that one of the worst problems our society imposed upon housewives was a degree of depressing banalization associated with the victim's sense of being imprisoned. It was also recognized that a lack of orientation toward moving continually, and happily to one's challenges in the real world, was a prime correlative of neurosis and worse. In other words, lack of outward-directness within the home correlated with infantile regression. (If one left two miners snowbound through a long northern winter, one expected in the spring to discover that either both had gone mad, or one had either simply murdered or murdered and eaten the other. Small is very ugly indeed, and so was the Nazi-international-connected author of *Small Is Beautiful*.)

In the soap opera, the relationship between home and real world is reversed from the healthy to the pathological. The world exists only within the "small, leaderless group" settings of the image projected to the addicted viewer. This is purely and simply brainwashing in every clinical sense of that term. The effect of such withdrawal from the outer, real world is literally schizophrenic.

In the early phase, Tavistockian principles of mass-brainwashing developed during the 1930s were employed to provide the trapped housewife and her daughter, by means of several daily hours of successive, fifteen-minute radio broadcasts, some assistance in creating a fantasy-life, imagining she were, happily part of a different family than the one she shared with her husband or the home in which she had grown up. Her daughter indulged in fantasies of adolescent courtship-relationships and dreams of the family she would become housewife of in time to come. Through heavy conditioning, this "entertainment" induced subtly, but effectively shifts in values within a large part of the population.

The immediate general effect of shifting a sense of reality from the real world into ever-narrower circles converging on the interior of the walls of the house or apartment, is to mystify the real world, and so make the problems of the real world relatively more frightening to the victim. This generates what is to be defined quite literally as a condition of dependency upon the soap opera, and associated acting-out of soap opera-like fantasy-life, a form of addiction.

Not *political*, one argues? Very much to the contrary, it is the essence of the political process within the electorate which is shaped by such methods.

First, the general effect is infantile regression in the mental life of the addicted viewer. This correlates with not only a fear of any change in the outside world which might affect the home, but a growing unwillingness to recognize such changes as they occur. Second, the persons and objects of the real world, except as they are members also of the artifacts and persons within the range of soap opera fantasy-versions of personal life, lose their quality of sensuous reality. Like the physician, lawyer and so forth within the soap opera as such, what he or she is in the real world is merely what he is reputed to be within the non-real world of the soap-opera setting. What the television screen, the household's daily newspaper, or the visiting gossip say to be the significance and value of objects and persons in the real world, becomes for the victim of psychological conditioning by soap opera the values which the victim will attribute to those objects and persons in real practice.

The political behavior of the electorate is changed to reflect this kind of brainwashing-effect, this behavioral modification.

Two kinds of examples suffice to illustrate that very specific kinds of modifications of political behavior of the electorate are induced by soap opera and related approaches to mass-brainwashing of the population.

First, during recent years, a sustained campaign was conducted throughout the nation, seeking rather successfully to condition the population into monetarist-doctrinal views by means of the simple fraud of saying to housewives, among others, that the administration of government fiscal and monetary policies could be more or less completely explained by comparing the U.S. federal budget and money-supply management to the housewife's management of a household budget. Either the promoters of this particular hoax were utterly ignorant of the ABCs of economics or they were simply hoaxsters: there is no similarity between a private household's budgetary problems and the budgetary, credit and monetary processes of our federal government.

The household budget is based on assumption of a fixed income and a fixed array of categories of needs. These needs have ranges of prices which are not controllable to any significant degree by any willful action of the members of the family. The object is not only to keep the sum of such necessary expenditures below the level of relatively fixed income, but to squeeze out some margin of saving and perhaps the proverbial "a few other little things," such as a family dining-out and a night or two during the month at a movie or something else of that general sort.

In the case of war, does a nation say to itself, we can not afford to equip and deploy an adequate military capability, merely because that would unbalance the budget? Does a nation say, "Well, I guess our commanders will just have to learn to win the war with a lot less. We can't let the fact that our enemy has twice the forces and better equipment, intimidate us into unbalancing our budget"?

Does a nation say, "If any of our pensioners starve as a result of our efforts to balance the budget, that would be terrible. I hope our pensioners show the self-reliance to survive without their pensions."

Those things ought to be immediately obvious. There is

another, more fundamental sort of difference to be considered.

The principal function of the debt of the federal government is not to cover deficits in "household accounts." Taxes must accomplish that. The business of government is to keep the level of production and circulation of agricultural and industrial goods sufficiently high that items of governmental expense can be covered by taxation without damaging the economy.

This growth of the economy is accomplished by two forms of governmental indebtedness. The preferred of the two forms is the printing and issuing of Treasury currency-notes, which the Treasury then lends through the national banking system to provide sufficient volumes of low-cost credit to ensure high rates of investment in the expansion and improvement of the production and circulation of, principally, agricultural and industrial goods. However, if the required investment-goods can not be produced within the national-economy, and if we lack a surplus in our balance-of-payments accounts, we must borrow funds to be used through national banking system lending, to enable our farmers and industries to buy abroad.

The credit-creating monetary function of the federal government, or, alternatively the federal debt used in place of new issues of lendable currency-notes, is the key variable of government's fiscal and monetary responsibilities. This involves a constitutional provision (Article 1, Section 8) which no housewife is permitted (or would be able) to invade.

In summary of this specific point, the most characteristic features of federal fiscal and monetary policy are elements which have no reflection in the functions of the family household budget. If we were to impose the supposed principles of the balanced household budget to federal fiscal and monetary policy of practice, our national economy would collapse.

The behaviorally modified portion of the population rejects such information out of hand. On what premises do they reject such elementary and important facts concerning the real world? They reject the truth of the matter because the truth involves a matter which exists *only in the real world.* It is a real world they have largely rejected, whose very claims to exist they view as suspicious, and which they wish would disappear, to leave their homes and families free of its intrusions. "What I know," the angered proponent of the balanced-budget constitutional amendment glowers menacingly, "is that the government is taking too much of my family income in taxes, and that I can't stand any more inflation. I'm not interested in hearing anything you have to say, if you're trying to sell me on not demanding a 100 percent balanced federal budget."

Where was such strange and destructive political behavior acquired? In significant part through the behavioral modification effects of soap opera.

The second point of illustration is of broader and more profound significance respecting the problem of our present national ideology as a whole.

Earlier, in describing the method of classical drama we employ here, we located the reflection of the divine potential of human beings. We pointed to its reflection in those self-conscious powers to change our consciousness as exemplified by fundamental scientific discovery, and also the active principle of those gradual and radical transformations in conscious values associated with maturation. We continue that point of discussion now, to emphasize the literally evil influence of behavioral modification of the sort soap opera tends to accomplish. This, we shall now show, is the most crucial issue presented by our current national ideology, the issue with a most direct bearing on the credulity we collectively exhibit in permitting British manipulation of our foreign policy.

From our line of exposition respecting this divine reflection in creative mental powers, it might be misjudged that we insist on certain social practices in our nation merely on religious grounds narrowly defined as religious. In other words, it might be misjudged that we are simply insisting that our people must express constantly that aspect of their natures which reflects the divine. We would not entirely reject such an argument were some other person to propose it; we would say to the proponent of such a view, "If you insist on looking at the matter in that way, your heart is in the right place, but you had better leave it to us to bring into being the direction of improvement you are right in desiring."

Nonetheless, such qualifying remarks duly registered, this notion of the divine is the efficient principle of Judeo-

Christian civilization, the *civilizing* effect of Judeo-Christian republican impulses. Without its efficient presence, our civilization must necessarily decay and collapse. It is the manner in which this divine creative power works, and indispensably so, in elaborating the development of society and the individual within society, which is the point to be grasped for practice of statecraft.

There are two, interrelated aspects to the elaboration of the divine in the properly informed practice of statecraft. The first aspect is existential, arising from reflections on the fact and implications of our mortal individual existence. The second is the elementary knowledge arising from discovery of a readily demonstrated principle, which shows us how we properly order the existence of a society of such mortal individuals. All classical Judeo-Christian republican statecraft has been premised upon these two considerations. These principles properly define the effective domestic and foreign policies of republics, principles which must be embedded and reflected in the judgments of the electorate as well as members of government.

The fact that we are mortal prompts us to despise hedonism. We must eat, and must provide ourselves the material preconditions for accomplishing our proper functions as something more than a mere animal; but irrational, mortal varieties of "inner psychological needs" we despise as gratifications shoveled into the grave with us. We seek to perform a larger Good, some Good to the proper advantage of mankind in some fashion over the course of generations yet to come. The difficulty posed to us in this way is twofold. Since society either nullifies or perpetuates the Good contributed by individuals, there can be no efficient perpetuation of individual Good without a Good society. To be Good, both the individual and the society must equip itself to know what policies of practice are in fact Good. This latter requirement defines the task of science, of reason. How can we know how the universe is ordered, that we may thereby pre-judge with confidence which policies of practice will lead in fact to Good consequences over generations yet to be born?

All that we can know with certainty at the start of any inquiry into what we call science is based on the empirical evidence bearing upon the power of the individual and society to sustain the existing population of that society, and to lay the basis for the future growth of society in such fashion that the individuals of the future acquire a greater power of this same sort than we exert in producing the preconditions for their existence.

We measure such a power in terms of what is best termed the potential relative population-density of society. Given land of relatively improved or depleted qualities of habitability, how many persons can be sustained on an average square mile of that territory merely by means of the productive powers of the population inhabiting that territory? For various reasons we have developed fully in other published locations, the maintenance of a fixed level of such a potential requires advances in technology. However, for reasons also elaborated in those published locations, the required technological progress means a requirement of an increased social division of labor in society, requiring an enlargement of the population as a whole. So, we shift our focus on the empirical evidence from simple measurement of potential relative population-density, to discovering the policies which generate either decreases or increases in such a potential. This notion of a "function of rising potential relative population-density" we show in those locations to be the unique basis, combined with astronomy, for the development of science from most ancient times to the present date.

The process of discovery which makes such technological progress possible is precisely that aspect of mental life we have identified as reflecting the divine. In exactly this connection lies the equivalence of the Socratic method to the scientific method. It is the exercise of an aroused and efficient consciousness of our consciousness, as we described the classical-dramatic method of elaborating this Socratic method, which brings directly into play that aspect of our mental life which has the power to change the ordering-principles of our ordinary levels of conscious behavior.

A science which defines its method so, as did Cusa, Leonardo da Vinci, Kepler, Leibniz, Carnot, Riemann, is indispensable, but not adequate if we limit this to what we narrowly define as scientific practice. Although science is the means for furthering Good, the object of Goodness is the development of mankind, the development of the nations in that direction which renders nations instruments to nullify wickedness and to assimilate and perpetuate the benefits of the Good.

Charles de Gaulle located efficiently the root of the evil of the French people under the Fourth Republic, as a state like that of calves chewing their cud unthinkingly in a meadow. To make citizens good, the nation a must have a higher purpose within the development of mankind as a whole. A nation must define for itself its appropriate place in the division of labor in furthering the moral condition of mankind as a whole. That nation, mobilizing itself consciously and efficiently to serve such a higher purpose, transforms the ordinary work of each of its citizens into a contribution to the accomplishment of that same purpose.

This is the bedrock of a form of nation and civilization morally fit to survive, an issue of moral fitness which coincides more or less exactly with the nation's and civilization's practical potential to endure.

The Judeo-Christian impulse expresses this in many practical ways of informing the consciousness of the individual in society. Two principles are most greatly to be emphasized for their bearing upon the relevant features of statecraft. The first, from the book of Genesis, is the injunction that man must be "Fruitful and multiply, and fill the earth and subdue it." The second, while articulated in a distinct way by such Judaic giants as Philo of Alexandria, is centered for Christianity in the opening verses of the Gospel according to St. John: the consubstantial unity of Godhead, Logos and Christ, from whence the so-called *Filioque* of the Catholic liturgy arises as the principal political issue defended, often with much blood sacrificed, from Charlemagne onward, against those forces seeking to impose their heathen "blood and soil" cults upon mankind as a whole. In both Philo's approach and in the principle of the consubstantial Trinity, the perfection of the potential divinity of life of each human individual is placed at the center of the practice of the individual and society.

If we are able, and must perfect our powers to do so, to account for such Judeo-Christian teaching in an entirely scientific way, this does not lessen the importance of that teaching. Without such teaching, man would degenerate into such a kind of beastlikeness as we witness in our Neronic "jet-setters" and the rock-drug-sex counterculture today.

This is the crux of the issue of national ideology today.

To the extent our citizens are estranged from mankind, from the notion of our higher national purpose to advance civilization as a whole, and, worse, narrowed in their consciousness in the way illustrated by the behavioral-modification effects of soap opera, they cut themselves off from the Good, and stultify that very attribute of themselves which reflects the divine. To employ the appropriate image of Dante's *Commedia* they fall lower in moral condition within the "Purgatory," to that cross-over-point at which they fall into the company of the *Washington Post*'s editorial staff, into the "Inferno."

As the scope of reality is narrowed for them, drawing in upon immediate community and family circles, the impulse for Goodness within those citizens approaches the point it is snuffed out of existence. At that latter point, hedonistic and irrationalist perceptions of individual and small-group "inner psychological needs" take command of their judgments, and a succession of phases of degeneration of their personalities proceeds, in the direction of the "Inferno's" Pit.

So long as the citizens so being narrowed in outlook retain their essential morality and rationality, the most immediately disastrous effects for statecraft are felt in the area of foreign-policy. Foreign things have virtually no reality for such citizens; they can tolerate an immoral or simply stupid sort of foreign-policy because their morality touches them only in those matters which are real, practical subjects of practice for them. They experience no twinges of conscience in the perpetuation of even an evil foreign-policy, because there is no comprehension of a sensuous reality respecting the matter for them. If a wicked government can keep the truth of an evil practice out of the sight of the citizens, to the point that the area involved is unreal to the moral citizens, the moral citizens will tolerate almost any monstrous practice by their government in that area of reality.

As the shift into the "Inferno" becomes predominant, then we begin to see popular toleration for such emulations of Nazi genocidal policies as the *Global 2000 Report* or promotion of medical policies representing in practice a re-enactment of Nazi euthanasia policies against our aged, on grounds of "cost-benefit analysis" of insurance-cost and similar considerations.

It is at such a critical point that bold, ruthless leadership to reverse such trends becomes indispensable if the nation is to survive. Only bold leadership by such admired and potent institutions, preferably from government itself, can turn the course of degradation around, and put the nation back into the direction of upward development. The frightened "little" politician, consulting opinion-polls, news-media editorializing, and those lobbying groups whose money and influence will determine a crucial margin in the next election, says, "I don't wish to be involved. Maybe you are right, but the people aren't ready for anything such as that you propose. Look, I've a tough election coming up, and so has our party. See me again after the election." So, the national ideology gripping both the elected official and the electorate defines the tragedy our nation is living out, perhaps near the close of the final act today.

Out of the Sports Arena, Into Reality

It is a good thing, from childhood on, to the point physicians might warn us we are overdoing this a bit, to subject our bodies to a purposeful education by means of stress, to develop and maintain those bodies as instruments more perfectly adapted to what the divine within us may require of those bodies. As we grow older, the best among our physicians practicing today may take one or two of us aside, to speak to us in the manner of the proverbial "dutch uncle," and to speak to us of the importance of an appropriate form and level of stressful activity, perhaps adding some information respecting the functions of potassium and ATP, and to cease salting our food.

A regular practice of climbing hills, if conducted in a proper frame of mind, is agreeable not only to the education of that instrument of mind we call our bodies, but may help in fostering a certain development of the mind. The word for this variety of exercise is “intrepid.” Not even memory of the real Colonel William Stephenson, as distinct from the myth, can spoil the word, intrepid, for this writer.

Two aspects of hill-climbing, or mountain-climbing, are to be underlined here, as bearing implicitly and usefully upon the subject of this report as a whole.

Once the objective has been adopted in a rational way, rational as to boundary-conditions of risk to be accepted, one must not stop, except at a risk-boundary, until the objective has been reached. If one must turn back from a boundary of that sort one day, one must return to the objective the next, and so on, until that objective has ultimately been reached, or until one has learned, by a process analogous to scientific discovery, that that was an improper objective. One must be ever intrepid in life in that sense, and one will profit from those exercises, such as hill- or mountain-climbing. in which one’s body and will are trained accordingly.

The second principle illustrated by mountain-climbing, most emphatically, is the principle of a necessary global overview of the defined task. One must not be such a fool as merely to hie off, letting one blind step follow another.

One must, from the outset, conceptualize that waiting mountain as a whole, in such a way as to define the intended process of successfully climbing it. This serves one as a global hypothesis, precisely analogous to a scientific hypothesis respecting the function this global hypothesis performs during the course of the undertaking. One must not continue blindly to a certain course of approach, merely because one has selected that earlier. One must be prepared to alter one's attack upon the objective by the same method of judgment employed for applying an hypothesis to scientific experiment and observation. It is the objective which is one's purpose, not any selection of means or pathways previously thought to be an appropriate approach to that objective. Sometimes, if a rigorously scientific comprehension of the experience demands this, the global hypothesis guides us through cumulative learning in the process of assault, to modify a choice of objectives, to, so to speak, "change the rules of the game."

Persons of such developed habits one must prefer among senior non-commissioned officers, as well as junior officers and unit-commanders. There is an approximation of *Entschlossenheit* in a rationally intrepid, global-hypotheses approach of the sort appropriate to mountain-climbing. Such qualities approximate the requirements of intelligence officers and political leaders.

The British oligarchical elite understands and applies this training-principle, but with one very significant point of difference. It would be instructive, that a seminar including in large part, reflective and capable military combat and logistics senior officers, compare British military command, to various levels and types of military operations, with exemplary cases of American traditionalist and Prussian practice. The British command tends to develop excellence for a certain kind of shock-troop deployment, but as illustrated by the case of Field Marshal Haig in World War I, or Montgomery in World War II, or Wellington at Waterloo and in command of the Mexican forces of General Santa Ana against Winfield Scott et al., the British repeatedly exhibit, with some few notable exceptions (like the early defeat of the foolishly commanded Italian forces during the first phase of the World War II North African campaign), a kind of strategic incompetence which has been repeatedly viewed contemptuously by traditionalist U.S. commanders. The manner in which General Douglas MacArthur outwitted the British in winning the war against the forces of Japan, is a single illustration of the point. This specific strategic incompetence of the British is reflected in a distinction in application of the training-principle.

The British win wars against capable adversaries only if capable Prussian or U.S. traditionalist commanders are given their head in conducting the war. Hence, a prudent President would never permit a war to be conducted according to NATO policy or under a NATO command.

Although the British appear to apply the training-principle we have cited--the notorious aphorism concerning the "playing-fields of Eton"--the variety of global hypothesis governing such training-activity has crucial distinctions in character, distinctions coherent with the bloodily monstrous incompetence of a Haig and set-piece lunacies of a Montgomery or Wellington.

Watch what we are doing carefully, dear reader, we are employing the Socratic method of classical tragedy once more here. Be prepared for abrupt demonstrations of the scientific validity of that method which is being developed here.

The excellence the Prussian command developed during the 19th century focuses our attention on that which is crucial within the American traditionalist military training and policy.

First, at the Battle of Jena, the forces under the command of Napoleon Bonaparte destroyed the Prussian Army and the Prussian state. Napoleon's forces destroyed much more. Napoleon's victory swept the 18th-century set-piece, or "cabinet " warfare training and strategic doctrine from existence on the battlefields of Europe. Napoleon, although in part an asset of oligarchical forces himself, destroyed the principles of war-fighting characteristic of the application of the oligarchical mind to military aspects of statecraft.

In a very deep sense, the new design of warfare engineered by the great Lazare Carnot from 1793 onward, had been placed in the hands of Bonaparte, producing a consequence analogous in all fundamentals to Alexander the Great's destruction of the military forces and political order of the Persian Empire. Without discounting Bonaparte's somewhat exaggerated reputation unduly, the essence of Jena was not Bonaparte's genius, but the genius of Carnot. This is no moot point, no mere matter of contested opinion. Without grasping the implications of the distinction we have emphasized here, there can be no competent grasp of any of the principal features of military and general history since 1793.

To comprehend the implications of Jena, including the new design of the Prussian state by the students and collaborators of Friedrich Schiller, one must grasp the world significance of the 1766 transatlantic conspiracy, organized and led by the titanic Benjamin Franklin, and the combination of worldwide forces which effected our great humiliation of the evil British at Yorktown, and the further humiliation of those British in the signing of the Paris Treaty of 1783. (If one imagines that the British oligarchy has ever forgiven us for that, one understands absolutely nothing of the mind of that oligarchy.)

Whence the genius of the Prussian military command from 1809-1810 onwards?

In the aftermath of the ruinous Thirty Years War of 1618-1648, the Great Elector of Prussia transformed the unlikely cabbage-patch known as Prussia into what became a great, feared European power during the 18th century. He accomplished this chiefly by an act of religious toleration which recruited French Huguenots and Jews to build a great culture in the northern regions of Germany, setting into motion a combined development of Prussia and

Rhineland Germany which extended as far south as the embattled outpost from whence von Cotta and Schiller came, Stuttgart. This set into motion the potentials of Gottfried Leibniz's driving influence creating in Germany a great, new republican force opposed to those contrary, oligarchical impulses tending to dominate the Prussian court, oligarchical impulses from Britain, from the Swiss Protestant precincts, and Venetian impulses mediated through the Austro-Hungarian and Bavarian oligarchies.

It was the oligarchical faction in Prussia which was discredited in the most devastating fashion at Jena. In this circumstance, a circle of the allies, co-conspirators and students of Friedrich Schiller, exemplified by Wilhelm von Humboldt, exercised their opportunity to seize leadership of, and to reconstruct the Prussian state and military policy according to a republican design.

This republican design had been forged out of the materials created by Colbert, Leibniz and their predecessors. It had been forged into becoming a new quality of world power for good through assembling itself to the common objective established as the adopted goal of that far-flung conspiracy which Benjamin Franklin forged beginning 1766: the conspiracy to realize the potentials of Cardinal Richelieu's collaboration with the Commonwealth (republican) party of England, the quasi-autonomous, republican English-speaking colonies of North America, to create a new, model constitutional republic, which would become, as described in the later words of Gilbert Marquis de LaFayette, a "temple of liberty" and "beacon of hope" for the republican forces of the Old World. In Germany, Friedrich Schiller, together with such musicians as Wolfgang Mozart and Ludwig van Beethoven, was the leading pro-American conspirator of the period of the French Revolution and its immediate aftermath.

From 1793 onward, the outstanding republican figure of science and politics of Europe was France's Lazare Carnot. Carnot applied French science and the experience and impulse of the creation of the constitutional United States to unleash the greatest single explosion of combined scientific, industrial and military development in the known history of mankind for any comparable brief period.

What Carnot had designed, subsuming in a more general way his revolution in war-fighting as such, placed in the hands of Napoleon, destroyed Prussia. Napoleon could be defeated only by Carnot and Schiller combined. The Prussian reformers' adoption of Carnot's principles of war-fighting design, and their employment of Schiller's studies of the Thirty Years War, including his Wallenstein dramas, to set, bait and close the Russian trap for Napoleon (despite that evil liar Tolstoy's account of the matter), destroyed Napoleon. Despite the successfully combined efforts of Venice, the Hapsburgs and British, at the 1815 Treaty of Vienna's sessions, in exiling Freiherr vom Stein from direct political leadership in Germany, the Prussian military, established by the reformers, became a prominent protecting institution for fostering the republican faction in Germany, even despite the power of Bismarck.

The global-hypothesis approach in the Prussian military

practice is exemplified by Schlieffen's strategic designs.

Schlieffen's design *for defeating Britain* under conditions France and Belgium became tools of Britain, would have won World War I against Britain and France but for interference in execution of the assault from the Prussian court. The final, war-winning assault was delayed on pretext of dynastic considerations, affording France the opportunity to rally and entrench, and for Marshal Haig to proceed with his attempt to depopulate the young manhood of Britain on the battlefields of France.

In World War II, the Prussian military under Nazi command executed the same operation successfully against France, but this time Hitler personally intervened to prevent the Prussians from destroying the British forces at Dunkirk and to divert the Luftwaffe into a strategically absurd engagement over the anti-aircraft shooting-gallery of London. Hitler had intervened to save the Britain of his beloved mentor, the anti-Semite Houston Stewart Chamberlain.

With a few, spoiling omissions, and the folly of accepting Jomini's Swiss point of reference, the model of Carnot was adopted by Commandant Sylvanus Thayer as the new, brilliant phase of development of West Point as a center for the technological, as well as military development of the power of the United States.

Meanwhile, Britain characteristically created an earldom for that bungling butcher Haig whose family gave us the Alexander Haig of recent State Department notoriety.

The folly of British strategic practice is embedded in that which directly impinges upon the minds and rules of the game for playing on the fields of Eton. We must never permit our population to be degraded to the level of British conceptions of sportsmanship. Winning games according to pre-set, oligarchical rules works only under conditions that no clever fellow, or simply the unfolding of circumstances, changes the rules in mid-game.

British command could never win militarily an honest war against a capable adversary. The British win wars, over the long run, by coopting Americans or Prussians to fight them, and then swindling the Americans and Prussians. The British exploit the implications of wars fought, preferably, by others. But, like their Venetian predecessors and teachers, the British play their real game for power on a different level than the present design of our nation's foreign and strategic policy even begins to imagine exists. With those words, we circumscribe the "Toynbee Factor."

Lest one doubt the empirical evidence we have assembled by means of reference here, consider this simple fact. Already, under Carnot, French masses of fire of newly designed mobile field artillery, and a reordering of the arms of battle to match, had proven conclusively what was proven afresh at Jena. Why, in general, have the British rather fanatically insisted on adhering to precisely those conceptions of warfare which were demolished on the field of battle over the period from the war with the United States during 1776-1683, and in more devastating fashion, by forces of Carnot, Bonaparte and the Prussian republican reformers, during the wars of 1793-1814?

Examine the Crimean War. Examine the obscenely outmoded deployment of British forces in the Boer War. Examine Winston Churchill's bloody folly in the straits during World War I. Examine the obscenely incompetent and bloody conduct of Field Marshal Haig during World War I. Examine Churchill's miserable insistence on the "soft underbelly" of Europe during the last world war--which, together with related British nonsense, extended the war at least one year longer than would have been the case had U.S. military leaders had their head in the matter.

More recently, this writer and his associates had the opportunity to observe from a most advantageous position the recent war-fighting in the South Atlantic. But for four conspicuous factors, Argentina would have given Britain the bloodiest nose since World War II experiences. These factors were, in order of importance bearing directly on the conclusion of that phase of the affair: (1) Argentinian leaders' fear that executing a battle-victory over British forces would trigger direct U.S. military deployment in full force against Argentina; (2) British hunter-killer nuclear-powered submarines plus combined forms of logistical and intelligence support to the British in this matter; (3) The political factor of the pro-British Tradition, Family and Property, "Blue Army" faction inside Argentina; and, (4) The late-phase equipping of British ground forces with U.S. weaponry more advanced than that presently supplied to our own forces.

Examination of some of the most conspicuous features of British naval and air task-force deployment is also instructive. What sort of an idiot constructs aluminum-based superstructure on a frigate deployed under modern conditions? In combat against Soviet forces, the entire British naval capability, excepting submarines, would vanish from further consideration within minutes of the outbreak of war-fighting. In serious war-fighting, the British might prove even to be a net liability to the military capabilities led by the United States; only a few items of British capability would be salvageable as auxiliary elements of a serious war-fighting deployment--a most invaluable military ally, indeed! The French military is, of course, a rather different proposition, as are the forces of the Federal Republic of Germany.

Consider also, a closely related and most important development among the eminently debatable features of our own and NATO posture. Firstly, according to the so-called "Kissinger doctrine," our essential strategic posture is one of strategic psychological warfare, not an actual strategic war-fighting capability, but only a doomsday capability. From McNamara onward we have drifted into what James R. Schlesinger, in 1976, aptly described (and also supported) publicly as the "aura of power," rather than the substance of capability.

Secondly, within this general setting of a literally lunatic strategic NATO doctrine overall, we have NATO MC 14{4, and the related, so-called Schlesinger Doctrine for nuclear-augmented theater-limited war-fighting in the gambited

European theater. In reality, any forward-based nuclear assault against the forces of the Soviet Union means immediate thermonuclear "knock-out" response against the territory of the fifty U.S.A. states. What is that utter lunacy of Schlesinger's, except the direct imitation, in a thermonuclear setting, of the same "cabinet warfare" doctrine demolished on the battlefield of Jena?

Now, we have the obscene folly promoted by our British convert, General Maxwell Taylor, a commitment to fighting wars to reduce population and seize raw materials below the Tropic of Cancer--indeed, if this is adopted, U.S. power is falling rapidly below its equinox. Maxwell Taylor's proposals, which some among our liberal congressmen appear to have been hoodwinked into tolerating, are not described with undue exaggeration as a scheme for fighting "limited," colonial wars of depopulation, relying on a drift toward such "Space Wars" gadgetry as electronically enhanced bow-and-arrow weapons-systems.

Under British influence, our drift in strategic policy first became absurd, and now becomes insane.

Admittedly, as we shall demonstrate more rigorously a bit later in this report, the British are not quite as stupid as some among their military policies might cause them to appear. Dr. Teller's and the Soviet development of deployable H-bombs presented the British with a double strategic problem. Within an H-bomb-dominated war-fighting regime, the British and Venice could not attempt to deal with the continental European "problem" as they had in orchestrating the eruption of World Wars I and II. This meant that actual war-fighting between the superpower alliances was excluded unless the Soviet Union could be induced to accept, with assuring indications they had in fact accepted this, a "limited nuclear war-fighting" option. The alternative to this arrangement would be the development of the more advanced forms of potential weapons-systems by which H-bomb bombardment could be destroyed (chiefly) in mid-flight. Except to the degree it was discovered that Soviet developments were moving in the direction of such systems, the British did everything possible, including exerting its veto-rights over U.S. research-and-development policies, as in the "Rudakov affair," to prevent serious work on advanced weapons-systems potentialities.

In short, British policy vacillates between Bertrand Russell's motives for peevishly walking out of Lord Alfred Milner's group in 1902--and Russell's policy after Soviet development of the H-bomb, and a policy of keeping ahead of the Soviets in the directions of advanced weapons-systems development, the Soviets are moving.

A total assessment of British military policies must include this consideration as a very weighty factor in determining the character of the policy as a whole. This is also key to the intrinsic absurdity of viewing strategic-arms-limitation negotiations as having any bearing on the issues of war or peace. These negotiations bear on Soviet desires to reduce the burden of arms-expenditures upon their economy, on which point some Soviet currents are most passionate. They bear, from the NATO side of the table, on a continuing, British-sponsored probing in search of a Soviet capitulation to the possibility of a "limited nuclear war" option, *an 18th century "cabinet warfare" option in the thermonuclear age!*

The aspect of this matter being developed here is the crucial role of "the playing-fields of Eton" in shaping British thinking to the effects described. Given the massive amount of time and emotion our population gives to commercial spectator-sports, it should be implicit for us that to the extent the image of those sports is characterized by a principle congruent with the "Eton principle," the thinking of our population generally, as well as our makers and influencers of policy, must tend to view a British-like approach to foreign and military policies as "natural," as a "common sense" approach.

What, then, is the difference between republican and British forms of sports?

As we emphasized from the outset of this present phase of our inquiry, there are aspects of sports and related activities which are of great benefit to the *participants* in those sports: the development of the body as an instrument of the creative powers of mind, through the forms of stress of body and will which are both health-restoring and which are governed by the principles of *intrepidity* and *global hypothesis*. Such sports and sports-like activities also benefit spectators on condition that the spectators project from themselves into the players those same principles: stress directed by the creative powers of mind, and characterized by intrepidity and the principle of global hypothesis.

The essence of such sports and sports-like activities is developing "a love for" kinds of physical (and "emotional") stress which are useful to service of the creative functions of the mind. Code words chosen for this might be "break-through," "new horizons," and so forth: words and phrases which reveal an implicit connection between sports-like achievements and creative scientific discovery.

In the "Eton" case, we have, of course, the factor of stress and a certain form of *intrepidity*. In such facets of the matter, British sportsmen--amateur and professional--and British military capabilities may appear sometimes to be outstanding in performance.

What is missing? What are missing are (stress subject to) the *creative powers of mind* and the *principle of global hypothesis*. *Position* dominates at the expense of *mobile development; positioned engagement* replaces the principle of global hypothesis of republican military strategy.

In a republican system, the sports-system is based on childhood and amateur sports and sports-like activities. These activities are ordered, by aid of guidance or "coaching," to emphasize, in effect: stress governed by creative powers of imagination, in which the accomplishment of the imagination is the source of joy associated with the achievements of physical stress directed by imagination. These are otherwise characterized by joy of becoming intrepid, and by the joy of succeeding by aid of application of a global hypothesis. At the top of the sports-system, so to speak, are the outstanding amateurs plus those professionals who reflect the highest standards of achievement according to again: imagination-directed stress for the purposes of the imagination, exceptionally well-developed powers of intrepidity, and a global-hypothesis-directed approach to solving the problems to be overcome in reaching the objective. It is in the knowledgeable witnessing of achievement of leading amateurs and professionals, in which amateurs focus upon this specific form of achievement, that spectator-sports have a beneficial function for populations.

The body is treated as if from the standpoint of medical science and the standpoint of Leonardo da Vinci respecting Platonic, harmonic ordering of the capabilities of living processes. The body's development of its capacities to serve an end determined by the imagination becomes a scientific experiment. The scientific subject of the experiment is, immediately the growth-potentials and associated bio-thermodynamical principles of metabolism under stressful energy-using activity. "If I wish to achieve this or that intellectual development of my powers in physical practice, how may I develop my body, through direction by means of stress, to provide me and to maintain such necessary capabilities for that mental purpose? What might those of us engaged in this spoil discover in respect to previously under-appreciated potentialities of this sort?"

The deeper implications of this point are more easily grasped by the reader by drawing attention to the proper meaning of the term "cowardice" in respect to sports and sports-like activities. To focus upon what is often denoted as "physical cowardice" is to miss the crucial point. *Fear of one's own creative-mental potentials is the essence of the matter*, the variety of cowardice associated with inability to act, in face of popular prejudice (for example), on the assurance of reason. Fear to exercise those creative qualities of mind which one anticipates will tend to impel one to act contrary to popular prejudice (for example).

In these respects, our political leaders and our people generally have become monstrously *cowardly* over the recent, post-war decades. We lack what Clausewitz attempted to circumscribe with his term *Entschlossenheit*. We have become, on this point, a nation *mortally incompetent* to fight war or to execute with resolution and promptness rationally determined policies determined to be in our most vital interests as a nation. The way we have accustomed ourselves to view commercial sports is a major contributing influence in promoting this drift into cowardice.

The Eton Principle is the principle of the Roman circus-arena under the Emperor Nero. It is a Hobbesian game, ordered according to that Hobbesian principle of self-degradation which Kissinger attributed to the British, and passionately embraced as his own, speaking in London on May 10, 1982. It is individuals or small groups ("teams"), "each in war against all." It is a game performed according to a fixed set of rules and successful cheating. Men and women are degraded into beasts, at best, rather clever beasts of prey. At the end, the Emperor Nero signals "thumbs up" or "thumbs down." So, in our British-influenced sports-practice, we retain the tradition of Nero, and this spills over into our daily life. "Thumbs up," the British say of their sports and life in general as well.

We have been transforming our professional sports into a parody of the Roman arena under Nero, the Eton Principle. We saturate ourselves as a people with such forms of valuation placed upon spectator-sports. The Hobbesian character of the game, and the anti-intellectual influence of strict "rules of the game plus successful cheating" becomes to a large degree our way of mental life. Winning, "by sticking to rules augmented by successful cheating" becomes increasingly our conduct of national and local elections, and this fact obliges our candidates to defer to those who control the rigging and alteration of election-results.

The effect of this upon our national character our national ideology, is very great. The British, smirkingly of course, have taken great pleasure in observing this fact, and in conducting, through the Tavistock Institute and its international psychoanalytical and other networks, numerous experiments and observations of this phenomenon, upon that experimental animal known to us as the American people. The British, particularly at the Tavistock animal-training center where Kissinger's education was completed, usually refer to this pathetic condition of our national ideology as the "Cowboy Ethic." It is, not so incidentally, the psycho-profile which Tavistock executives reported to this writer's undercover investigators as the basis for their manipulation of President Ronald Reagan and his California circles. The British, and accomplices including both Kissinger and Haig, have observably followed that Tavistock script, and our administration has been repeatedly successfully manipulated by exploitation of the script specified by Tavistock.

The Hollywood "cowboy" is a mythical being. That cowboy never really existed until cowboys began to watch Hollywood movies. Place the Hollywood cowboys and Indians, the Hollywood cowboys and rustlers, and so forth, in Nero's Roman arena, and the nature of the myth ought to be clear to all of us immediately. It is the Hobbesian principle, expressed as intrepidly winning the game, "being a winner," by a combination of appearing to play entirely according to the rules while successfully cheating.

It is most instructive to compare some of the "classical" Hollywood cowboy-epics, such as the *Rio Bravo* featuring the late John Wayne, with the more recent *Urban Cowboy*. These are each an image of ourselves, of our acquired national character. Yet, although the two cited cases have a generally common character, the contrast between the two exhibits the manner and the degree to which we have degenerated as a people since the "classical period" of the 1950s and early 1960s.

The British, who have abused us, corrupted us, and now mock us as "the unofficial colony," overlook one very important fact. We have the power to change ourselves, to become once again what the 1787 Constitution and the circumstances of its creation exemplify. We, the gladiators, need not forever reenact once more that bloody show which amuses our British Neros. We gladiators can awaken our minds, and charge out of the arena, back into reality. We can slay Nero.

3.

Meet Arnold Toynbee

During the Second World War, a very distinguished Senator and leading military officials reflected on the observed fact that each time the United States thought itself to introduce some policy to its ever-loving British ally, the British had advance knowledge of this policy, and had completed and did present a fully-staff-elaborated set of countermeasures to prevent the American policy from being executed. Worse, returning to home-base from such conferences, the American officials would find elements of the U.S. government already fully deployed to sabotage the U.S. proposal, and to impose the British counterproposal.

One of the most notable instances of this sort of British practice was the bloody, immoral exercise Churchill conducted, deliberately sending Canadian troops and others to die in a deliberately botched mission, Dieppe, which the British intended to be a bloody fiasco. The point of this particular obscenity was to persuade the United States that an assault on the north of the European continent was a "mistake" at that time. So, the British gave Hitler a year more in which to pour more concrete along the northern French coastal defenses than has perhaps ever been poured since in any single undertaking.

The Senator and the military officials had good cause to wonder at many developments falling under the same general category.

Broadly speaking, the British oligarchy always seems to win, in a process which the British amuse themselves to describe, tongue in cheek, as "muddling through, somehow."

The problem here is not merely the British oligarchy as such. The British are a special sub-section of a larger entity, complementing a "Central European" oligarchical collection of aristocratic and rentier-financier "families". These are essentially the outgrowth of the ruling families of Venice. Excepting the different but connected case of Peking China, an ancient oligarchical system waving the Communist flag, the British oligarchy (with its Commonwealth extensions), plus the colonial "families" of the United States' branch of the British oligarchy overall, represent a special function within the oligarchy as a whole. At times, the internal life of the alliance among oligarchical "families" displays its intrinsically Hobbesian characteristics, with a rash of mafia-like waves of assassinations and counter-assassinations, and associated devices of squabbling over one of the issues which emerges over on that other side of the fence from the human race generally. This larger indication is to be borne in mind as we continue to focus upon the British aspect of the collection here. By "British" we usually mean, as the context implies, the larger collection. Moreover, this applies with special force to assessment of British capabilities against the United States, including most emphatically Swiss finance.

The British oligarchy does not "muddle through." It is *pragmatic* in method of application of its policies, but there is nothing random-like in the development and deployment of those policies as such. The British oligarchy is a lying, ruthless, fanatically single-minded band of criminals, vastly knowledgeable, and obsessed by such centuries-old objectives as completing the obliteration of the United States as a sovereign nation-state. Pamela Churchill Harriman's stated commitment to ripping up the Constitution of the United States reflects merely a corner of overall British policy concerning us.

During 1978, the British reacted publicly against certain of the efforts of this writer and his associates. The nature of the issue, as the reader shall soon see for himself, was such that we at first could not understand such a rapid, rather violent and public reaction of that sort on a matter of historical issues relating to times so ancient. Our curiosity was aroused, to say the least. Our sustained curiosity led us to a range of discoveries, during the course of which we discovered the significance of what had been earlier for us merely an amusingly curious fact. What prompted the British to place the historian Arnold Toynbee at the head of British foreign intelligence during a most-crucial period? What special sort of knowledge and skills did Toynbee the historian represent which suited him particularly for that sort of responsibility?

In fact, the case of Arnold Toynbee merely illustrates a broader phenomenon within the British Secret Intelligence Service's policy-shaping activities to back earlier than

Britain itself, back into the Genoese, treasonous faction within Elizabethan England, the faction around the Cecils which brought James I to power in 1603 through such bloody intelligence-operations as Cecil's Francis Bacon's corruption and destruction of the adolescent Earl of Essex. David Hume is a predecessor in the type of policy-shaping function performed by Toynbee. So was Walter Scott, Hume's successor at the Edinburgh headquarters of SIS. A related function was performed by the British agent Montesquieu in France, at a lower level by the British agent Voltaire, by the British-Swiss agents in charge of the French Encyclopaedia project of the 18th century, by the putative one-time competitor, the historian Edward Gibbon, of William Pitt the Younger for the hand-in-marriage of the daughter of Jacques Necker, the notorious Madame de Staël, (Necker was the British-allied Swiss agent who destroyed the finances of France, Volcker-style, triggering the French Revolution, and the political backer of the Jacobin Terror, the Duke of Orleans, Franklin's old enemy.) Toynbee merely exemplifies this sort of tradition, but with a special feature of emphasis added.

We interpolated, during our examination of the sports question, that the British operate against us in dimensions of *efficient practice* which are unknown to the content and adoption of the foreign and military policies of the United States. It would not be inappropriate to say that the British hoodwink us repeatedly and cumulatively by "coming up on our blind side." The nature of that "blind spot" in our national character generally is illustrated by the resentment among numerous readers of this report against our style and our emphasis upon certain classes of phenomena. Most of us believe that looking at matters in the way we do in this report is variously "outrageous," "not practical," "pretty weird," and so forth. That demonstrates our point about the British exactly. That popular resentment against the style of this report indicates the typically American "blind side" against which the British deploy their usually and cumulatively successful work of destroying us inch-by-inch.

This is the key to the problem which attracted the remarks of the distinguished Senator during the course of the last world war. Until we both see our national "practical" ideology as an ideology, recognize the "blind side" implications of that ideology, we can not see the aspect of social processes toward which efficient British oligarchical actions are addressed.

The British, left to their own military devices, would lose every war fought against capable adversaries. The British appear to have lost an Empire spanning most of the globe in the form of colonies and semi-colonies such as China. Yet, in this process of appearing incapable of winning wars of importance, in this process of seeming to lose their imperial power, amid the putrifying rubble of their Thatcher-ruined island, they appear to be taking over most of the world, including us.

We are riding, seated next the British, in a conveyance of some sort. In every game played within that conveyance, our characteristically "American" way of solving "practical problems" can outmatch the British every time. Yet, the British are defeating us, even to the point of making our nation Britain's fawning slave. How is this done? "You see, dear fellow, we are controlling the conveyance which we are about to send over the edge of the cliff. Must leave you now," and our British acquaintance, our ever-loving ally, departs our company, leaving us to our doom.

Precisely on what level do the British operate against us? "What is this conveyance to which you referred just now?" The "conveyance," dear fellow-citizen, is our national culture, our evolving (downward) national ideology.

It we have astonished our readers considerably earlier, we are about to "really shock the pants off" most among you with what we do next at this point in our report. Be patient with us on this point: as you shall see rather quickly, your patience will be richly rewarded. The included benefit will include the needed redefinition of the fundamental strategic problem now confronting us, and a subsumed solution to the perplexing problem of Communism.

We take your attention back a short distance to mid-1978. Repeatedly, the British press attacked us obliquely but prominently, denouncing some implicit, mysterious agency which was circulating ideas about ancient history which, the British informed their readers, they were obliged to denounce prominently and promptly in a most vigorous fashion. Subsumed as part of this general deployment by the British were the activities of a miserable little, decaying ex-journalist, I. F. Stone, writing in the *New York Times* from Greece, and later demanding the execution of Socrates on the lecture-stump in the United States. (We believe even the wicked little I. F. Stone knew at the time that Socrates had already been executed about 2.400 years ago. With fellows like Stone, one can never be quite certain on some points. Perhaps Stone regarded this writer as a reincarnation of Socrates. If Stone suspects me of metempsychosis, he may be assured that the only psychosis involved is his own.)

This public effusion of venom and Stone-throwing in our direction was complemented by some rather nasty-minded private actions of a secret-intelligence variety, in which the implications of Socrates were communicated quite efficiently to us as the point of the matter.

We first situate the issue prompting this bilious explosion of British flatulence, and so situating the matter in respect to the preceding development of this report, we turn directly to the issue itself.

It should not be required that we demonstrate the point that history is a history of conflict. Karl Marx was sweepingly wrong; history is not a "history of class struggles." Struggle, yes, but not defined in terms of "classes" as Marx insists on his view. Conflict between what, then? Between various assortments of forces? On the surface, perhaps so. It is not only an error, but the most dangerous error a republic could perpetuate to assume that the immediately apparent conflicts between nations and so forth necessarily embody in themselves the determining issues of the real conflict in process. Therein lies the tragic inadequacy of our anti-Soviet ideology. What underlies, stands behind and above, and permeates the forces unleashed in the form of the general struggles characterizing entire periods of history as a whole? It is on this point, our national-ideological self-delusion on this point, that the British have had us, have sent us rolling down to the edge of the precipice, during this post-war period. What is the basic conflict? Does each age and region of the world experience a peculiar form of conflict, more or less unconnected in characteristic features from that of a preceding period--as Karl Marx argues fallaciously? Or, is the entire sweep of known history and known pre-history the unfolding of a single issue of conflict?

That states the nub of the question of statecraft.

For the past 2,500 years and somewhat longer, the entirety of the conflict within Middle East and European civilization's development has been only one underlying issue. Early during this 2,500- year span, the conflict was in the form of wars between Greece and the Persian Empire. About 2,000 years ago, with the eruption of the ministry of Jesus Christ during the time of Philo of Alexandria, as the opening verses of the Gospel according to St. John establish this, the republicanism of Greece, its scientific method, its science of statecraft, was subordinated to Christianity, an arrangement as this is elaborated by St. Augustine. That configuration as elaborated by St. Augustine, defines Judeo-Christian republicanism. For 2,000 years to date, the solely determining conflict within European civilization, including our 1776-1783 war with Britain, has been a struggle of the forces of Judeo-Christian republicanism against the law, the immorality, and the religious outlook associated with the Republic and Empire of Rome.

These two periods of conflict are of one piece. The issues defining the conflict were elaborated in the written form surviving for scrutiny today during the 4th century B.C., during and immediately following the lifetime of Plato. The issues between Christianity and Nero, between us and Britain in 1776-1783, are the identical issues for the outline of the matter in Greek-language correspondence written during the 4th century B.C. from the island of Rhodes (chiefly).

The center of the opposition to Plato's faction during that period was a group of pagan-priestly and rentier-financier "families" called during that time and other periods variously the "Phoenicians," "Chaldeans," "Magi" ("The Magicians"), or "Mobeds." At that time, until Alexander the Great conquered that city, they were based at Tyre, but were otherwise spread throughout the Persian Empire, as priests and tax-farmers, as well as controllers of commerce, controlling the Persian monarchy and its satrapies from within. They also controlled, in mainland Greece, the Phoenician colony of Thebes, and nearby and allied to Thebes, the Delphi Temple and Cult of Apollo.

The strategic problem occupying these Phoenicians' attention at that time was the persisting failure of the

Persians to conquer mainland Greece. Greek culture and military science, fostered for about four hundred years by the Cyrenaic Temple of Amon (the most ancient and highest form of advancement of Egyptian culture), could not be matched militarily by the Persians. If there had ever been doubts on this point, the march of "The Ten Thousand" Greek soldiers through the heart of the Persian Empire back to Greece left no margin for quibbling on the point.

In this setting, these oligarchical priests and usurers concocted a scheme they entitled "The Western Division of the Persian Empire." They assigned their agent, King Philip of Macedon to conduct a two-step operation to bring this proposed empire into being. First, aided by subversion and provocations by such paid agents of Philip as Demosthenes and the Delphi cult's Aristotle (the "check-stubs" survive to the present date), the Greek states were to be provoked into wars with Philip one by one, much as Delphi had orchestrated the long Peloponnesian wars earlier. Once Philip had conquered Greece piecemeal, he was to lead an army of approximately 25,000 Macedonian and Greek troops, through Western Anatolia, down to the vicinity of the Cilician gates, to fight a prearranged battle with the Persian forces there. During a negotiated truce in the midst of that prearranged battle, the Persian ruler would be treated to "crisis-management" influence by the Phoenicians. The ruler would award to King Philip that portion of his empire to the west of the Euphrates River plus a corresponding western portion of Anatolia. Philip was then to extend the newly-gained empire westward to conquer the entire Mediterranean region. This would constitute the "Western Division of the Persian Empire."

The political order inside this new empire was prespecified in letters from Rhodes. The internal social and political order was to be what was alternately named the "Persian Model" or the "Oligarchical Model." Those specifications define the proper, generic usage of the term *oligarchism* down to the present time.

The conflict of these ages has been the struggle of the forces of *republicanism* against the forces of *oligarchism.*

A few additional historical observations are required to situate the broader definition of oligarchism.

On approximately the eve of Philip's departure to take command of the troops already encamped in Anatolia, he was assassinated. Plato had died earlier, but Plato's Academy at Athens, the think tank and command-center for Greek republican resistance against the Persian Empire and the Phoenicians, was very much alive and in full force. They picked a protégé of the Temple of Amon, one of Philip's sons and the enemy of Aristotle, Alexander, to become King of Macedon. The combined, allied forces of the Academy and Temple of Amon won the near-civil-war over the Macedonia succession.

Staffed by representatives of the Academy and aided by the intelligence-services of both the Academy and the Temple of Amon, Alexander quickly consolidated his position in Macedon, and left to take command of his father's waiting troops in Anatolia.

He liberated the Ionian city-states, restored their constitutions, and created for his growing domain the first modern form of central treasury and currency system, marching, reenforced by Greek Ionians, to defeat the Persian satrapal and imperial forces in successive battles, including the prearranged battle. The prearranged offer of the Western Division was made as the Phoenicians had planned. Alexander rejected the offer, and continued on to conquer Phoenicia, destroying Tyre with direct assistance in this from the same Temple of Amon which organized an insurrection overthrowing Persian satrapal rule in Egypt. After secret counsel with the priests in the Temple of Amon, Alexander proceeded to the battles in which he destroyed the Persian hordes, and in the succeeding developments, established his own empire.

In the document sometimes referred to as the testament of Alexander the Great, there is outlined the plan for the completion of the great republican city-building program Alexander had begun on such an astonishing scale during the few years of his rule.

There are two known attempts to assassinate Alexander by poisoning. The first, unsuccessful attempt directly involved the nephew of Aristotle, with evidence that Aristotle (whose botanical skills were chiefly those of a trained poisoner) had prepared and forwarded the toxin. The second attempt succeeded. (There are documents which attempt to discredit surviving records concerning the fact and circumstances of the assassination, but the later manufactured denials are probably hoaxes in that they refer to conclusive evidence premised on a temple which did not exist until decades after Alexander's death.)

The Macedonian generals, most of whom had been political allies of Philip in the "Persian Model" plot, tore apart the empire, dividing it into satrapies according to the Persian Model. However, the destruction of the Phoenicians' power by Alexander prevented the projected Western Division from being set into motion until the plan concocted during the 4th century B.C. was finally accomplished with the launching of the Roman Empire according to those specifications as to "Model."

Rome, according to Livius, had been controlled by the Rome branch of the Temple of Apollo from earliest historical times. Rome had conquered its Italian-speaking and Greek neighbors by the same methods the Delphi temple had employed in orchestrating the Peloponnesian Wars and in Philip's piecemeal conquest of Greece. St. Augustine's commentaries on Roman culture are to be referred to for more on this matter.

Under the Empire, Rome underwent depopulation as a result of Roman social and economic-practices. The moral decay was more rapid, as the case of Nero exemplifies. In 313, Constantine moved the capital of the Empire to the center of the reduced population of the Empire as a whole, Greece. Unable to crush Christianity, Constantine attempted to coopt it and corrupt it from the top, through such instruments as the Arius he made Bishop. The Roman oligarchical families attempted to flood the church hierarchy with retreaded priests from pagan cults.

Christianity was assaulted now from within the Church as also from without.

Within Byzantium, the oligarchical families attempted to destroy Judeo-Christian republican impulses by repeated attempts to outlaw the Greek language. The fight for and against the teaching and literature of classical Greek complemented the fight over the religious issues and issues of statecraft.

The central point of attack against Christianity was against the co-substantiality of Christ within the Trinity, the keystone in Apostolic Christian doctrine for the sacredness and divinity of the potential within the human person, and for the development of that potential through ordering society to that effect: republicanism. St. Augustine emerged as the rallying point for defense of Christianity throughout the world. Augustinian Christianity the defense of Christ's co-consubstantiality (the *Filioque* of the Latin Catholic liturgy), became the central political issue. It was no mere religious dispute in the sense ignorant persons often regard it. On this distinction hangs every feature of Christian civilization, as to statecraft in general, as to public and private morality, and as to economic practices by implication, such as the outlawing of usury as an abominable wickedness to be crushed wherever it appears.

Wars were fought to defend Western civilization against efforts of Eastern Rite's oligarchical currents in its hierarchies to stamp out the *Filioque*. These pseudo-Christian priests launched wars as distant as invasions of France during the 8th century A.D. The formal split between Catholics and Eastern Rite in 1024 A.D. was merely an inconclusive culmination of this continuing struggle.

The Byzantine oligarchical families had two principal colonies, analogous to the Phoenicians' Thebes and Delphi earlier, in Italy: Venice (primarily) and Genoa (secondly). As upsurges against the oligarchical rule erupted in the Greek-speaking populations of Byzantium, Venice's role as a secondary world-capital for the Byzantine oligarchy developed. With the rise of the Paleologues, Venice became the world-capital for the Byzantine oligarchy and its allies among the surviving remnants of old imperial oligarchical families, such as the Colonnas, in Rome. It was Venice which organized the Ottoman conquest of Constantinople in 1453, in repayment for which Venice and the Eastern Rite ran the Ottoman Empire increasingly from the inside, as the Phoenicians had controlled the Persian Empire from the inside earlier.

It was Venetian-Genoese political operations, complemented by Volcker-like usurious practices of Lombard bankers such as the Bardi and Peruzzi, which nearly destroyed civilization over approximately a century from the mid-13 into the late-middle of the 14th century. It was during this period that Venice promoted the rise of power of the Hapsburgs in Austria and the Holy Roman Empire. The Hapsburg Austro-Hungarian Empire is a Venetian puppet to the present date, including extensive Venetian operations, many run through Vienna or Bavaria, into old Austro-Hungarian regions of Eastern Europe.

One further historical observation respecting the medieval period situates the point whose mention by us drove the British agencies indicated into the astonishing, cited outbursts of 1978.

The new design for civilization outlined by Dante Alighieri materialized in the form of the Golden Renaissance of the 15th century. This Renaissance established the first modern nation-state, France under Louis XI, triggered the creation of a second, Tudor England, and unleashed the cultural revolution whose achievements are the high points of European civilization as we know it from the subsequent period.

Once again, the oligarchical forces, with regained strength, moved, chiefly by unifying the Genoese-controlled House of Charles the Bold of Burgundy with the Hapsburgs, and securing Charles V the succession to the combined Austro-Hungarian, Burgundian and Spanish domains. From the Peasant Wars in southern Germany (circa 1525) and the Hapsburg sack of Rome 1527, until the defeat of the Spanish Hapsburgs by forces led by Cardinal Mazarin in 1653, a semi-dark age descended upon Europe, consolidating oligarchical power in Britain, but for the brief period of the Commonwealth--the Commonwealth Party being our English political heritage. With the defeat of Colbert, Mazarin's political heir, in France, it became the rallying of the republicans of Europe around Franklin, beginning 1766, which restored republicanism as a coherent force until approximately the 1870s, when, during approximately that latter time, oligarchical forces led by

Britain reassumed monetary and political hegemony over most of the world.

Through this sweep of history, oligarchism has a consistent precisely defined character and essentially unaltered world-outlook. It is centered around the notion of world-rule by a collection of powerful priestly, aristocratic and rentier-financier "families." These families exert material power by controlling institutions of government and by accumulating the vast real-estate, mineral-rights, and rentier-financier holdings through which they loot society and society's production of wealth by means of rent and usury: President Franklin Roosevelt's adversaries, "the economic royalists." They are opposed to a general cultural development of populations, prefer a bucolic to an urban-centered form of society, and seek to perpetuate their rule by dividing society into political micro-entities, attempting to promote differences in local dialects and religions as a means for fostering such divisions within society into micro-entities.

Today, for example, there is a cluster of central European oligarchical families, the forces immediately behind such entities as the Club of Rome, World Wildlife Fund, and the Hapsburg Pan-European Union. The strategic policy of these circles, as the Pan-European Union most explicitly, is to bring into being the variety of "blue-shirt" fascism developed by the founder of the Pan-European Union, Richard Graf Coudenhove-Kalergi. This utopian scheme is best quickly described as "Malthusian world-federalism," embodying general goals and designs identical to those of the Anglo-American World Federalists. This includes the promotion of "separatist movements," such as Bretons, Basques, Alsatians, Corsicans, Sardinians, Tyroleans, Sicilians, American Indian tribes, and what-not, throughout the world. To use these "separatist movements" to aid in breaking all existing nation-states into collections of micro-entities. Regional groups of such semi-autonomous micro-entities are to be grouped under a regional over-government, having the general political character of a Persian satrapy. A federation of these regional satrapies forms a world-wide super government, overlapping a dictatorial monetary agency. All of this is to be controlled by a federation of oligarchical "families" of aristocratic or rentier-financier or combined characteristics.

This brings us to the point on which we and Toynbee work from opposite political directions, his *oligarchical* and ours *republica*n. Every feature of the policy-shaping structure of the British oligarchy, and British Secret Intelligence Service, is based on the oligarchical point of view typified by Toynbee's approach. Every policy-shaping criterion in the practice of the writer and his immediate associates is determined by the republican outlook and objectives directly opposite to those of Toynbee et al. Except for certain forces more or less closely associated to the Catholic Church, to the best of our knowledge the writer and his associates are presently the only agency in the world defining its political-intelligence outlook and practice from the classical republican standpoint. There are other republican currents, but except as just noted, those currents do not maintain the kind of attention to fundamental considerations which was more or less commonplace during earlier centuries of modern European civilization.

Within the scope of the variety of historical reference-points we summarized just before this point, our ability to trace the pattern of oligarchical activities and characteristics of oligarchical world-outlook and behavior poses a profound problem to any serious historian. When and how did oligarchism emerge as a well-defined and very "hard" form of current in human society? Toynbee asks himself the same question, but approaching this subject from the opposing political standpoint, he also asks himself: How did this blasted republicanism come into being, and how do we not only crush it out of existence, but ensure that it never erupts again in the future?

Neither we nor the late Toynbee require immediately an exact answer to such questions, but we must have some general notion of where the answer might lie. The importance of that knowledge is not limited to our curiosity about very early pre-history. That is a fascinating inquiry in its own right, but there is a much more immediate and very practical issue of contemporary political-intelligence at stake in getting approximately the correct answer to the questions posed. Establishing a *correct approximation of* the answer to the questions provides us reference-points through which to deal with evidence from the long sweep of verifiable history bearing on the conflict. Without such a reference-point certain crucial issues of interpretation of known history can not be resolved.

This can be restated fruitfully thus. Without such reference points, we can not resolve certain questions bearing on the laws of human behavior, questions which bear directly and significantly upon policy-decisions confronting us presently. The late Arnold Toynbee from his vantage-point and we from ours.

The answer to the question has been known for a very long time. However, we could not accept the answer provided by Plato and other ancient literary sources out of hand. The question has been, could we prove one way or the other that Plato and the other relevant sources are either spinning myths, or merely mistaken accounts as to date and so forth, or that these accounts of the matter are presently verifiable by aid of objective, presently available empirical evidence? Beginning with Johannes Kepler's work on the ancient Vedic calendar, into similar work continued into the early 19th century, chiefly around Karl Gauss's orbit, crucial philological evidence as well as astronomical evidence indicated Plato's account to be at least essentially correct.

Then, somewhere during the 19th century, about the same range of developments the son of the great Schliemann was mysteriously murdered, Plato's and other accounts were widely attacked as absurd, as if the earlier accumulation of near-conclusive verification referenced by the philologist A. Boeckh had never existed.

During 1977 and 1978, in connection with background researches conducted to aid a new English-language translation of Plato's *Timaeus*, we dug into this matter of the Atlas culture afresh. We sorted through a mass of ludicrous cultish stuff on this area, and isolated the sources of verifiable scientific merit. We published a summary of certain features of this material which we thought would be of interest to a popular readership. The explosion of flatulence from Britain came promptly in response.

Beginning most emphatically with John Ruskin's Pre-Raphaelite Brotherhood accomplice, Benjamin Jowett, Britain has produced a mass of fraudulent translations of classical Greek literature. The most crucial features of the classical Greek texts are mangled to say in English what they do not say in Greek, or even to supply meanings directly opposite to the original text. This has been covered up, in a manner of speaking, by basing the standard Oxbridge Greek/English lexicons on the putative meanings of terms associated with sources including, predominantly the hoaxster Jowett.

For example, in the *Timaeus*, the entire conception developed depends on Socrates's assigning the name "Composer" to God, which leads the subsequent main line of discussion to discuss the laws of the universe from the standpoint of harmonic principles of composition, anticipating in principle the later founding of modern mathematical physics by Johannes Kepler. In fact, the *Timaeus* has been the principal stimulus to the development of modern science from the 15th through the 17th century, as it was used in a similar fashion by St. Augustine earlier. Without putting the English text into order, to preserve Plato's original meaning of crucial terms for conceptions, it is next to impossible for the English-speaking reader to make any real sense of the *Timaeus*.

The Atlas-epic issue encounters the same problems with the British today as attacks on Jowett's fraudulent translations. British scholarship is intimately aware of the verification of Plato's account of the "fall of Atlantis," but is determined to keep this evidence away from the attention of others who might draw the appropriate conclusions bearing on present-day policy-making from this evidence.

The fact that the British were virtually in a panic over our references to these connections indicated to us that the British viewed such material as having a very practical, if merely implicit relevance for the most crucial strategic-political issues of the present period of developing crisis. This obliged us to recognize the real significance of Toynbee's and related British historiography, and thus to recognize exactly what sort of a vital role that historiography performs in the shaping of British policy-directions today.

The reader should not lose from the back of his mind that all of this seeming detour has a very practical bearing upon the shaping of U.S. foreign policy. It is not only our concern to remove the potentially fatal "blind spot" from our policy-outlook. The particular point immediately before us as we consider this essential background-material, is that we are concerned to adduce scientific knowledge bearing on the way in which nations are controlled by a sustained manipulation of national cultures over a period of decades or longer. We must become conscious of the efficiency of the methods the British have employed to shift our national character by their manipulating the direction of evolution of our popular culture. We are also concerned to indicate the proof showing the consequences toward which we are headed rapidly, unless we become conscious of and reverse the effects of British manipulation of our culture. There are other practical implications flowing from understanding the answers to the questions implied in the listing we have just given.

With that, we turn now to identify the reference-point in question, and so to indicate its significance for modern political science and U.S. policy-making. You will find this next sub-topic most amusing as well as leading to a very relevant, practical point.

The Atlas Epic & Its Political Implications Today

Three ancient sources, the Egyptian priest Manetho (3rd century B.C.), the Roman historian Didorus Siculus (1st century B.C.), and Plato (4th century B.C.), provide us our principal, surviving literary sources for a seismic upheaval in human society dated to approximately the 11th millennium B.C.

These reports, transmitted into literate times by a combination of oral-traditional epic poems and calendars, locate the principal site of this upheaval as either in or in the vicinity of present-day Morocco, in a site occupied by a people *self-identified* as descendants of an Atlantean culture into the period of the Roman Empire. The kernel of the epic tradition bearing immediately upon our concerns runs thus.

Preceding the upheaval in the Atlantean kingdom about the 11th millennium B.C., revolutionary advances in astronomy and in the introduction of agriculture were accomplished by a city-builder king named Uranus, the epic figure whose name is used to designate "sky" in Greek. Uranus had two sons, Chronos and Atlas, who co-administered a far-flung domain. It was among the children of Chronos's wife and his concubines that the war erupted. The children of Chronos's wife were called "Titans" after the maiden-name of their mother. The faction constituted of the children of the concubines were called "Olympians," and were led by Zeus. Prometheus, one of the Titans, allied conditionally with the Olympians against the tyranny imposed by two of his Titan siblings. Then, Prometheus was the victim of the Olympians.

Furthermore, the Atlanteans of Roman Empire times insisted that the Olympian pantheon and its cognates around the world were a gigantic hoax. The Olympians had deified themselves and imposed this hoax upon superstitious peoples they had colonized, is the gist of the matter.

Did it actually happen, or did it not? The Greek dynastic accounts listed in a surviving fragment of Manetho's records verify the account of Didorous Siculus. Plato's account is reported as originating with the Temple of Amon. The British have tried to shave years off Manetho's list of dynasties, lopping off some thousands of years of Egyptian civilization in the process. The evidence supporting the case that something very much like that did happen is overwhelming.

The crucial supporting evidence is of two interdependent categories, actually overlapping as well as interdependent: philological and astronomical. The whole range of evidence bearing upon this dates back to before 40,000 B.C., as we shall identify the proof for that. Correlated with this is that the entire period from about 40,000 B.C. to about 4,000 B.C. is the span of the last phase of glaciation and glacial melt of the last Ice Age. During the general period of melt, covering more than 10,000 years, the sea-levels rose in a S-curve fashion, trickling along into about the 2nd millennium B.C., but essentially completing the melt about 4,000 B.C., according to a survey of generally accepted studies on this matter.

The hardest evidence, on which proof of the other evidence depends, is astronomical. The *Rigveda* is the key reference-point from which other work on this approach began among modern Europeans. Kepler, at the turn of the 17th century, was the first to prove the accuracy of the calendar of the *Rigveda*. The teacher of Karl Gauss generalized the findings to that date, including his own, in 1797.

The range of ancient calendars dating from pre-literate periods of human society are defined in respect to four principal sets of cycles. The progression of the position of the equinox with respect to fixed constellations--which ancient calendars locate as one degree of arc for seventy-two years. The time required for shift of the earth's geographic North Pole to return to any stated original position. The corresponding cycle for the magnetic pole. The complete cycle--hundreds of thousands of years--for the solar system to complete a cycle, in its orbit within the galaxy. Naturally, no one plotted a complete set of data for repetition of several solar galactic orbitings or anything of that general variety. However, the ability of a pre-literate culture to develop calendars of such proven accuracy and sophistication does provide crucial indications bearing upon the questions we have put before ourselves here.

At the turn of the present century, the great Indian politician-scholar Bal Gangadhar Tilak published two books of important bearing on this matter: *The Orion* (1893) and *The Arctic Home in the Vedas* (1903). Tilak focused principally upon two notable features of astronomical and related references in the *Rigveda* and Persian Avesta. First, in *The Orion*, he dated the origins of the Vedic poems to not later than 4,000 B.C., by virtue of the poems' positioning events in central Asia at the time the equinox was in Orion. In the second book, he correlated the fact that the ancient Vedic calendar is an Arctic region calendar astronomically, with the Avestic references to an ancient Indo-European homeland in a land where the sun shone once a year and from which they were driven permanently by ice and snow. In addition, he correlated the fact that Vedic pantheons include deities associated with the Arctic calendar. This presents the hypothesis that the Indo-European culture maintained an oral tradition of great precision (relatively speaking) from approximately 40,000 B.C. or earlier.

We have a similar kind of situation with the old Mayan long-cycle calender, and with a calendar associated with an advanced pre-Columbian city-state culture in Colombia. We have the post-800 A.D. Olmec decline into a short-cycle calendar, indicating implicitly the general long sweep of decay of Meso-American cultures leading into the disastrous Aztec degeneracy.

Through aid of work accomplished by classical Sanskrit scholars working in the Humboldt-Bopp tradition, and work from a different tack added to this from discoveries of this writer and his associates, these resources were able not only to prove the astonishing fidelity of certain kinds of epic poems transmitted by oral tradition over thousands of years, but to account for those principles of the mind which explain how such an accomplishment is lawful. The transmission of calendar- astronomical information by such modes of communication is a crucial part of the objective verification. On that basis of verification, we are able to use certain selected other features of these epics with scientific precision.

These epics tend to have a central tendency of social-functional character. By and large, they are astrological epic poems, a string of astrological homilies used in a manner implied by the use of *mantras* to the present date. Our names for months and days of the week are an outgrowth of such practices. There is a superimposition of deities upon the calendar and, in each case, corresponding planet or constellation. Events are correlated within the system so broadly defined.

The coincidence of such an epic "system" with a very sophisticated astronomical design of the associated calendar is the variety of "Rosetta Stone" on which we focus in selecting our empirical-conceptual reference-point for further explorations in such matters. (The principal other, supplementary working-tool we employ is the conception of prosodic modes, which serve both as a composition-mnemonic device in any efficiently oral-transmittable form of epic poem, but are modes which have other very important implications of a kind not directly bearing on our more bare-bones point of interest in this report.)

This broadly identifies, thus far, the nature of the evidence, without venturing into the book-length treatment the subject deserves were it to be represented for something more than the very specific purpose of our inquiry in this report. We shall pick up on a few more important bits of evidence, as we develop the case a bit further, after stating our essential point next.

We are informed to divide pre-history into three broad categories. First, there is a large, catch-all category concerning which we propose to say nothing here. This is followed by the first period of immediate relevance to us, the pre-Olympian age typified by Uranus in the Atlantean account reported by Diodorus Siculus. This age we identify as the "astronomical age," during which astronomically sophisticated calendars were developed, probably to the maximum degree of refinement as to scientific principles they ever reached thereafter until modern times, not ignoring the qualitatively more advanced astronomy in pre-Ptolemaic times than is represented by that wretched, oligarchical hoax concocted by Ptolemy Soter. The great crisis ushers in an irrationalist "astrological age" of the Olympians, in which the calendar is preserved and observations are often continued, but in which the scientific point of view needed to produce such calendar-designs is more or less suppressed. This astrological age is the origin of *oligarchism.*

For many reasons, we are obliged to associate the astronomical age with a far-ranging maritime culture. The existence of sophisticated ancient calendars which include an accurate measurement of the cycle for a complete series of shifts of the earth's magnetic pole is an interesting case in point: this feature of the calendar proves systematic employment of the navigational compass among those who designed such calendars. The sophisticated ancient calendars including this feature are otherwise principally navigational instruments for transoceanic travel.

Of course, a culture which measures the complete cycles for the separate and combined shifts back to any starting point for both the magnetic and geographical north poles of the earth proves itself to have known that the earth is approximately spherical as a whole. A people who design a calendar including provision for cycles respecting the solar system's orbit within our galaxy, a feature of the Vedic calendar on which Kepler focused special attention, know that our solar system does orbit within this galaxy. Moreover, on the basis of facts relating to these calendars' antiquity, we know that such astronomical knowledge was possessed by some cultures well before the Orion equinoctical period, before 4.000 B.C. Respecting the Arctic origins of the Indo-European language-group, only a culture living in the Arctic region can produce an Arctic calendar, unless it is a modern culture much like our own, which it was not.

The Diodorus Siculus version of the account of the ancient culture of the Atlanteans living in the vicinity of the Straits of Gibraltar (for whom the Atlantic Ocean was named), reports that Uranus brought agriculture to the previously uncivilized Atlanteans. This would date the development of agriculture to no later than the 11th millennium B.C. Existing evidence, although limited in amount collected, nonetheless suffices to prove conclusively that agriculture was developed before approximately the 8th millennium B.C., about the same time, according to the account of Manetho, that colonists from the shards of the former Uranian kingdom established the first dynasty of Egypt.

Moreover, the Atlanteans of the period of the Roman Empire insisted, the Uranus-culture was based on cities. We know a significant amount about much-later cultures of the general social morphological characteristics of a maritime culture of the Uranus type. The most recent instances date from the 2nd millennium B.C., from the city-state sites of the Peoples of the Sea.

These Peoples of the Sea appear to have reached a high-point of importance in the Eastern Mediterranean during the same period as the Hittite iron-working culture in Anatolia, and predominantly, insofar as our knowledge accounts for any part of these peoples, they were the Achaean Greeks, who had well-established close intercourse with their Indo-European cousins, the Hittites. The problem associated with this phenomenon is that it appears to be a broad maritime culture, which may have been diffused among several peoples, in addition to the Achaeans.

This culture, which used oared sailing craft (sometimes copper-bottomed) almost identical with the design of Viking ships later, ranged all around the Mediterranean littoral and into the North Sea, including Helgoland and its vicinity. This is the variety of craft which the *Odyssey* identifies (as to crucial features of its performance) as used by Ulysses and his crew to voyage through the Straits of Gibraltar and down across the Atlantic Ocean into the Caribbean region. The *Odyssey's* detailed specifications as to the lapsed time and other features of the transatlantic journey are exactly reproducible for such a voyage made with such a craft. Generally speaking, the origins of such voyaging in human culture, using approximately the same technology, would have to be the general level of culture associated with the astronomical-age culture on the basis of the crucial-scientific implications of the internal features of the calendars themselves. Some such varieties of cultures would have had magnetic compasses and corresponding charts on board, and would otherwise have navigated with about the same sort of astronomical observations we would associate with the maritime technology of 17th and 18th

century European civilization.

The 2nd millennium city-sites of special interest to us in reflecting upon the Atlantean urban-centered culture under Uranus are those sites established by Peoples of the Sea in which there are no fortifications to the ocean-side, but notable fortifications facing inland.

Such evidence references our attention to one of the best-documented cases for Meso-American pre-Columbian early culture, the Quiché Maya culture centered in Guatemala, which left its epic recorded for us in part in the form of plates of gold, discovered by Alexander von Humboldt, very much in character like those exhibited at the Mormon museum, as attempted reproductions of the account of Joseph Smith, in Salt Lake City. The oral tradition was recorded in Latin approximately 1550 A.D., a transcribed account generally identified as the *Popol Vuh* of the Quiché Maya.

This case of the Quiché Maya assists us greatly in correlating surviving fragments, such as the *Chilam Balam*. With aid of such sources and correlated archeological facts, we establish securely the impact of both trans-Atlantic and trans-Pacific maritime cultures, associated with calendars of the indicated category of sophistication. A comparative study of Vedic and Avestic, Atlas-linked and Meso-American (down into Colombia, Peru, and Bolivia) materials guides us to some admittedly rather broad, but nonetheless incontestable knowledge of long-wave patterns of human behavior in ancient, pre-literate cultures.

The "hydraulic" urban-centered culture of the ancient Mayan sites and sophisticated "hydraulic" sites in Colombia are among the most important and conclusive varieties of general facts to be emphasized in such connections: the spinning-off of sophisticated agriculture from colonies of a sophisticated ancient, pre-literate maritime culture is among the key considerations.

With aid of two varieties of improved analytical apparatus developed by this writer and his associates, the one bearing on certain aspects of philology, the other a revolutionary advance in economic science, we are now able to peel away several additional layers of the archeological-philological, "onion"-like riddle of pre-history. With aid of the LaRouche-Riemann method of computer-assisted economic analysis, we are now able to correlate relative population-densities, the energy-throughput per square mile of a culture, and the characteristic features of technology of a culture, and to do so conclusively, with aid of a relative handful of appropriate varieties of information. On the basis of previously well-established and these additional elements of analytical apparatus, we now know a great deal about the general, lawful features of this sort of pre-literate culture we are examining here.

For example, if the habitable area of the earth today were in the pre-inhabited condition we would assume from our knowledge of such conditions, the total human population of the world at any one time, in a simple hunting and gathering mode, could never have exceeded ten million persons. The possibility for increasing the potential relative population-density of society correlates approximately with the amount of energy used per-capita by a culture. This translates into the correlative parameter: energy-flux-density (e.g. in calories or watts) per square mile or square kilometer of areas of human habitation. The best performance which might be achieved prior to large-scale application of heat-powered machinery and chemical fertilization would require that for each average person living in an urban site, there must be ten to twenty persons engaged in agricultural production in that society. So, on the basis of known urban sites from pre-literate periods, such as Harappan sites in northwest India and Pakistan today, we can determine with an indicated degree of exactness the total population of those cultures, and the approximate agricultural yield per hectare available for cultivation in that culture. Knowing also the general upper and lower limits of possible per-hectare performance such cultures might possibly accomplish, a scattering of urban sites of a culture informs us a great deal concerning the area subsumed by the associated culture as a whole. Also, as in the pre-Columbian Inca case, or the initially astonishing population-density of Quiché Maya culture at approximately the time of Spanish conquest, and earlier, we can infer within broad but conclusive and very informative terms, the general level of culture achieved, using the known correlation between potential relative population-density and energy-flux density.

This approach aids us in a most important manner as we take into account the changes in climate and sea-level known to have occurred over not only the period of rise and ebb of glaciation, from about 40,000 B.C. to about 4,000 B.C., but also traumatic shifts in climate and crucial seismic developments, such as the Krakatoa-like explosion of the island of Thera, into the late 2nd millennium B.C. The changes in climate in central Asia, finally forcing the mass migrations of Indo-Europeans during approximately the century 2,500 to 2,400 B.C. (at the latest), the desertification of the Arabian peninsula, and progressive desertification of the Sahara region, and so forth, are notable features of the developments directly affecting African and Eurasian culture during the approach into the historic period proper. (Large ancient city-sites of Indo-Europeans must be extant in central Asia, of--probably Semitic--sites in the Arabian desert, and other important sites in the Sahara, are among the cases of varying degrees of certainty we must infer from the existing evidence.)

The existence of an extensive maritime culture developing an astronomical-age culture in the 11th millennium B.C. presents archaeology with a definite, and crucial problem in ancient geography. We are confronted with search for ancient coastlines and island sites up to hundreds of feet beneath sea-levels today. We are also confronted, quite significantly, with the large river-systems and post-glacial lakes which either vanished or exist only in vestigial form today (such as our Great Lakes system, which is a vestige of the massive system existing during the period of highest-rate of glacial retreat), including a relatively recently-died river in the Punjab-Pakistan region, and extensive ancient river systems of the Sahara. The problem of defining the habitable areas of the ancient world during various intervals is compounded by the irregularities in the patterns of both glaciation and melting, including the possibly catastrophic effect on a culture which is hit abruptly by avalanches of mud and stones in the kinds of monstrous and sudden floods which must have occurred at various sites during the period of relatively rapid rise in the world-wide sea-levels. Orbitting satellites now assist us greatly in dealing with such problems.

When this sort of set of geographic and climatic considerations is applied to the analytical knowledge and facts otherwise available to us, some broad, but conclusive and very valuable (for today) generalizations confront us.

The pattern, directly opposite to the working-hypothesis of Thor Heyerdahl, is of a maritime, astronomical-age culture, based on the urban sites indispensable to the astronomical work of such an age, which spins off agricultural development, including the development of riparian forms of "hydraulic," inland-turning colonies. In the early phase, fishing was necessarily the point of emphasis in production of food. This obliges us to focus a certain degree of emphasis on coastal sites near the mouths of large ancient river-systems. (In this connection, the changes in geography through silting attract our attention as a crucial variety of problem.)

It is perhaps indispensable to interpolate another point of scientific argument at this point, to the purpose that the conclusive evidence supporting what we have just stated not be underestimated.

The LaRouche-Riemann method has enabled us to prove not only the correlation between energy-flux-density and potential relative population-density. This analytical apparatus proves conclusively that the direction of acquisition of added sources of energy consumed for the maintenance and reproductive growth of the population of a society shapes the direction of development of that society. The corollary of this for today's policy-making is, that if we wish to achieve economic growth, we must vector research and development bearing upon development of production along a path of research which increases the quantity of energy for society in both per-capita and per-square-kilometer terms of reference, and must also direct that research and development toward point-sources of applicable heat-energy corresponding to a series of increasing energy-flux-density. It were more precise to report that the pathway of economic development, and constant improvement in the individual's conditions of life, is a pathway of progress in applied research and development which corresponds to a world-line of *absolute negentropy*. In the simplest valid explanation of this point concerning *absolute negentropy*, we define such negentropy in the following terms of reference.

In ordinary thermodynamics, we divide the entire energy-throughout (or, work-throughput) of a process into two principal sub-categories. The first is the portion of the energy-throughput which the process itself must consume internally to avoid "running down." This component of the total energy throughput we name, conventionally, the *energy of the system*. The remaining portion of the energy-throughput as a whole we often designate as *free energy*. This is the portion of energy available, after meeting the internal needs of the process itself, either to do work on some part of the universe external to that process itself, or to raise the level of organization of the process, if the free energy is applied to transform the process which produces it.

Therefore, the elementary operation performed in thermodynamics is a measurement of the ratio of these two sub-components compiling the totality of a process's energy-throughput. We measure the changes in this ratio as the process advances forward in time. If the ratio declines over time, we describe the process as functionally *entropic*, as a process whose corresponding description in terms of an appropriate mathematical statement of a function "exhibits entropy." If the ratio increases over time, we say that the mathematical function describing this process adequately exhibits "negative entropy." For convenience, we shorten the latter term, and say "negentropy." All living processes are negentropic, with morphological-geometrical proportionings of their patterns of growth and articulation of form according to what are described as *self-similar* patternings of a mode derived from extracting the Golden Section out of the implications of the so-called five Platonic solids.

Many kinds of processes might be described as negentropic. Only one variety of such process is actually negentropic in the proper sense of that term. Hence, for this case we employ the term *absolute negentropy*.

Without going into the detailed proof of this point, we describe what is most crucial in the distinctions of any mathematical function reflecting absolute negentropy. We define such processes only on the basis of defining empirically a definition of the process which satisfies the most unique principle of proof for all mathematics: *closure.* We must rigorously define the process under consideration in such terms of empirical reference that it defines a closed thermodynamical system both as to mathematical form and in empirical fact. Therefore, the definition of absolute negentropy depends upon identifying those kinds of empirical phenomena of a process for the case that all of the free energy which is not wasted is applied efficiently to transformation of the organization of the process itself. Only those transformations which maintain or increase the negentropy of the process are negentropic transformations.

In such a closed system, any negentropic transformation which increases the negentropy of the closed process also increases the energy flux-density of the energy of the system. This appears to defy a never proven, but merely asserted "law," called the Law of Conservation of Energy: absolute-negentropic processes *at least appear to* create energy. All living processes satisfy the mathematical-functional specifications of absolute-negentropic processes. All systems of such characteristics are describable adequately only by means of resort to Riemannian functions, as problems associated with the defining of such mathematical functions were finally solved--after centuries of preceding advancement toward this point--by the overlapping work of chiefly Bernhard Riemann, Karl Weierstrass and the 1871-1883 work on transfinite functions by Weierstrass's former student, Georg Cantor.

This should not be intellectually frightening in any proper way. Although Riemannian functions appear monstrously difficult from the vantage-point of a purely-algebraic approach, they are readily mastered, and could be mastered by a properly educated high-school student, from a purely-synthetic-geometric approach to mathematics.

It has been this writer's most notable scientific discovery, effected some decades past, that economic functions describing a society undergoing successive levels of economic growth are uniquely Riemannian functions. Society as a whole reflects the same special class of ordering-principles otherwise characteristic of living processes. This applies not only to the kinds of processes by which societies grow, but the considerations determining the way in which wrong policies cause them to die. Indeed, the impact of the oligarchical principle on societies is identical in form to a bio-thermodynamical definition of cancer--for which the mathematical biophysics of the late N. Rashevsky of Chicago University is a fair-to-middling approximation even to the present date.

The unique success of economic forecasts using the LaRouche-Riemann method, consistent success against complete failure of all published governmental and private econometric forecasts, is centered in the fact that the econometricians failed most fundamentally because such econometric methods are intrinsically incompetent to cope with the kind of phase-change the economy has experienced successively since the introduction of the Volcker measures during early October 1979. This is a problem readily mastered by employing Riemannian functions, whose characteristic feature is their attention to ordered series of so-called "non-linear" phase-changes in a process otherwise defined functionally as continuous. The more general point to be made in this connection, the point bearing directly upon both the immediate and general topic of the report, is that social processes (both in economic and social terms of reference) can appear to be "linear" only during relatively short intervals. All economic and cultural processes are characteristically, functionally defined correctly only if they are defined as a Riemannian functional continuum, characterized by directed series of successive phase-changes.

In studying modern or ancient society, our primary actual or implied measurement is a function defining a directed series of phase-changes of either an entropic or negentropic series, as the social process is either, respectively, increasing or decreasing the potential relative population-density of the society under prevailing policies of practice. This function correlates with shifts in the relative and absolute composition of those demographic features of the society reflecting shifts in the broadly defined social division of labor. These shifts are correlated with changes in energy-flux-density, usually on several interrelated levels of approximation of this. We consider energy-flux-density per square kilometer, per-capita, and point-source energy-flux-density of heat-sources employed.

It is from this standpoint that we can examine the characteristics of a society on the basis of demonstrating that on one side of the process, the economic and associated social development is emphatically an emphasis on fishing, and on the other side a marked shift into emphasis upon agriculture. Conversely, the morphological characteristics of a culture, such as the correlation of urban and maritime-calender morphologies, enable us to state conclusively on the basis of such crucial varieties of empirical evidence, that the one culture is a reflection of fishing as a principal source of energy for that society's maintenance and reproductive characteristics.

The same reasons which turn our strategic focus to oceans, islands, fishing and so forth today were operative in the astronomical-age culture and its astrological-age sequelae. Life did not develop out of the oceans, for the simple reason that living processes produced the oceans as well as our present atmosphere, but it is those oceans, and the "invention" of chlorophyll by living processes, which define those parameters of our biosphere upon which human life depends today, and define what we must reproduce in orbitting, Moon and planetary colonies in intra-solar system space during the coming century. Out of the oceans, so to speak, civilization was born. This oceanic birthplace of the astronomical age defies the culture of the astrological age--despite the mad, wicked ambitions of theosophical Isis-Urania cultist Aleister Crowley, and his cult-converts Aldous and Julian Huxley, to bring back the heathen worship of Satan (Dionysus) in his proposal to launch an "Age of Aquarius" during this present century.

Friedrich Nietzsche, that lunatic, evil, existentialist arch-Nazi, who also proposed, in alliance with Crowley, the launching of a dionysian "Age of Aquarius" to trample out both Jesus Christ and the rationalism of Socrates, will, we are determined shall become the case, also be drowned from continued political existence in human culture in the oceans which gave birth to the astronomical age.

Nietzsche and Crowley, like Arnold Toynbee, were profoundly well-educated, on exactly those decisive points of knowledge of how to shape history in the large which we foolish Americans, with our pathetic obsession against "theory," reject as relevant, efficient knowledge. Nietzsche, Crowley, Toynbee, or any similar fellow would agree at once with the importance and accuracy of what we are reporting, and each of them would resolve to murder the writer as soon as possible after reading this report. If we Americans ever begin to grasp the practical importance of what is being presented in this report, we shall promptly unleash a kind of republican power which will quickly come to rule the world forever. It is not the writer that such wicked fellows fear, not the writer as such; it is you they fear, that you might be informed of such matters of decisive strategic importance. For that reason, and that reason alone, wicked fellows on approximately the same level of knowledge as a Toynbee would promptly dedicate themselves to shutting this writer's mouth and smashing his typewriter, if not by a wall of political-social containment, then by removing the potential "contamination" at its source. That is the only reason wicked fellows *at that level of knowledge and responsibility* have taken this writer's work as seriously as they do in practice.

We need not guess how much of this Nietzsche, Crowley or Toynbee actually knew. They practiced an oligarchical version of precisely such knowledge.

Perhaps not the part which bears upon Riemannian physics, although Lord Rayleigh, Bertrand Russell and others, beginning the 1890s, launched a world-wide campaign to eradicate the influence of Riemann's work, culminating in the hooligans' assault upon science, in the name of "science," around the time of the notorious Solvay Conference of the 1920s. This particular inquisition has a long history, predating the British campaign launched in the 1890s, with the coordinated effort, centered around the British agent Helmholtz, and deployment of that "Mutt and Jeff" team, Leopold Kronecker and Richard Dedekind, most directly against Weierstrass and Cantor during the period beginning the 1860s.

Bertrand Russell's heirs, including the Harvard-based History of the Exact Sciences project, are still to this day composing fraudulent, published papers, purporting to discredit Riemann, Cantor, et al., into the present period. The physics-standpoint we have adopted--Kepler, Leibniz, Carnot, Gauss, Dirichlet, Weber, Riemann, Weierstrass, Cantor, et al., they hate almost as venomously as they hate this writer himself.

Nonetheless, that significant qualification noted, insofar as this report presents accounts of history, current, modern, medieval or ancient, the kind of oligarchical adversary we have identified as at the indicated level of knowledge and influence knows them to be fact. The writer's leading adversaries agree entirely with this writer respecting the map of the historical terrain on which we fight to destroy one another. They also agree as to the cultural and religious principles of the *oligarchical method.* This method they practice with a degree of informed precision, and employment of appropriate classical references as models adopted for *their modern efforts to destroy the United States of America, largely from within.*

There is no need to guess at what they do or do not know; their public practice, their consistent practice proves conclusively both the nature of their policy and the variety of knowledge they bring directly to bear to shape even the fine details of that policy of practice.

The scientific names for those "practical Americans" who reject such levels and scope of knowledge are "victim," "slave," and "credulous, hoodwinked dupe."

The most immediate point of focus, for this writer and for the Toynbee factor in British intelligence's Grand Strategy, is the relevance of the Atlas epic, as a reference-point, for analyzing the crucial features of the process leading in a more immediate way into the eruption of Alexander the Great's process of destruction of Phoenician Tyre and the Persian Empire. Our oligarchical adversaries' purpose in this historical research is to design an effective cultural strategy for corrupting and destroying those features of culture which characterize the potential reemergence of a Golden Renaissance-like revival of well-organized republican insurgency against oligarchism. This writer's concern, like that of Leibniz, Benjamin Franklin, Lazare Carnot, and the leading republicans around Schiller in the Weimar Classic circles of the Humboldt brothers, is directed to precisely the end totally opposite to those of the British oligarchy's intelligence-service and of the European-continental "Venetian" black oligarchy.

They are searching for a "new Adolf Hitler": I am determined to kill such a "new, 'charismatic' Adolf Hitler" before he is born. This is the gist of the matter.

We shall now proceed to complete the discussion of the Atlas Epic's significance by turning more directly to the characteristic features of the two opposing forces, referencing the evidence to be added out of literature from the ancient classical period.

The Oligarchical Doctrine of "Blood and Soil"

What is the motive of the British for insisting so obsessively, so touchily, so promptly, that the events reported in Plato's references to Atlantis "never happened"? How would the modern world, on which their Grand Strategy is passionately focused for practical results, be different for them if the facts bearing on the existence of a pre-"astrological," astronomical-maritime culture were simply debated in the ordinary way among scholars, scientists and the general reading public looking over the shoulders of those scholarly and scientific circles? *What practical harm in that?*

The practical, *strategic* issue is essentially this. If it is believed that those modes of thinking, of social and individual behavior which are characteristic of early astrologically-ordered oligarchical cultures are in some sense a "natural" reflection of "human nature," then, this selected body of evidence, applied to the promulgated teaching of history, religion, and so forth, will lure the credulous mind into accepting that version of "human nature" and "human understanding" summarily argued-out in the writings of David Hume.

Under appropriate cultural circumstances, the standpoint represented by Hume's writings can be brought to a deeper degree of moral degeneracy, that of Jeremy Bentham's "hedonistic calculus" and Bentham's and James Mill's followers among what the British themselves label "19th century British philosophical radicalism." This "radicalism" then serves as the characteristic feature of a method for destroying culture and its institutions, leading toward the preconditions for launching enterprises such as Nietzsche's and Crowley's, now overtly in progress, launching of an "Age of Aquarius", to destroy civilization, during this century.

If, however, it is known that the astrological age's culture and oligarchism are "unnatural," having the same general significance for human culture and individual belief as cancer represents for the human body, then, such facts considered, mankind will arise to eradicate oligarchism, as Plato's republicans attempted to do, and as the active principle subsuming Judeo-Christian republicanism continues to attempt into the present date.

They would regard astrology as what it is, a Satanic, cancerous infection, by which the morals and minds of individuals and entire cultures are destroyed, and would regard as the obscenity it is, the current of argument and policy traced from Francis Bacon, Hobbes, Locke, Hume, Bentham, the 19th-century utilitarians (Mill, Jevons, Marshall), and that spawn of Hell, the Pre-Raphaelite Brotherhood of Oxford University's John Ruskin and the lying hoaxster Benjamin Jowett. They would recognize, rightly, that the marginal-utility dogma of monetarism is not merely absurd and destructive economic policy; they would recognize that there is a specific element of evil--Jeremy Bentham's radical hedonism--embedded in that dogma as its axiomatic foundation. They would recognize that same evil as the ordering-principle imparted to British Socialism generally, Fabianism, Bertrand Russell, and the circles and political heirs of Lord Alfred Milner ruling Britain throughout this century to date.

They would recognize that it is British empiricism as such which most efficiently expresses this evil, and that it is such imported British empiricism, aggravated by the pragmatism of William James and John Dewey, which has eroded away the morals and culture of the United States.

In the classical Hellenic period which more or less concludes with the assassination of Alexander the Great, the epic histories predominating in Greece were of principally two categories. The one, the Phoenician-Cadmus version associated with Thebes and nearby Delphi, is an ugly, irrationalist outlook on nature and man. This embodies all of the characteristic features of the oligarchical world-outlook, and is exemplified by the case of Hesiod. The second is best labelled the Egyptian or rationalist view, signifying, more narrowly, the alliance of republican Greece with the Cyrenaic Temple of Amon. The paradigms for this latter outlook are Aeschylus and Plato. This latter world-outlook on science, history and statecraft, is the body of classical Greek republican knowledge assimilated into Christianity in the degree and manner St. Augustine elaborates the point.

The most essential point of distinction between the two, opposing currents of literature is the Phoenician emphasis on "blood and soil" as both the self-interest and ordering-principle of human behavior. The rationalist current, exemplified by the figure of the Socrates whose murder was cheered by the wizened liberal I. F. Stone, is the divinity of the creative aspect of the individual mind.

Nero's arena expresses the essence of the oligarchical or Phoenician principle. The combatants, the members of society, are seeking to win over another in a universe whose characteristics are fixed rules subsuming successful cheating, as abruptly modified by caprice of that embodiment of an Olympian deity, Nero. As the other "gods" in the spectator's ranks influence Nero's caprices in the matter of events in the arena, so the combatant may hope to appeal to the influence of one of the lesser "gods" and to so, he may hope, direct Nero's capriciousness to his advantage. ("Oh, Nero, make this one a seven!") "Human nature" is permanently fixed; the laws of nature, the "arena," are fixed, and Isaac Newton sadly confessed to his readers that his doomed universe was like a clock whose mainspring was running down. There is only hope in the caprice of the gods (i.e., the oligarchical families' power and capriciousness). Be, therefore, a Stoic, or, cease all worrying about Fate, and be, like drugged, satanic zombies of the Rolling Stones, or Oscar Wilde, an Epicurean.

Apart from such recreations as "jus primae noctis," or a maiden raped or boy sodomized by night on whim, the Phoenician "gods" (e g., the oligarchical families) have time to secure themselves the wealth and power to sustain themselves in such noble recreations. These pursuits of power and wealth, most emphatically power, are chiefly religious, absentee landlordism, and tax-farming, the latter the ancient form of modern rentier-financier usury. Pagan religions, based on the astrological design for the principle of "blood and soil," are used to control the mind of society. Landlordism prevents others from having rights of ownership of valuable aspects of nature and provides the oligarch with a parasitical form of income, ground-rent. Tax-farming, and its outgrowth, usury, enables the oligarch to acquire without cost that which he does not yet own, by means of ground- rent from lending of money. Religion must defend the source of the oligarchs' material power, ground-rent and usury.

Interference with such oligarchical practices, prerogatives and institutions provokes the oligarchs immediately into a murderous frenzy. The existence of republicanism so adds to the basic repertoire of oligarchical ideology an eruption of an added dimensionality. To account for this, we must glance toward that against which the oligarchs are reacting with such homicidal malignancy.

At several earlier points during this report, we have returned to the subject of the creative principle in mental life. We correlated this with the principle of composition of classical tragedy, then, later, returned to treat this same point in another context, and located the same phenomena with respect to sports and qualities of military command. At a more recent point, we have introduced the conception of negentropy. If the reader will now recollect those earlier treatments of this matter, our immediate task here is greatly foreshortened.

The notion of processes ordered in the manner of absolute negentropy, and the ordering-principle characteristic of productions of the creative aspect of mental processes, are congruent mappings of reality. This requires at least a brief explication now.

The possibility of continued development of society, even the existence of society over the longer term, depends upon a negentropic ordering of the aggregated behavior of the society. If the human mind were so ordered that it could not alter the behavior of members of society to such an effect, human existence *as human existence* would be impossible. In that very specific and rigorous sense, the inability to successfully change the characteristic behavior of members of the society in that specific way would represent a profoundly *unnatural* condition for a human personality. In other words, a human being lacking such characteristic attributes of mental life would be considered to be rigorously defined as *clinically* insane. (In fact, such an approach is the only proper approach to defining a state of insanity, or to properly adduce the etiology of a psychopathology.)

The natural and sane behavior of human beings is thus expressed socially, respecting effects of such behavior for society in the large, by the kind of behavior associated with discovery, assimilation for practice, and teaching of technological progress, of a sort which fosters the perpetuation of a negentropic function in the ordering of society's development. However, technological progress as such merely exemplifies the more general principle involved. We earlier elaborated the deeper issue and purpose of society, for which technological progress is merely an indispensable mediation. Nonetheless, although technological progress is merely an indispensable aspect of the sane activity of a society and its members, it is also indispensable to employ technological progress as the "hard," empirical standpoint of reference for examining mental behavior's role in this progress.

This implies that a Riemannian function outlining the condition for absolute negentropy in technological progress is an echo of the internal ordering of the creative processes of the human mind. This is more or less exactly the case, as Riemann himself insisted it must necessarily be the case, in his commentaries on the work of Herbart. (Here, we have struck upon the reason the British hate Kepler,

Leibniz, Riemann, Cantor and so forth. As soon as they recognized this implication of Riemann, Weierstrass and Cantor, the oligarchs reacted with a wont to kill.)

From a clinical-psychological standpoint, as the late Dr. Lawrence S. Kubie recognized such a connection, the kind of self-conscious alteration of the ordering of consciousness which we summarily described earlier, is the empirical location and empirical correlative of all creative-mental activity. This signifies the added point, which Kubie did not propose, that the kind of creative changes in ordering of human practice represented by scientific discoveries leading toward increased potential relative population-density, negentropic changes in human practice, must be in some way congruent with what we can define empirically, from a psychological-clinical standpoint, as creative mentation.

Plato's Socratic dialogues provide the solution to the question so posed. This solution is provided literally, at least on principle, by what the content of the dialogues provide the reader. The solution is also presented on another level: the demonstration of the power of the Socratic method as such. These two aspects of Plato's work (compared most appropriately with Aeschylus's dramas) aid us in adducing the most crucial point of this entire report. We take the second aspect of the matter, the power of the Socratic dialogue as such, as our first next sub-topic.

The reader was already given the point earlier, that the classical tragedies of Shakespeare and Schiller exemplify with a practical, efficient excellence the principle of the Socratic dialogue. The spectator's consciousness, adopting for itself the function Kubie assigns to the psychoanalytical *preconscious*, has been caused to become conscious of its own ordinary, everyday level of simple conscious behavior. In psychoanalytical terms of reference, the preconscious has been made conscious. By means of the comedy composed according to Socratic principles, the preconscious is made to laugh at the follies of the simply conscious mind. By means of classical tragedy, a more powerful motivation is given to the preconscious made conscious.

The motivated preconscious is a preconscious consciously motivated to act, it must change simple consciousness: it must change something more profound than this-or-that isolable prejudice; it must change the way in which simple consciousness thinks. It must alter the "axioms" underlying the ordering of conscious thinking. It must alter the philosophical world-outlook of the same person's own conscious thinking.

This locates the general kind of phenomenon upon which clinical inquiry must focus. It is the surge of joyful emotion at a valid discovery effected by the kind of arrangement within mental processes we have just identified once again, which is one of the more readily identifiable correlatives of the variety of process toward which we are pointing.

Nonetheless, we have not quite yet gone far enough. The kind of creative activity we properly describe as "fundamental scientific breakthroughs" does not occur within exactly the configuration we just have described. By the same principle, preconsciousness can act upon preconscious judgment in a manner analogous to the mode by which preconsciousness alters the way of thinking of simple consciousness. This is the location of what we properly identify as creative discovery, creative thinking.

This account of the "location" of creative mentation is identical to Plato's development and employment of the notion of the *hypothesis of the higher hypothesis*. This is the kernel of what foolish critics of Plato describe pejoratively as his *idealism,* and the point of issue at which the most sophisticated varieties of attempted criticism are directed against what is described as *Platonic realism*. We shall shortly identify the proof that such criticisms are absurd.

In Plato's dialogues taken as a whole, the Socratic method repels all attempts to make a distinction between what modern opinion compartmentalizes more or less absolutely as the arts and the sciences. The Socratic method insists, by virtue of its practice, that the laws of the mind, the laws bearing upon ordering of relations in society, and the lawful ordering of galaxies, planets, pebbles and so-called "elementary particles" are one and the same. Moreover, as the work of Cardinal Nicholas of Cusa, of Leonardo da Vinci and his circle, of Kepler, of Leibniz, of Riemann, et al., have specifically proven the point, Plato's scientific method is correct, and uniquely so. Thus, in that manner, the entirety of Plato's dialogues is proof of the universality of the way in which the creative processes of mind are ordered by the Socratic method.

As we now turn to the matter of the specific content of Plato's writings, before turning to the completion of the proof we have promised, we must situate the implications of this for the conflict between Christianity and the oligarchical cults of the astrological world-outlook.

The most immediate point of intersection of Plato's science with the very center of Christian theology is most immediately located in the juxtaposition of the opening verses of the Gospel according to St. John with the *Timaeus* dialogue. This is directly accessed by comparing the principle of the *Filioque*, the consubstantial Trinity, with the consubstantiality of the Composer, the Absolute Good, with the notion of the hypothesis of the higher hypothesis in Plato's work. Here, we locate the issue which motivates certain wicked, nominally Catholic and other black-oligarchical families of Europe to wish to assassinate the Pope today. It is what might be described by some as the rock-bottom issue between republicanism and oligarchism.

Plato shows that the notion of the hypothesis of the higher hypothesis has an empirical object, in the same sense that simple consciousness has rocks, trees, and so forth as its objects. This higher objectivity is the lawful elaboration of creation as a whole, not simply as an elaborated series, but rather the principle subsuming that series. In other words, the transfinite corresponding to the elaboration of creation as a whole. This is the Logos, both

Plato's notion of the Logos and the Logos of the Christian Trinity.

This Logos is the principle of composition of the universe, the principle expressing the activity of the Composer. That Christ also embodies the Absolute Good and that his activity is also the principle of composition of the universe, is the specific distinction of Christianity. That this principle, this principle of composition, can guide man to perfection, toward atonement with the Absolute Good, is in Christianity, the "imitation of Christ," and the correlation of the creative aspect of the human mind as the reflection of the divine.

The writings of Philo of Alexandria should be consulted by those who doubt that the same method is implicit in Judaism.

This interpolation advances us toward the proof in reach, and also serves to situate the issue between Christianity and oligarchical families more precisely.

What is the proof, then, that shows a scientifically verifiable basis for treating the Logos as the proper object of the creative powers of the human mind? To state the matter in that form is half way to answering it.

How do we prove that the reflected form of the Logos, and of the creative processes of mind, are negentropic? Essentially, as we have been proceeding here, we first define the task which creative mentation must solve. This task is a negentropic function, a succession of discoveries whose consistent feature is an increase in the negentropy of society. Then, we must indicate that what the mind knows through such a process of discovery, by viewing that process of discovery itself as an object of conscious reflection, is in congruence with its negentropic result. By correlating the willfully preconscious transformation of preconsciousness with the notion of the hypothesis of the higher hypothesis, we have implicitly accomplished that task. The remaining obstacle to be overcome, the obstacle which usually arouses the greatest degree of intellectual cowardice, is to make conscious the proofs that the tangible, practical objects of simple consciousness are a projected reflection of reality, rather than reality in itself.

We merely summarize the proof required.

During Plato's lifetime, his collaborators at the Cyrenaic Temple of Amon proved that only five regular polyhedrons can be constructed in Euclidean space. All fundamental accomplishments in modern European science are based entirely upon the implications of that discovery. These implications are the central topic of Plato's *Timaeus*. The commentaries on this and upon the added contributions of Archimedes, were taken as topics by Cardinal Nicholas of Cusa. All the fundamental achievements of modern science were set into motion, at first directly and then indirectly, by Cusa's treatment of this matter.

Plato recognized, correctly, the the fact that visual space-time was so ordered that only five such solids could be constructed, signified demonstration that the geometry of our space of vision is bounded, and bounded in a manner directly refuting the axiomatic assumptions of René

Descartes later, or also the Royal Society of Locke, Hooke, Newton, Boyle et al. From this, Plato adduced two working-principles.

First, that the world of visual space-time is not an accurate representation of the work in which efficient cause is located *ontologically*, but that, the space-time we see--our bounded *discrete manifold* of particles appearing to act upon one another at a distance--is not otherwise unreal. To employ modern language for describing this, this discrete manifold of visual space-time is a more or less faithful, but distorted projection of the ontological reality which causes its appearance and of which it, this discrete manifold, is itself a subsumed part.

Second, Plato adduced that the way in which the discrete manifold is ordered reflects directly the same geometrical principles by which the entirety of Euclidean space is bounded, the principles reflected in the uniqueness of the five polyhedrons of Amon--the so-called *five Platonic solids*. By examining with special emphasis the regular polygons of which the Platonic solids are constructed, Plato adduced what Kepler demonstrated later, that the inscription of those polygons within the circle divides the circumference of the circle in portions corresponding to the ordering principle of a twelve-note, octave scale centered on the principle of the fifth. (The elementary system of well-tempered polyphony existed during Plato's lifetime.) From this standpoint of reference, Plato judged that the universe as we see it, the discrete manifold, is ordered according to the harmonic implications of the Platonic solids. (We shall omit proving the grounds on which Plato concluded this as a *necessary* solution.) Hence, the *Timaeus* is dedicated to the subject of the Composer (Absolute Good) and lawful composition of the universe.

With aid of crucial mediating work by Leonardo da Vinci, Pacioli, Durer, et al., Cusa's treatment of the implications of this problem was partially realized by Kepler. The work of Leonardo et al. to this effect includes two points which must be cited for clarity about the basis for Kepler's hypothesis. First, Leonardo, Pacioli, et al. reconstructed the spherical proof for the uniqueness of the five Platonic solids, and from this, together with exploration of the anomalies of Albertian perspective, developed a new conception of visual space which is the distinguishing feature of compositions of painting of Leonardo, the School of Raphael, and so forth: to represent important relations not as we view them naively, but as they are without anomalies. Second, as a correlative of this, they demonstrated that implicitly all living processes are ordered morphologically in self-similar proportionings congruent with the Golden Section adduced as the most characteristic limiting feature of the bounding of Euclidean space.

Kepler proved Plato's conclusions as to the fact that the universe seen in the discrete manifold is composed harmonically. The harmonic ordering of the orbits proved the principle empirically on the scale of the solar system. Kepler embedded in this proof one notable added feature, identifying the harmonic values of the orbit of a planet which must necessarily have existed but had been necessarily destroyed. Gauss was the first to prove that the asteroid belt has precisely the harmonic orbital values for the destroyed planet--orbit specified by Kepler.

To merely subsume the mass of further development on the basis of Kepler's founding of modern mathematical physics by means of this identified proof, we leap to the outcome of this development, Riemann. Riemann, in a dissertation composed for his qualifying habilitation to become Professor at Göttingen University, solved in principle the chief problem left unsolved by Kepler's proof. Kepler had proven, in fact conclusively, the essential argument of Plato's *Timaeus*: the discrete manifold is an harmonically composed, bounded projection of the reality located in a higher, subsuming continuous manifold. Riemann was the first to prove what the ontological-geometric character of that higher order universe is. In a unique experimental design, predicting the method of generation of accoustical shock-waves, in 1859, Riemann selected a method for testing empirically his notion of the specific character of the continuous manifold from which our discrete manifold of visible space-time is generated.

That continuous manifold is absolutely negentropic, and has the kind of transfinite ordering of negentropic processes according to the Socratic method. The fundamental, negentropic ordering of the continuous manifold does concur with Plato's notion of the Logos, as that notion was developed by means of the Socratic method.

What we have just completed summarizing is the kernel of the issue in every aspect of formal knowledge, defining the core-issue of the irreconcilability of republican and oligarchical ways of thinking about the universe and man in that universe.

To make this a bit less formal in appearance, to bring the astronomical questions down to earth, so to speak, the following is perhaps the most efficient point of reference to employ.

If we reduce the statement of existence of society to the form in which it is a statement consistent with the scientific principle of closure, we are obliged to state it as the closed, negentropic, functional description of a process, as we outlined this approach earlier. In this representation of that process, the empirical reference of the experimental observation is the *work* represented by an actual or implicit (virtual) increase in the potential relative population-density of society. All of the activity of persons in society which does not bear upon that *work* may appear to have the form of work-activity, but is merely analogous to what we term *virtual work* in elementary instruction in physics to students. (The work being done by a silently-standing three-legged stool is the paradigm for "virtual work.")

The location of the work actually accomplished, in terms of closure, is the injection of negentropy into society's activity. In practice, in the short-term, the improvement effected may involve relatively greater emphasis on pre-existing forms of relatively more advanced technologies, for example. In the longer run, the stock of available relatively advanced technologies must be qualitatively improved by scientific and related discovery. In the final analysis, the only source of net work accomplished by society and the individuals within it is those scientific and related discoveries which increase the negentropy of society, in terms of increases of potential relative population-density.

As the Book of Genesis prescribes: Man accomplishes work as he fulfills the injunction to "Be fruitful and multiply, and fill the earth and subdue it." To fulfill that injunction, for society and man within it to continue to exist, scientific and related forms of (negentropic) discovery must transform the existing practice of society and its individual members. To exist as man, man must exercise the divine potentiality of negentropic creative powers within each individual. So, the consubstantiality of the Trinity complements, and is implicitly required by this cited injunction of the Book of Genesis.

This work, this negentropy, is work upon what? What is the object for this work? Upon what object does man work? Man works upon the lawful ordering of the universe as a whole. What he fancies himself to see in the discrete manifold is not unreal, but not adequately real. He is like a workman watching the work of his hands in a highly distorted mirror-reflection. What is real in the reflection is that it is a reflection of the real. Hence, the shadows in the wall of the darkened cave, as an image Plato offers his readers. So, St. Paul's observation that we see as in a glass darkly. The error occurs not as man recognizes the objects in the mirror as a reflection of reality, but when man's mind mistakes the real reflection for the reality reflected. We do our work in the lawful composition of the universe as a whole. The content of that work is creative mentation in the form of negentropy. When we peer into the mirror, it is that negentropic reality we must instruct ourselves to see as a reflected reality.

The general function of what we call culture is implicitly defined by what we have developed to this immediate point of our report. (We are now preparing to descend downhill, from the Empyreal peaks of astronomical knowledge, into those humbler foothills, on which lower peaks our nation's foreign policy is composed.)

The essential, practical function of classical forms of composition of music, literature, and the plastic arts is to express the Socratic principle as we have defined it here. The purpose of this is, in a rather obvious way, to orient the mental life of individuals and social intercourse into that ordering of mental life and social practice which coheres in principle with the proper work of mankind. Yet, it is higher. As creative work reflects the divine, as that which distinguishes us essentially from a cow, so we must desire to become more human in ourselves and with one another, by occupying an increasing portion of this brief mortal living of ours with that which coheres with the divine.

Why do not all persons wish to live as truly human? How can a human being become so unnatural a thing as an oligarch? And. why do oligarchs hate humanity with such bestial ferocity? Where, from within the ranks of new generations, are new oligarchs recruited, like mythical changelings, to perpetuate their parasitical, cancerous species from the ranks of our children?

The classical treatment of this problem occurs in Plato's *Republic*, in the writings of St. Augustine, and is elaborated as the single subject of Dante Alighieri's *Commedia.* We find the oligarch in the "Inferno." Not simply because all sorts of nasty, wicked people inhabit that place, but for a more rigorous, profound reason of principle.

The three-canticle *Commedia* is the application of the principle of the Socratic method to elaborate two kinds of maturation in a single mode. It is, in principle, an account of the process by which a newborn infant is transformed into a perfected form of adult. The final, hundredth, Empyreal canto expresses the completion of maturation. It is otherwise a statement of a principle of maturation which may be applied to an entire society or section of that society. Implicit in the representation of an ordering-principle for such maturation is a key to understanding what occurs if this maturation is aborted, or the direction reversed. In this third aspect of the matter we find the oligarch.

The newborn infant is, we have noted, a bawling, irrational existentialist, a destructive anarchist with a divine potential for maturation. What, then, occurs if this maturation is aborted, or the process of maturation reversed? The result we often recognize as the "infantile" child, youth or adult. In the same sense, we recognize that all psychopathology is of the common quality of "infantile regression."

Imagine now a mature adult, with the conscious powers of an adult, but a philosophical outlook which is a parody of an infant. With that analogy, we approach the etiological definition of an oligarch: among the ranks of the criminally insane, and more commonly, simply within the category we rightly distinguish as the *criminal mind.* We examine our oligarch as of this latter type, and then proceed to differentiate the real oligarchical mind from the pure-and-simple criminal mind.

By an insane person we mean a psychotic, a condition we associate with some specific sort of delusional element in the ordering of the victim's consciousness of the discrete manifold as representation of a realm of social practice. We need not, for our purposes here, explore the matter further than that: we can now focus upon the criminal mind, as distinct from the criminally insane, or insane in general.

We distinguish the criminal mind from the insane person (criminally or otherwise) in that the criminal mind is described as "fully conscious of what he is doing and of the practical consequences of those actions." He is insane in a specific sense: he is *morally insane.* This moral insanity is generically of the "substance" of infantile regression. It is some expression of what we otherwise identify, in formal terms of reference apart from a clinical setting, as a philosophical anarchist, an existentialist, or, to catch the full flavor of the matter, a *radical existentialist.*

We distinguish among the ranks of criminal minds in general according to special features associated with their criminal impulses. In all cases, what truly confronts us is not a criminal passion for a specific hedonistic sort of goal, even where obsessions of that form may appear to be the controlling feature of their behavior at a particular point of observation. The essential feature of the criminal mind is a disposition for a certain category, or categories of criminality. The criminal mind requires certain categories of criminal activity as his compelling "inner psychological needs." Without these specific kinds of "pleasures," existence itself becomes intolerable for him. It is the manner in which these categorical sorts of criminal "pleasures" are defined for him, which differentiates the one variety of criminal mind from another.

The general problem of categorization is broadly illustrated by comparing two kinds of dangerous anarchists: the first is the individual anarchist assassin; the other is the Nazi, who is philosophically the same general sub-category of criminal mind as the anarchist assassin, *but the latter abhors the former*, and perhaps vice versa. The evil fascist character of Hermann Hesse's *Steppenwolf* helps to illustrate the distinction. Steppenwolf is the prototype of the worst sort of Nazi, but he could also embody exactly the same impulsions respecting the facts of evil he performs as an individual outside of, and with a certain hostility to the Nazi organization.

The first level of categorical distinction to be considered in attempting to differentiate the oligarch within the ranks of the criminal mind, is the distinction between individual and social categories of criminal dispositions. The individualist among criminal minds may occasionally perpetrate crime in the accidental pack of criminality, but he does not need a *pack* psychologically; it may or may not be a means to an end, but not the end. The social category of criminal mind is defined by the need to execute his dominant criminal category of "pleasure" in a pack-form. Without the pack, the same sort of criminality has significantly less pleasure for him.

The oligarch is a special variety of the pack-criminal mind. His passion is to execute concerted destruction against an entire society, and to perpetuate that destructive pleasure by continuing to torture the society once his pack succeeds in establishing rulership over it. Friedrich Nietzsche is the best paradigm for this kind of pack-criminal mind. Nietzsche's putative assertion of individual action is a fraud on his part. He does not propose individual action; he proposes to eradicate the memory of Jesus Christ from the human species, and to bring into being a world-order of worship of Satan (Dionysus), a world-order of Chaos Nietzsche names " The Age of Aquarius," together with Crowley of Britain. These are not individual acts, this is a distillation of that pack-criminal mentality, the essence of a highly informed oligarchical mind.

The oligarchy's disposition for murder and torture is monstrous, but its essential object of hatred is not to murder and torture, although torture is relatively more proximate than murder to its essential appetite. What the oligarchy wishes to destroy is the creative potentiality of the human mind.

Imagine an evil, oversized pre-adolescent boy, who promptly murders any school-teacher who commits the offense of causing the brat to learn a new conception, a conception which the brat's sordid consciousness reacts to as an attempt to "change my mind." This is, approximately, the kind of hatred which governs the oligarchy as a whole. It is the kind of criminal mind developing in the child who reacts with venomous desire to kill, like Steppenwolf, against "Anyone who tries to force me to grow up," against "Anyone who tries to fool with my mind, to try to change me from what I am right now." The oligarch's perverted pleasure is to "deschool" the human race, down to the level that race, as his prey and subjects, retain barely the faculties needed to perform a fixed sort of assigned service to the oligarch.

The oligarch can be sly about this. He may even collect classical culture for himself and his "elite friends," but he will not tolerate an active form of classical cultural activity ruling *him*, ordering developments in *his* society. He may gloat over patronizing art or science, and may delight in exhibiting such things as *his possessions*. He will kill in homicidal rage if any force threatens to subject him to an ordering of society according to the creation of such a culture.

"Blood and soil," characterized by irrationalism, are the qualities of the infantile mind. "My mommy! (My Great

Mother)" the enraged child of arrested moral development bursts out in a way so incongruous for his age that there is something incestuously obscene, think the adults and older children witnessing this. "This is mine!" the "disturbed" variety of child erupts in a way which witnesses might find also obscene. We are witnessing perhaps, a potential Nazi, or a potential trusted errand-runner for an oligarch.

These are lawful phenomena corresponding to the pathology and etiology of persons who are like oligarchs in these respects. This is not yet an adequate definition of the oligarchy or oligarchism.

The differentiation of the oligarchy is the *oligarchical system*. Rather than eruption of the sort of pack-criminal mind we have described in some "spontaneous" manner from within a predominantly healthy society (e.g.. "Purgatory"), the oligarchy and its oligarchical current of servants and camp-followers is *perpetuated across successive generations as a cultural movement.*

The oligarchical culture, the cultural tradition rooted in astrological-age culture, is an evolved, "pre-packaged" design with two principal sorts of describable consequences. It is, in its first effect, a "pre-package" system, a culture for transforming he or she whom it significantly infects with its full force into an unhuman changeling, an oligarchical personality. It has also acquired a second specific kind of impact; it embodies recipes designed to eradicate its enemy, republicanism, wherever it encounters that enemy.

This latter aspect has two features. First, it embodies what may be regarded as the "genetic model" for the infected oligarchical mind's ostensibly instinctive hatred against personalities and cultural impulses which reflect republicanism. The oligarchical mind acquires a built-in disposition for detecting and reacting, as a species to its natural enemy, to republicanism. In the second feature, the oligarchical culture has built into the design a corrosive method of injecting a cancer-like development into the tissue of republicanism. The latter is the problem on which we focused attention in the opening portions of this report.

Our employment of descriptive terminology to catalogue these features of oligarchism is not intended to substitute for an analytical treatment; we have merely catalogued that for which we must now account.

All of these catalogued features of the oligarchical system--all of those features we have identified at various points of this report up to this point--are permeated by a common, central, active principle. Shall we call this principle the anti Christ? It is the principle which meets every Apostolic Christian theological specification for the Satan, whose name, not accidentally, is merely a variant of the same entity otherwise known as the Phrygian pagan god Dionysus. Whatever you may prefer to call this principle, it is the principle of infantile regression, hostility against the higher functions of the "preconscious" corresponding to the notion of the hypothesis of the higher hypothesis. This hostility functions within the mind as an inversion of that principle of conscience seen in the mental life of the republican.

It is the structuring of this principle by oligarchical culture--the oligarchical system--which is crucial to the working of this principle in its oligarchical expression.

This structure meets the requirements of coherence with the oligarchical principle by its restrictions on the manner in which the oligarchical mind can conceptualize physical space-time. Nietzsche showed himself to be well-informed by choosing the names of Apollo and Dionysus for these two oligarchical frames of space-time reference. Nietzsche popularized the mind-deadening dogma, that all art-forms and the works produced in these forms must be classified primarily as either Apollonian or Dionysian.

For example, once during a radio-broadcast interview in the United States, that product of Hapsburg oligarchical culture, the late conductor Bruno Walter insisted (one might wish to say "with his bare face hanging out at the time") that the difference which the conductor must know to exist between the music of Beethoven and Brahms, is that Brahms "is Apollonian," whereas Beethoven is "Dionysian." Such an admission explains why, in available recordings known, Walter never demonstrates an understanding of the musical ideas embedded in a work of Brahms or Beethoven, and why his performances of Brahms are only "less bad" than his Beethoven. Take that as an illustration, so that we may avoid proving the principles of musical ideas as such here. What is to be illustrated is this following, important point.

The oligarchical doctrine, earlier than the literate age, has insisted that the world is ruled, in the final analysis, by the two "gods." Apollo and Dionysus. Oligarchism will tolerate the existence of Christ by name only on condition that the name of Christ is employed as a disguise for an Apollo (or, Horus) hiding behind. These two "gods," Apollo and Dionysus, are rival sons of an incestuous old homicidal biddy, the Great Mother.

During the 1920s and 1930s, the Great Earth Mother often referred to Apollo as "stinky," because Apollo, before going out to parade himself in front of prospective male bed-companions for that next night, would bathe, fix his hair so, and that sort of thing generally. Apollo was a nasty character if he caught you by surprise in an alley, but in public Apollo was the image of an upstanding, respectable fellow, a person of absolutely no morals--at least, no good morals. Apollo's urbanity adopts a substitute for morality: this substitute is named "ethics."

During the same time, Earth Mother referred to Dionysus as "my stinking, dirty louse," or words to that general effect. Nonetheless, these vile words Mother always spoke in a way which Dionysus recognized secretly as Mother's way of expressing--well, endearment is not the proper word for anything involving Mother--shall we say, the least homicidal of Mother's lustful impulses. In fact. Mother--this "Ma Barker" of mythology--recognized that Dionysus resembled herself spiritually a bit more than Apollo did.

Great Mother loving both her sons, she gave each a turn running the universe, in perpetual alternation. Taoism? Yin-Yang? Of course it is; who but the same filthy gang as produced the Chaldeans, the Magicians shipped that sort of filth into China millennia past, to destroy China from the inside, to destroy the ancient culture of China? Manicheanism? Naturally, if you believe there is any difference in principle among Hesiodism, Arianism, Manicheanism, Monophysite varieties of lunacy, you expose the fact that you walked out of the theater without waiting to discover what would be shown to you during the second act of the play. This Manichean alternation is the pivotal point on which the arch-Nazi Nietzsche based his own and the theosophists' plan to destroy Christ and civilization, by introducing an "Age of Aquarius" during this present century.

The oligarchical doctrine often represents itself as a kind of substitute for the canticle-categories of Dante's *Commedia*. In that sort of spiritual consumer fraud, Apollo or *Apollonian* is projected as the state of "Purgatory," and Dionysus assumes his own proper domain, the "Inferno." There is no "Paradise."

This sort of substitution was not cooked up by Nietzsche. It is based on the same ancient oligarchical trick which cooked up the worship of Isis, Osiris and Horus as a substitute for the consubstantial trinity. Admittedly, that nasty trick was smuggled into German Protestantism by (chiefly) the influence of Ludwig Feuerbach's *The Essence of Christianity*, in which Mary's name is used as a disguise for Isis, and Isis is then substituted for the Logos (Holy Spirit), using this fictive Mary, within the Holy Family, to replace the Trinity. Isis is an Egyptian name for the Anatolian Great Mother, the Mother of Apollo and Dionysus.

The oligarchical approach to such myth-building involves the variety of problem to which Socrates refers in Plato's *Republic*. Socrates plays a deservedly mean trick on the Phoenicians, as he underscores "Phoenician" at that point in the dialogue. According to Phoenician myths (lies), says Socrates, the human condition is divided among golden souls (the highest condition), silver souls (a slightly less valuable stuff), and. down to iron or brass souls (a most regrettable condition in which to find oneself). Then, Socrates, after listing such Phoenician categories, reports that there are three categorical conditions of development of, not genetic distinctions of mankind, which he will and does explain: the three categories of the *Commedia*. This brings us now to the point of indicating the reason for the reference to Bruno Walter.

In a truthful version of the general kind of Phoenician myth to which Socrates refers, one would expect a hierarchy of Hercules, Apollo and Dionysus, in which Hercules would be associated, as the epic myths do associate him, with Prometheus's uncle (or, father?) Atlas. We emphasize again, that reference to the Atlas Epic, the Atlantis Battle of Olympians against Titans, is an indispensable point of reference for formulating successful hypotheses in exploring the manner in which the oligarchical system functions internally and against the world outside itself.

Look again at the implications of Bruno Walter's absurd dogma. The republican faction of Europe was known among those with a classical education as *Prometheans*. The classical image employed as reference for this usage was principally Aeschylus's. In the Christian view of the Apostles, Prometheus is an image of what might be associated variously with St. Peter combatting the Magis' effort to spread a form of pseudo-Christianity in Rome, or the role of St. Paul in the mission to the peoples of the world, or the profundity and awesome power of the mind of St. John. These are the kinds of images usefully referenced to project a sense of what the Prometheus-image signifies.

Admittedly, like the case of the fellow who stole your new winter coat from the rack while you were briefly occupied elsewhere, the name *Promethean* has been misappropriated only with decreasing frequency during recent decades. (You see, as a result of our national ideology, many of us can no longer afford to buy new winter coats.) Despite such hoaxes and blunders, what the term *Promethean* ought to signify is very precisely understood among those sharing a classical cultural background.

Shelley was becoming, self-consciously, a Promethean as his premature death approached him--unlike that degraded witch he married, the author of *Frankenstein* and other evils. *Frankenstein* was intended by the authoress, and publisher, and this was then known by readers generally, to be an anti-technology, Malthusian libel against the memory and continuing influence of that "modern Prometheus," Benjamin Franklin. Mary Wollstonecraft (she is unworthy of the name "Shelley") subtitled her propaganda-tract, *Frankenstein* ("Dr. Franklin"), "Modern Prometheus." The published references to Franklin as the Prometheus of the 18th Century, including those of Forster and Immanuel Kant, abound in that period.

The one figure of the entire half-century, say approximately 1775-1825, with whom the Promethean outlook in personality *and in work* is most assuredly identified, most ruthlessly self-identified, is Ludwig van Beethoven. A voice is heard addressing this writer now: "I mean, after all, Bruno Walter was a very busy conductor, I mean, you know, a person to become a successful conductor, I mean such important orchestras, you know, doesn't have time, I mean, well, basically, you know, reading about a lot of other things. I'm sure Beethoven must be Dionysian."

For a Bruno Walter to describe Beethoven as a Dionysian is to prove that either Walter was lying, or that he was sufficiently ignorant of the principles of musical ideas to believe the sort of trash he was spouting. Listening to available recordings of Walter purporting to conduct Beethoven appears to settle the matter in favor of Walter's musical-idea illiteracy. It was not personally Walter's fault, perhaps, that this occurred; he had the misfortune to have come from a successful career developed in Hapsburg Vienna. Like many Austro-Hungarian intellectuals, his mind was oligarchical, reducing him to the musical equivalent of a talented Osiris.

This bears directly on the principal point toward which we have been pressing here. The kernel-principle of oligarchism determines a definite "structural ordering" of the oligarchical mind. This is a "structuring" which determines not so much exactly what an oligarch will think, but how he will think it, whatever it is. If Walter's mind were structured oligarchically, according to an Apollonian or Dionysian mental mapping, no amount of technical accomplishment as a musician, nor any amount of added loving intention to master the music of Beethoven would have led Walter to grasp the essence of any Beethoven symphony, its musical idea.

No accomplished conductor wishes to conduct from reading score, just as only the requirements of ensemble performance would permit any musician to perform a work as finished performance from reading score. There is an extremely urgent principle at issue in this fact, a principle which is crucial to understanding the mental map of the oligarchical mind, and to understand the more finely detailed features of the process by which the oligarchy has been destroying the United States from within, by degrading our national culture.

A musical idea, or a poetical idea is, first of all, a kind of idea which is associated only with the unit-composition as an entirety. This idea is characteristically indivisible, in the respect that the idea can not be represented by any portion of the composition less than the composition as a whole.

The mere addition of even all the parts of the whole composition could not represent the idea. At this point, most people become quite agitated. "What is all this nonsense? You mean, we can't hear it, we can't touch it, but you insist it's there?"

Pause! Now reference your attention for a moment back to our earlier discussion of what the late Kubie would have classed as "two layers" of the "preconscious " functions of the mind. Now, from that standpoint of reference, look at a score of music for any single important classical composition not as a collection of notes, but as a sequence of "footprints" of a musical idea. By retracing those footprints in the proper fashion, we produce the musical idea for an audience (and ourselves). To avoid digging into the principles of counterpoint, we emphasize merely that score is a "footprinting" of a process of development. In brief, contrapuntal statements in music generate musical paradoxes. In a classical composition, there are usually one principal paradox and various secondary paradoxes associated with a unit of musical composition. The process of solving the secondary paradoxes, leading toward a general solution of the principal paradox, is the process of development from which a definite musical idea is recognizable as associated with a unit-composition as a whole.

To restate the matter appropriately: A musical composition corresponding to a musical idea is analogous in one respect to a scientific proof: the idea is communicated only at the point the proof has been completed--no earlier, no later.

To think in terms of musical ideas or poetical ideas, one must employ the same principles of mental life we introduced to this report with reference to the principle of classical tragedy. A great musical composition is one whose musical idea corresponds necessarily to the order of mental life associated with production of fundamental scientific discoveries. It is this task-oriented aspect of mental life which is the basis of reference for defining a Promethean personality, in the sense Shelley, for example, would have recognized the appropriateness of the appellation to a Franklin or Beethoven.

Now, we situate this, the central feature of all music worth reproducing, as the principal task the conductor or performer must solve. All of the technical proficiency of the conductor and performer, all the musician's other knowledge means almost nothing musically, unless the application of those skills results in a proper grasp and presentation of the musical idea of a composition. By dealing with the Bruno Walter paradox in this fashion, we define the reference point in contrasting conception, to attack directly the structural features of the oligarchical mental mapping.

The conductor, for example, does not memorize a score merely to demonstrate his memory, nor even to avoid the need to turn his glance away from the orchestra or chorus to read a piece of the score. Nor does the mere memorizing of the score have anything to do in and of itself with the musical idea to be presented. Having the notes "entirely in memory" has nothing in itself to do with communication of musical ideas. The late Arturo Toscanini possessed a prodigious memory and conducting skills, with aid of which he beautifully embalmed the corpses of Beethoven symphonies.

"First, Bruno Walter, now Toscanini! What has all this suspicious and probably irrelevant kicking of some of the world's most honored conductors to do with our foreign policy?" That reaction would be consistent with the nature of the national ideology by means of which we are destroying ourselves.

We are focusing, it should not be forgotten at any moment, on how the systematic erosion and degradation of our nation's cultural life was used, deliberately, by the European oligarchy and its domestic accomplices, to destroy our nation from within. The case of Bruno Walter points our attention to the major problem the importation of Hapsburg culture has represented for us in many aspects of our national life. The case of Toscanini points more narrowly to the vileness, and conscious malignancy he himself exhibited over an extended period in his conscious efforts to eradicate musical ideas from performances.

The relevance of the Toscanini affair to our general undertaking here has several interdependent aspects. His was an oligarchical mind, reenforced by his association with the oligarchy. He was the instrument of a certain circle of the international oligarchical "families," and his adopted function, as he himself avowed this intent, was to eradicate the methods of performance and conducting of performances by which musical ideas are communicated.

There was a musical-homicidal side to Toscanini which is not to be explained, but may of course correlate with, his famous displays of bad temper. His vendetta, from the 1920s onward, against both Wilhelm Furtwängler, and Furtwängler's closest musician-collaborator, Vienna's Heinrich Schenker, is the clearest, and one of the dirtiest cases of an undisguised oligarchical effort to wipe out the basis for continued existence of an entire facet of the culture of civilization, in this case the continuity of transmission of classical musical composition. We have accused Toscanini of nothing in respect to music of which he did not repeatedly accuse himself. To understand Toscanini in the flesh on this point, is to view personified the oligarchical gnome working inside the mind of the person being transformed into an oligarch.

There was a nakedly manifest side to Toscanini which reminds one of the nasty little fascist of Herman Hesse's design, Steppenwolf.

A brief summary of the background to a post-war aspect of Toscanini's evil vendetta against musical ideas is needed to leave no one in doubt of the accuracy and appropriateness of the point being developed by aid of this case. During the Nazi period, Nazi boss Hermann Goering picked up a young conductor, Herbert von Karajan, as his protégé. In due course, von Karajan, a member of the Nazi party, was boosted by the Nazi gang in Berlin, toward challenging the policies and position of Furtwängler, Nikisch's successor as head of the Berlin symphony. The nationalists rallied to Furtwängler against von Karajan. It was the late 1930s, and the Nazis did not yet sense themselves strong enough to proceed with killing off the Prussian elite, as they did as rapidly as they dared during the course of the war. Furtwängler won that issue.

During the immediate post-war period, an Anglo-American faction, featuring Hans Haber and that obscene old Isis-witch from the American Museum of Natural History, Margaret Mead, used the fact that Furtwängler had beaten off the Nazis' efforts to advance von Karajan, to argue that this was a demonstration of Furtwängler's complicity in the Nazi leadership. Karajan, after a discrete interval, now gained Furtwängler's post.

Arturo Toscanini, who knew that the whole accusation against Furtwängler was a wicked fraud, did not miss the opportunity to join such despicable creatures as Margaret Mead, to put a dirty knife into Furtwängler at such an opportune moment.

To believe that Toscanini was a mere dupe of anti-Fascist passions is nonsense. Toscanini belonged to the circle of oligarchical families which had placed Mussolini in power and which continued to control him until the end of the matter. Toscanini's objections to Mussolini were quite simple: it is one thing to send a gang of rowdies to smash up something or other; this does not mean that the man who hires and dispatches the rowdies then takes those rowdies home to live with his own family. As for Dame Margaret Mead herself, clomping about the upper corridors of the Museum, thumping that great horned staff of an Isis-witch, her anti-Fascist passions must be measured against her key role in promoting within the United States her own preferred versions of the Nazi youth-counterculture and Nazi "eugenics" doctrines.

Calling Furtwängler a "Nazi" for his opposing the advancement of the Nazi protégé and Nazi von Karajan, was merely a lying cover-story for an attempt to assassinate musical culture.

The clincher against Toscanini (from 1920s onward) and against Hans Haber and Mead on this issue, is that they lumped in the frame-up against Furtwängler, his collaborator Heinrich Schenker.

Schenker had been a collaborator of Johannes Brahms, and the last great musicologist of Europe in a line beginning with St. Augustine, continuing through the gigantic Bishop Zarlino, and culminating in Beethoven as its pinnacle to date. It is clear from his writings that Schenker did not grasp the full import of the poetic principle of composition in music, the secret of Beethoven's method of composition (in particular). Nonetheless, like the magnificent Pablo Casals' conducting in his prime, like the somewhat different attack by Furtwängler, musicology relies to this day on Shenker's work as the best approximation of location of the poetic principle of composition in music. Each time Furtwängler was in Vienna, he would take the first opportunity to get over to the house of his friend, the composer-musicologist Schenker. There, according to independent reports of surviving figures among witnesses to such proceedings,

Furtwängler and Schenker would collaborate in the effort to perfect some crucial detail of performance of, chiefly, a work of Beethoven.

During the 1930s, following the Nazi occupation of Austria, Schenker's work was largely suppressed as a matter of Nazi music policy. Schenker's Jewish widow was hied off to a Nazi concentration-camp, and died during the war at Auschwitz. To this date, the same set of scoundrels who vilified Furtwängler and Schenker as Nazis in the domain of musical culture, repeat over and over the refrain that Schenker was a Nazi.

What is it, then, which a great conductor (or, other accomplished musical performer) does which requires him to seem to conduct from memory? In first approximation: musical ideas can not be reproduced effectively if the musical score corresponding to that composition is performed literally. This does not represent a foot-in-the-door-opening for what often passes for the "performer's liberty to interpret." The conductor or performer may improve in performance over the kind of performance the composer heard in his mind, but this is valid only if the performer presents the musical idea the composer has specified in a better way than the composer himself imagined at the time of the composition.

The best comparison is the comparison of the original discoverer of a fundamental scientific discovery and some teacher who attempts to present the same, exact proof, as the discoverer presented it. While adhering rigorously even to every word the original discoverer employed, the teacher's delivery of the discoverer's written text may be more efficient a delivery of those words, in respect to the efficiency of the students' rapid comprehension of the discoverer's intended point, than the discoverer might have accomplished reading his own words himself.

In either case, music or a teacher reciting a crucial proof to a classroom, the performer's consciousness must be directed not to the successions of words or notes, but must be focused upon the single idea associated with the composition as a whole. He must direct the reproduction of each word or note in reference to the musical idea to be produced by all of the notes as a process. Each successive note must be performed in such a fashion that the *potential* for reaching the musical idea is increased by that note. It is by gauging this increase of potential against each particular note's performance that the conductor or performer "brings forth" the musical idea of the entire composition at the conclusion.

To ensure that we have not permitted ourselves to be misunderstood on this particular point. A musical performer or conductor has no "freedom," no available margin of interpretation for "expressing myself" in the treatment of the composition. It is the composer's musical idea, and only that idea, which must govern every note's performance to the finest degree that a shading of interpretation might he definable. The musician must discover the one and only range of interpretation of each note's performance, a value which is almost never the literal interpretation of the note on the page, nor even a literal interpretation according to classical conventions. There is always a necessary, slight variation from the indicated norms of score and conventions. These slight nuances, insofar as they are required to generate the musical idea emerging from the developmental characteristics of the unit-composition as a whole, are either grasped in performance or the musical idea fails "to come across" either entirely or in some meaningful sense of such failure.

There are two ways to destroy the developed capability of musicians and audiences to "hear" such nuances as increasing of potential leading to a distinct musical idea. One is Stravinskyian "neo-classicism;" the other is producing smeared pages as purported musical compositions, as Stockhausen. The one is an apparently rigorous, formal-logical, mechanical-like preciseness. This is the method by which Apollo prefers to kill minds. The nuance of rigorous creative development is destroyed as Toscanini beautifully embalmed Beethoven symphonies. The other is the method of Madame de Staël and the Romantic school she nurtured amid the stained linens of her Lausanne, Switzerland bedchamber: Stockhausen is of the next-to-most-recent of the generations of the spiritually illegitimate descendants of the de Staël: by unleashing the irrational, arbitrary nuance in both composition and performance, as Franz Liszt and Richard Wagner do this, Dionysus is unleashed from such locations as the phalanxes of Wagner's and Hitler's interpretation of the musical achievements of ancient Nuremberg. The first is the method of Toscanini: the second is the attempt to interpret a Beethoven symphony as if it had been composed by Stockhausen, the policy and craft of Leonard Bernstein.

This has shown us an aspect of the method used to destroy the culture of the United States. The example so given, we now proceed to elaborate the general principles illustrated.

The Great Mother's two sons, Apollo and Dionysus, are the same, Dr. Jekyll and Mr. Hyde. They do not exist, of course, but they have an efficient existence nonetheless: the oligarchical system behaves as if they did exist. Yet, since in even that form of existence, each is but one of a pair of Jekyll-Hyde masks, even within the oligarchical system, they are but different personas for that common thing they disguise. She that they disguise is known variously as the *Great Mother, Isis*, and so forth, each and all identical to what St. John identified as the *Whore of Babylon*. She exists, this Whore of Babylon, in the sense that the oligarchical system behaves as if she did exist: as long as the oligarchical system exists, she will exist in that sense, and it will continue to be as if she were an efficient being. There is nothing mystical anywhere in this whole, obscene, oligarchical system. There is only a pervasive mystification of a every earthly, and thoroughly evil, cancer-analogous social process.

This is the common truth behind all versions of the same, common oligarchical system's mythologies: Taoism, Yin-Yang otherwise, Manicheanism, and the Age of Aquarius scenario now in process of destroying the United States from within.

We have employed the term "structure" to underscore the point that the analysis of the ordering of the mental map of the oligarchical mind is best accomplished, for all purposes, by studying the mapping of those mental processes as a problem posed to us by a perverted paradox of Euclidean space-time.

The oligarchical universe is Nero's arena extended to infinite perspective, in the worst possible sense of a "mathematically infinite." It is the worst implication of René Descartes's version of physical space. (After seeing that his friend's, Spinoza's dangerous blunders were a product of an evil influence embedded in Descartes' system, Gottfried Leibniz undertook to destroy Descartes' influence. The treatment of Descartes on this point by Leibniz is extensive, and is easily referenced without doing more than pointing to that fact here.)

In this system, there are things, many things. In this system, a thing set into motion continues to move with that initial linear velocity except as inhibiting action hinders this, an arrangement which does not occur in the real universe, in which latter the bounding principles of physical space determine the distribution of action in the discrete manifold according to principles of harmony.

In the oligarchical system, the amount of work available at any time in the universe as a whole is the maximum amount of work which will be available at any time in the future: unless Nero intervenes into the arena from outside it. There is no direction, or design to the universe but entropy and descent.

In this universe, there are only things, such as oligarchs. Thingness is "irreducible," but some things can be reduced to their constituent, ultimately irreducible things. This is called substance, reality, fact.

Things interact with one another, out of Hobbesian motives and in a Hobbesian way. However the harmonic relations which appear to occur in the course of such interaction are not real, but only statistical, only ephemeral constructs of the mind. No matter what occurs in the universe, only things are substantial, are real. ("There's nothing wrong with Junior's mind; the only problem is that he is a thing which stuffs too many things into its mouth.")

The universe is merely such an interconnection of things.

There is nothing else, except Nero and his pantheon, sometimes disguised as Fortuna, whom we worship by a religious rite often called Gambling. Within the limits of the Almighty Ergodic Theorem, which rules this universe, Nero and his pantheon have an ephemeral margin of statistical error, through which to intervene capriciously to alter the direction of flow of work in part of the system as a whole. Nero's capricious interventions are called "accidents" or "random behavior," which is our way, say the oligarchist theoreticians, of maintaining the rules while actually successfully cheating. In manners statistical, all oligarchists will probably lie, probably all of the time.

That, broadly speaking, is the general outline of the universe according to Apollo. There is no causality in

Apollo's universe, but only the ethical principle of keeping up the appearance of causality in the disguise of the Middle Term of the Syllogism. There is no law, there are only Ethics and prevailing opinions; and, no science, but only plausible explanation as prescribed by the principles of Isocrates' School of Rhetoric. (This is all adequately covered in two writings attributed to Aristotle, his *Nicomachean Ethics* and his (unexpurgated version) *Politics*.)

How, then, does Apollo become Dionysus: how does Dr. Jekyll become transformed into Mr. Hyde?

There is a very simple, parlor-trick demonstration of how Apollo is turned into Dionysus. "Do you not agree that our universe is 'interconnected'? Is it not true, that if A is connected to B, but also B to A? I will prove this. If I proceed from A to B, then I can proceed also from B to C. From C, then I can proceed to A. Therefore, B leads to A. There is no direction in the universe of interconnectedness . . . ." From that starting point, which may at first appear to be a harmless, if specious, insignificant trick, the victim can be lured into the contemplation of The Great Complexity of It All. If the victim can be induced to extend this exercise sufficiently, a "lost in space" state like psychosis is readily induced. The operator who has lured the victim to that point is now situated to manipulate the victim's will in such a way as to produce effects which might seem Magical to the uninformed.

How could the victim of such a trick find those moorings to sanity which would protect him from the effects of such tricks?

The characteristic feature of this problem might be termed the "problem of the conception of limits," the problem of conceptualizing "infinity." We emphasized earlier that what we see is a discrete manifold, a subsumed feature and reflection of the higher-order physical space by which the discrete manifold is bounded. We indicated the fact that all fundamental progress in modern science--from Cusa, through Leonardo, Kepler, Leibniz, Gauss, Riemann, and so forth--has been achieved on the basis of exploration of this boundedness and its provable implications.

Now, along comes some Magician, of the species with which St. Peter had to deal in the form of the pseudo-Christian cult of Simon Magus at Rome. He points to the discrete manifold, which we ought to know is a looking-glass of a special sort, albeit a looking-glass built into real physical space. The Magician says, "I will prove to you that what you see is the only reality. Come with me into the Looking-Glass, and I will show you that it is infinitely interconnected, with no possible limit. Are you so cowardly you will not put matters to this Test as I propose to you?" You are "lost in space," drawn into an infinity which does not exist.

By such tricks, tricks to dupe the victim into believing in infinite Interconnectedness, the axiomatic absurdities of the Cartesian-Hobbesian universe are exploited, by use of deductive methods. If you accept the non-existent universe as real, then you must accept those formal-logical conclusions which are most directly derived from an induced state of believing in such a universe.

These Magician's tricks center in pseudo-reason, in such forms as syllogistic deduction representing itself falsely to the credulous as Reason. This trick lures the dupe into the world of Apollo. Apollo welcomes the recruit to the place of syllogistic law and order: "All will be explained to you by means of the syllogism." With that, Apollo winks. The credulous dupe being received deludes himself again: he imagines that Apollo is winking at him. Apollo is looking across the dupe's shoulder, to wink at Dionysus in the mirror on the opposite wail. Night, and Chaos will come at the close of the day.

Evening approaches. The recruited dupe is looking into Apollo's eyes, as Apollo has requested. The dupe is becoming acquainted with that Great Secret, he is proceeding toward the discovery of The Great Complexity Of It All. The happy novice is almost half way to Infinity, he imagines. Night falls. He is "lost in space." He calls out, "Apollo, where am I?"

"You are with me," replies Dionysus.

"Infinity" has revealed itself to be "The Infinitesimal." Apollo's world of seemingly orderly statistic probability was in fact densely packed with leaks, tiny holes of Chance, of utter irrationality.

"Wait! Are you saying that Aristotle describes a kind of universe which is really nothing but a collection of tiny holes filled with absolute chaos?" Precisely, dear reader, except for one qualification. Aristotle says nothing about the real universe. Aristotle is a radical nominalist; it is the names for things that are his only reality. Aristotle duped credulous people into believing he was discussing the universe: all the while, he was describing nothing but the inside of a crippled mind's consciousness. The crippled man whose consciousness Aristotle describes to you is, if you accept what Aristotle teaches you, *yourself!*

"What is this shrinking? It's just a metaphor, right?"

It is not merely a metaphor; metaphors, being of a higher degree of closeness to reality than literal meanings of common terms, are never to be called "merely." Poetic ideas are metaphors, so are musical ideas. People are taught to believe and practice nonsense concerning metaphors. People are taught that metaphors are simply a matter of using the name for one thing to describe an entirely different thing, to no other purpose than adding color and elegance to conversation. Metaphors are properly names for *conceptions of processes of development*, for the mind's taking its own experiencing of such a process of development, that experience, as the object for consciousness. Such objects are, like any simple sort of named object, either real or false, or something in between.

This "shrinking" is to be understood formally in these terms of reference. The relations among things in Aristotle's universe are the relationships of a Hobbesian universe. This is the import of Aristotle's definitions of existences and their fixed attributes: every "elementary particle" has its specific "inner psychological needs." By becoming small enough, one falls into being Hobbesian man, into one of the *holes*, called *substantial objects* or *things*, in Aristotle's imaginary, nominalist's universe of consciousness. The psychoanalytical explanation for the "shrinking" and degrading effect of the experience of the spiritual exercise of the Infinite And Beautiful Complexity Of It All--about as *beautiful* as sodomic rape of a chicken by a cassocked goat--is elementary; but before turning to that elementary point, we explore the problem a bit more.

Examine, at least very briefly, a strange thing about the manner in which most people use the English language. The emphasis is almost always on the *nouns*. The correspondence of *noun* to *thing* is the way most children are drilled into thinking all the way through to senility. In the real world, reality does not occur as fixed things, if something were to be able to remain absolutely fixed, like an immovable boundary, human beings could not directly experience that boundary in the way we distinguish objects. We experience only that which is being changed, or which we are actually or implicitly changing. The words used to identify change are *verbs*. It is in the transformation of the discrete manifold characterized by verbal statements of transformation (i.e., an experienced process of transformation), that we identify the nature of sensuous reality for sane persons. How, then, did this *insane* emphasis upon the noun emerge?

The great ancient philologist, Panini, insists and demonstrates that the Vedic-Sanskrit language is an elaboration of the use of the verb, that nouns are eggs laid by verbs. We experience (verb) a process; that process becomes an object (noun) for us by conceptualization of *experiencing*, as *experience* (noun/verb). Since 19th and early 20th century classical philology has demonstrated the ancient, common Indo-European language-stock, this means that Celtic, Italian, Germanic, Slavic, Greek, as well as Farsi, Hittite and all but one of the local dialects of the sub-continent are descended principally from a language with the same original characteristics as the Vedic. Are we, once again, faced with the same problem as in the overthrow of the astronomical age by the astrological age?

In every formal respect, the psychological shift away from the reality of the verbal idea to the lunacy of nominalism fits precisely a shift from a rational to an astrological-irrational world-outlook.

When did the nominalist degeneration of languages begin? This writer proposes no answer to that nagging question at this time. No matter; the nominalist degeneration of a language, converging on the monstrous evil of Chomskyan and related practices of "linguistics," does map to the astrological system. Panini warns that some dirty work of that sort was afoot during the 1st millennium B.C. Later during that same millennium, the Peripatetics and their circles are known to have produced the first known written grammar in which the Aristoteleans' nominalist schema is superimposed as a variety of Nicomachean Ethics upon language, to produce the worst features of the Latin known from the Republic and Empire literature.

The ordering of consciousness in a nominalist fashion--in which the name for the thing is made the anchor for a "sense of reality" as located in "fixed objects"--is the root of schizophrenia in language-processes. Pathological mental states are associated with the association of strong emotions labeled "guilt," "anger," and "fear" with nominalist mental organization. Ignorant, or disinformed opinion usually argues that it is "guilt," "anger" or "fear" which is the seed of mental disorder; there is nothing insane in human emotion--insanity lies not in emotion, but in the directing of emotion by lunatic ideas. All nouns are implicitly lunatic ideas. It is obsession with nouns which characterizes schizophrenia. Emotion may be employed by the schizophrenic to project an obsession violently upon the "outside world." The obsession may, on the other hand, violently suppress an appropriate use of emotion. The obsession is attached to both names (images) for objects of experience, and includes objects which could not have been actually experienced in the insane mind's way of relating them to other experiences.

The delusional aspect of mental disorder requires the principle that "Mother isn't peeking" when a small boy heads for the forbidden cookie-jar. The "preconscious" function must be either deceived or locked away.

The Hobbesian man can be produced by various methods for degrading a human being. In respect to the kind of trick we referred to, the degeneration of the personality by means of such a spiritual exercise (exercising), it is the fear associated with the "lost in space" experience which is to be identified. Becoming "lost" in such a tangle of objects (nouns, noun-like images) is the location of the feared object. (The object is a predicate, which always occurs in one of two of each of available genitive, dative or accusative cases. The mind experiencing the predicated objective is always the subject, the same subject which directs the acting, the unleashing of emotion to accomplish shaped work.)

The commonplace use of such spiritual exercises by contemporary Magicians is to reduce the victim of the trick to a state of intellectual and moral malleability. The Magician threw the victim into the imagined terror of the Infinite ("lost in space"). Certainty vanished, confidence in rational powers of the mind vanished. In place of confidence in rationality, the victim returned, shaken in intellectual self-confidence. If asked, "Do you still believe in a rational order of things?" the victim would give a nervous shrug, and reply, "Yes, of course I do, but you must never overlook the fact that the world is very interconnected." That response is characteristic of the victim who has been brainwashed by a Magician employing the variety of trick we have described. The victim has become slightly superstitious: he is afraid not to read the horoscope published in the newspaper lying folded open on the waiting-room table. Seeing the Magician looking over at him and smiling, the victim asks almost plaintively, "Pisces?" The Magician smirks, shakes his head back and forth three times, very slowly, and then leers as he says, "No, not Pisces: Aquarius."

The fearful obsession with objects, a pathological state merely significantly accentuated by the spiritual exercise, is the essential form of the delusion in the victim upon which the astrological system depends for its power and sustenance.

The fixation upon noun-images pulls emotion (energy) away from the *natural* mode in which any sane human being would think. A sane adult (or adolescent) human being thinks not in terms of noun-images, but in terms of *verb-images*, in terms of processes of reality, not such ephemeral footprints of processes as things. *Verb-images, process-images*, are in mathematical physics what the 1871-1883 work of Georg Cantor defines as transfinite conceptions.

These are *classical dramatic conceptions*, the experience the mind of the spectator takes as its object for consciousness in seeing the tragic process unfolding for its consciousness on stage. All reality, all real experience is transfinite in this way.

If, then, an *anti-conscience* is developed, if the preconscious functions insist that all alterations in simple consciousness must be ordered according to the nominalist principles defended by Aristotle, then, to that degree the individual's soul is dead; reality has to that degree, ceased to exist for him, and that within himself which can act consciously for Good in reality has been either simply killed or is being tortured in the basement of the prison; his mind reacts to stress by changing itself hedonistically, entropically--he descends.

Here, we are at the heart of the matter, bearing directly upon the making of our nation's foreign-policy.

Our problem is not that we make wrong policy in some succession of isolated cases. Our problem is not the bad eggs which our chickens keep producing; our problem is bad chickens. We must peer into that hen-house which is the mind of each of us, and remove those biddies which are fouling the premises. It is not the mere eggs, the nouns, which must be changed, but the hens of conscience which produce bad judgments.

How is a wicked or otherwise defective conscience produced? It is produced by a process of anti-maturation, a process of psychological conditioning, through manipulation of a controlled environment. The controlled psychological environment of a society as a whole is its culture. The easiest way to destroy a people is to control its environment of *entertainment*, and to employ the hedonistic principle, the oligarchical principle, to gradually shift the values of pleasure and pain attached to that slightly altered entertainment. Within a mere decade, if a people is undefended against such an operation, the values that people and its representatives in government will apply to the less-entertaining business of government and business will conform to the shift in values effected through the medium of entertainment.

It is by chiefly British control over our nation's major news media and entertainment media that our culture has been degraded, and we made slaves whose pain is not to be whipped.

At the core of what oligarchical conditioning has done to our national character, to produce our tragic national ideology, is the popularization of a pathological sort of misconception of the very important noun, *freedom*. It has come to mean not only "freedom to do evil." It has come to mean, almost, in the United States what such "freedom" meant to the Nazis. The Nazis copied Nietzsche's slogan: "All is permitted!"

If something looking like a dozen rejects from a casting-session for a film version of the Rolling Stones comes strolling into the back yard, "and begins eating my chickens alive, I may fear to find myself served with a decision by one of these new-fangled judges we have nowadays. I might find out that my waving that shotgun in their direction was me 'using excessive force' and, moreover, that was their way of conducting their regular tribal ritual, and I was acting like some fascist trying to deprive them of their religious freedoms."

To a normal, sane mind, *freedom* is the exercise of the divine potentialities of mind, and the political right to discover, and to promulgate every attempt we make to contribute to the Good. The right to participate in changing society negentropically, is the only ultimate definition of freedom that is not *Dionysian*.

To the oligarchist, "freedom" is nothing more than the arbitrarily allowable margin of statistical error, in morality, in matters of felonious practices, in choosing between foods and poisons, or in guessing one's wife's sex. "Freedom" has become: "Do whatever you like, but try not to be caught at it." It is not long to go before our national ideology and judicial practice overtakes the Nazis': "All is permitted," if but those who have seized power in institutions but desire it.

The acid of this anarchist doctrine of "freedom" corrodes everything. We deregulate those institutions which will collapse in chaos if they are not properly regulated: we are beginning even to deregulate what was rightly defined as felony not so long ago. "Freedom" will exert its Magical Power and we shall have "Paradise."

"Hey, Mister, explain to me how this free-market magic works . . . Look, buddy, thanks for trying to answer my question, but what you said doesn't explain anything at all."

The other returns the rebuke with a glow over his own face, smiling knowingly, almost angelically, the forefinger of his right hand pressed lightly against both lips. He moves the finger a half inch forward from his lips: "It's really very simple. You simply have to accept the fact that the world is very interconnected." There is a pause, and the speaker's head tilts just slightly to an angle: "Perhaps I should explain what I mean by 'interconnected'?"

So, the oligarchical body-snatchers, reach out seeking to capture, brainwash and destroy another soul.

"Freedom?" *Freedom for what*, and against what? Without science, the very word "freedom" can be transformed into the chains of slavery, as we have been destroyed with aid of use of that word.

Our weapons are classical culture's advancement on every front, especially in education and entertainments, combined with knowledge of who the oligarchy are and what we must do currently to destroy their force. We must nourish the proper objects for that which is divine, protect and nourish that divine potential in each person and destroy that which would destroy this. That is the essence of the policy of republican statecraft. The rest is science guiding the elaboration of that essence into practice.

4.

The Soviet Paradox:

Leibniz Versus Bentham

For most readers, including senior elected and appointed members of the federal government, much included within what we are about to report now will shock and deeply anger. The anger will be directed most notably at such figures of the U.S. intelligence community as Jay Lovestone, Sidney Hook, and James J. Angleton, who have known a great deal of what we report about the Soviet leadership all along; "Why have they been lying to us?" some will direct their anger against Lovestone and others.

What leading members have been told, in better-quality background briefings on the Soviet leadership, Communist parties, and so forth, is probably loaded with secondary errors of fact and evaluation, but the overall picture might be nonetheless a fair caricature of the fact. It is the areas which have been either entirely or almost entirely suppressed, which constitute the infuriating aspect of the business. Those crucial omissions are easily recognized as proof that much of U.S. A. Soviet policy has been violently contrary to what most senior members of government must have manifestly believed to be fundamental interests of the United States.

The ironical part of the same point is that most Soviet circles today do not know much of this crucial information, or they have ideological reasons not to wish to know certain aspects of their own history, much as they do not wish to know or believe some of the most crucial facts of our history and national character.

That forewarning given, we proceed to the matter first at hand.

Earlier, we identified a fundamental Soviet Paradox, indicating that the United States can not conceivably define an effective foreign policy toward the Soviet Union unless the nature, causes and practical implications of this Soviet Paradox are understood. We now situate the facts of the matter in the setting of our preceding analysis of oligarchism; that is the key to all of the paradoxes, principal and secondary, of the Soviet Union, and of Communist and related parties as an aggregation, around the world.

We begin with an incident from the 1920s. Once we have defined the immediate implications of that incident, we go back in history to account for the process leading into that incident. Once the incident is understood in light of the historical developments reflected in it, we are prepared to proceed, as we shall, to assess the strategic impact of that for today and tomorrow. In conclusion of this topic, we shall outline not an exact U.S.A. Soviet policy, but something more durable, more valuable; a method and outlook for developing policy in this matter.

Whether Josef Stalin said it when and exactly as the best documentation indicates, what he said on that occasion--according to the account--represents a truthful and accurate report *from Stalin's own standpoint.* The whole weight of evidence confirms that to have been his viewpoint during that approximate period. During a meeting of the Soviet leadership of the faction-torn 1920s, Stalin announced that the real cause for the factional furore was a deep, underlying difference in philosophical heritage, dividing the admirers of Leibniz from the political heirs of Rousseau and Bentham. That statement, properly interpreted, is the key to the Soviet Paradox to the present date.

Stalin's famous adversary, Leon Trotsky, agreed with Stalin's reference to Bentham, announcing his own warmth and indebtedness toward Bentham in his autobiography, *My Life*, published a few years later. Like many of the prominent exiles returning to Russia after February 1917, Trotsky was one of those "left-social-democrats" attached to oligarchical patrons during most of his adult life. The evidence is conclusive and of vital strategic importance even today. Stalin's own connection to Leibniz was formally more delphic than substantial in matters of philosophy; he belonged, culturally, to a broad, multi-faceted Russian nationalist tradition as revived by the impact of Peter the Great's successful implementation of the program of economic development designed for Peter I by his advisor, Gottfried Leibniz. From the reference-point of this sort of secondary or tertiary version of the Leibniz heritage, Stalin s words are entirely accurate, and point to the heart of the Soviet Paradox to the present date.

Most of the leaders of the Left and Right oppositions in Russia and in the Communist International, from the 1920s and 1930s, are fairly characterized as more Rousseau and Bentham than Karl Marx. To understand how this functioned, we must shift our attention from the literary to the practical domain. It is impossible to understand the Comintern, many among the existing Communist parties of today, or the operative features of the Soviet Union then or now, without focusing on the implication of the figure the Soviet leadership would most prefer to pretend never existed. The point in this case is the most celebrated spy of the 20th century, whose person was one of the fattest points of intersection of many things, the latter including the First World War itself, during the interval 1893-1918: Odessa-born (according to best information) Alexander Helphand, the most famous super-spy of modern history, “Parvus.”

Parvus is the key to the secret of Trotsky, or Bukharin, Radek, Riazanov, Rakovsky--to most of the leadership of both the Left and Right Oppositions of Russia and of the Comintern. The Moscow Trials of the 1930s were not entirely a hoax. Parvus bought and sold many prominent and semi-prominent figures walking in the footsteps of Rousseau and Bentham. He could afford to buy, he was probably the highest-paid spy in history, “The Fat Man,” the Rossini of all Venetian spies throughout history.

Parvus has been suspected of being an agent for almost everyone. He did, in fact, receive an estimated 30-40 million Reichsmarks for fees and expenses from the German intelligence service during the 1916-1917 period.

By 1893, he was already a collaborator of the Fabian Society. He was famous as a wealthy Black Sea grain-trader. He was an arms-dealer for the British Vickers' interests. All that and other celebrated fact and fable are secondary. Parvus was in the Venetian service, most notably, of the Volpi di Misurata who orchestrated the Balkan Wars, starting World War I almost single-handed, the creator and owner of Libya, and the creator and controller of the fascist government of Benito Mussolini, as the "Italian Schacht."

These Venetians, in concert with the British, orchestrated the 1905 Russian Revolution, with Parvus on the scene directing his asset Trotsky. The same forces, with German help enlisted, launched the February 1917 Russian Revolution, and were apparently in control of the continuing destabilization up to Lenin's October Revolution of that year. For this and related reasons, Parvus is a painful subject in Moscow, as Lenin was most embarrassing to Parvus and his backers at the point it began to be clear what Lenin was actually setting into motion.

Each time our government, or the Soviet leadership overlooks the lesson of the Parvus case, that government makes a fool of itself in foreign policy. Then, the self-blinded governments become mere gladiators combatting one another in Nero's arena, with Nero orchestrating the conflict, working toward the virtually simultaneous destruction of both.

There are three interconnected features of the period from Catherine the Great through World War I which bear most directly upon the history of the Soviet state and Communist parties over the period 1917-1953, the period of Lenin and Stalin. In all of these Venice and its satellite-nations and Britain were in close collaboration, as they are globally today. Venice with its immediate satellite-oligarchical families, and the Anglo-American oligarchical families allied with Venice to the present day, are the principal adversary of the United States, playing the "Soviet Card" against us, and, simultaneously, the "NATO Card" against the "Soviet Empire." The three items of most direct bearing are, first, the British-Venetian "Great Game," of which we consider only the highlights of the indicated period, second, the modification of the "Great Game" with the formation of the group of John Ruskin's heirs around Lord Alfred Milner at the onset of the present century, *the geopolitical doctrine*; and. third, the creation of the anarchist, socialist, communist and fascist motions by Britain and the Venice-centered oligarchical families.

If the reader will bear in mind relevant points of history we have treated earlier during this report, it will be sufficient, to begin our analysis of the "Great Game," to define the structural features of 18th-century and later Europe bearing directly on the case in terms of only the most crucial outgrowths of the 15th century.

The Issues of the Golden Renaissance

As we noted earlier, Cardinal Nicholas of Cusa, already, as a young man, the deciding force in the reconstitution of the shattered Papacy (e.g., *Concordantia Catholica*), was the principal organizing-figure of the 15th-century Golden Renaissance, pulling together the Augustinian Neoplatonic current to perfect the program earlier set into motion by Dante Alighieri. From this impetus, the modern form of sovereign nation-state, modern science, and the entirety of the renaissance of classical culture developed into the middle of the 19th century have emerged. This, and the institutions associated with it, are the immediate targets for destruction by the oligarchical families.

The oligarchical families, weakened by the bankruptcy of the Lombards during the 14th century and related developments of that century, pulled themselves together during the economic revival of the early 15th century, and launched the process of attempting to destroy the work of the Golden Renaissance, the process which those oligarchs now hope to bring to a successful conclusion before the end of the present century.

The first major victory gained by the oligarchs was the destruction of the Paleologue monarchy in Constantinople in 1453 A.D. This was organized by Venice, with aid from its partner Genoa, and crucial assistance from within the hierarchy of the Eastern Rite. These forces entered into an agreement with the Turkish Sultan, Muhammed the Conqueror. The Eastern Rite hierarchy ordered Greeks not to assist the Paleologues; the Venetians and their Roman accomplices supplied the Turkish forces with artillery and gunners; and, 4,000 Genoese mercenaries, hired to assist in defense of Constantinople, opened the gates of the city to Turkish troops during the night.

In return, the Eastern Rite was given administration over all non-Muslims in the Ottoman Empire. The Venetians were given large amounts of former Byzantine territory, and were given the administration of the Ottoman intelligence service (the dragomans). The Venetian grip over the interior of the Ottoman Empire increased with each crisis of the Empire.

Venice launched a major build-up of its Hapsburg puppets, working with its Genoese partners to take over the finances and Queen Isabella of Spain, gobbling up Portugal, and developing Switzerland and Burgundian interests as Venetian Genoese assets. With the death of Ferdinand, the Venetians and Genoese took over Spain. Spain, Burgundy, Austro-Hungary were united under the Venetian puppet Charles V, for whom they purchased the position of Emperor of the Holy Roman Empire (aided by the German assets of the Venetian bankers, the Fuggers). The Hapsburg sack of Rome in 1527 followed the orchestration of the 1524-1525 Peasant War in Germany. In Western and Central Europe, only the two nation-states established by the Golden Renaissance, France and Tudor England, represented potent resistance to Venetian power mediated through Venice's (chiefly) Hapsburg puppets.

The defeat of the Spanish Hapsburgs by Mazarin, set back Venice, and, as we noted, the 1766 rallying of European republican networks around Franklin realized what Colbert and Leibniz had set into motion as new potentialities.

Venice, with British collaboration, through control of the

Netherlands, and so forth, launched during the 18th century the vast operation properly known as the "Great Game."

The game was launched by assassination of the husband of Catherine the Great, and the rise to power of Potemkin. Venice, which controlled both the Ottoman and Hapsburg empires, embarked on a project of destroying both empires, but in a fashion which would bring all of continental Europe down into ruins in the process. To accomplish this, the intended result, Russia must be destroyed first in this process.

Russia, contrary to today's popular mythologies, had outpaced Britain in industrial economy by about the time of the American Revolution's completion. The program Leibniz had devised for Peter the Great had been a success. Russia was later slid into backwardness again, until Czar Alexander II launched a major, successful industrialization-centered program following the Crimean War. With the 1905 Revolution, whole regions of advanced Russian economic development were in ruins, and Sergei Count Witte "safely" ousted from power.

The "Great Game" centered upon drawing Russia into a policy of "warm water port" access to the Mediterranean, and engaging a Russia so oriented into a Pan-Slav ("blood and soil") commitment to the Balkans, putting Russia between the Austro-Hungarian Hapsburg forces and the controlled disintegration of the Ottoman Empire. The motion toward World Wars I and II was already defined by the time of Catherine and Potemkin.

The Testament of Cecil Rhodes, John Ruskin's protégé, gave the final impetus toward the two world wars. The Anglo-Saxon world-empire must be brought into being by subverting the United States, and engaging the European continent in a larger version of the 1618-1648 Thirty Years War. Ruskin's and Rhodes's heir, the executor for Rhodes's estate, Lord Alfred Milner, complemented Volpi di Misurata in Venice. The mutual destruction of France, Germany, Russia, Austro-Hungary, the Ottoman Empire, and subversion of the United States, would produce the ruin, the chaos in which an oligarchical world-rule based on malthusian world-federalist ("Persian Model") design would be brought into being.

The socialist, anarchist and communist movements were intended to supply the erosive, mass-based dionysiac rabble from within, the "new' barbarians." Marx and Lenin exemplify that development within 19th-century radicalism which turned in directions contrary to the desire and intent of the oligarchical authors of those movements--the oligarchical creators of the anarchist, socialist, communist and fascist movements. This is key to understanding the paradox.

We turn to this third point next, thus outlining all of our cited three points in a general, fundamental fashion, before examining in greater detail the historically local matters bearing more directly upon the shaping of our current foreign policy.

Political Radicalism

Although this writer is a member of the Democratic Party and a leading figure of a rapidly growing, if highly contested faction in the ranks of Democrats nationally, honesty and patriotism oblige him to insist that we of the United States will never free ourselves from the kind of degenerating slavery to which we are presently subject, until we strip away the popularized myths, and face the simple truths respecting such key historical figures as Thomas Jefferson, Aaron Burr, Andrew Jackson, and the wicked, Edinburgh roots of New England Secessionist varieties of former and contemporary radical conservatism. It is our national blindness to such matters of our own history which prevents us from looking at those features of the 19th-century radical movements which are the trail leading one to understand the Soviet Paradox.

It must be insisted that there is no excuse, in respect to facts of the matter, for patriotic Americans today to consider Thomas Jefferson, Andrew Jackson or Aaron Burr exactly a national hero.

Of Thomas Jefferson, as of an Othello nobler than Jefferson himself, it must be acknowledged that Jefferson performed our state some notable service. Of Jefferson, it must be judged from balance of the evidence, that he was actually dedicated to many among the political objectives to which he advertised himself as committed: perhaps that is the feature of Jefferson which renders him a relatively moral giant, looking backward from what our public life has become. Jefferson was consistent to that point even as he defined Negroes as a lower-than-human species, but to be treated humanely. Jefferson was consistent to that point in leading what Washington, Hamilton and others viewed during the 1790s as a treason so foul that Washington and Hamilton were prepared to go to war against France because they believed, wrongly, that France was behind the spread of the insurrectionary Jacobin Clubs sponsored by Jefferson throughout the United States. Jefferson, meanwhile, consulted on such projects with such leading figures of the British Secret Intelligence Service as Jeremy Bentham. *The details of the matter are in large part in the published collections of Jefferson's correspondence.*

Meanwhile, during 1796-1797, a leading, Edinburgh-based executive for the British Secret Intelligence Service, John Robison, sank his hooks into the leading circles of Boston and New York City (among other locations of our nation). Robison published a book which was more recently republished for complication of the minds of the credulous by the John Birch Society, *The Roots of Conspiracy*. The book is a lying hoax from beginning to end, but was a cleverly composed and very effective hoax at the time. Even Washington and Hamilton, as well as President John Adams, believed it passionately at the time. Under Inspector-General Alexander Hamilton, we developed quickly one of the most respectable armies and naval forces of the world of that time--which Jefferson and Madison destroyed in time for the War of 1812, originally in preparation for a projected war against France.

The masthead of a semi-weekly newspaper published by

some among the writer's associates, *New Solidarity*, carries each issue a quotation from Alexander Hamilton: "It was by the press that the morals of this country have been ruined, and it is by the press that they shall be restored." If one reads our nation's press during the relevant period, one understands the passion of Hamilton's mind as he steered the creation of the *New York Post*, hoping to fight the British crowd around the Bank of Manhattan of Baring's representative, Aaron Burr.

During the first decade of the 19th century, as Jefferson tore down the credit, economy and military institutions of the United States, under guidance of that apostle of Adam Smith's "free trade," Gallatin, the response among the senior of the surviving leading patriots of 1766-1789 and their sons was to curse the earlier ruinous credulousness of themselves and their fathers. Assembled around the prudent but determined John Marshall, the circles of the Cincinnatus Society organized the secret-intelligence service assigned to defend us against and to aid in destroying the Britain which had been the great mother of Robison's Apollonian Anglophile conservatism and Jefferson's Dionysian Jacobinism. But for that prompt, if a few years' belated correction of our error of strategic-intelligence assessment, this nation would not have survived into the middle of the 19th century, let alone the 20th.

So, out of the Federalist Party's ruins, around such as John Quincy Adams, emerged a party resolved never to resume the errors into which President John Adams and the

Federalists generally had fallen under the impact of Jefferson's radicalism and Robison's lying seductions, the American Whigs. It is that Whig current, unfortunately, itself not exactly impervious to corruption and penetration, which, as that party in its own name, or as the Whig currents developed in the Democratic and Republican parties later, contributed everything which has worked for good in those respective parties' contribution to our national Good.

This writer is proud to present himself to the readers (most of whom ought to have known this long before) as a continuation of that American Whig tradition. He and his associates today may be better informed on many matters than our Whig predecessors, but without the accomplishments of those predecessors we could not have received the basis in knowledge to which to add our contributions to the continued growth of that knowledge. We who stand with adequate consciousness of that Whig tradition know proudly, and with a certain appropriately patriotic ruthlessness, that without our forebears among the Whigs the great "beacon of hope" established by Franklin's co-conspirators would have been doused more than a century ago.

Any person who resumes that American Whig standpoint today, on condition that outlook is adequately informed as to the developments in the world about us, is rather uniquely qualified to see quickly and relatively clearly the problems of method and outlook properly imposed upon our foreign policy by the Soviet Paradox and its implications. If this writer and his associates, over a period of more than a decade to date, have been obliged to function in the mode of the model of the secret-intelligence service of the 19th-century Whigs and their collaborators among the circles of the Marquis de Lafayette in Europe, this has *not* been, *unfortunately*, under assignment to organize ourselves so by any official branch of our nation's intelligence services. Guided by the philosophical standpoint represented to our Founding Fathers by chiefly Leibniz, and informed increasingly by the written record of our nation's architects and the great Whig-led international intelligence service, we have acted as informed private citizens should, us Franklin did, to adopt for ourselves that essential task which no other institution appeared to be maintaining.

On the Russian Question, in particular, we view the contemporary expression of that matter with a mind's eye informed by Leibniz, by Franklin, and by our 19th-century Whig leaders. We are informed by passions aroused in memory of the Great Deception of the late 1790s, the Great Betrayal of the 1876-1879 Specie Resumption Act, and the Great Undoing which Henry Kissinger has smirkingly embraced as the British shaping of our nation's post-war foreign-policy-making.

Our nation requires no empire, nor any other arrangement among foreign governments of the sort euphemistically called client-status, or, more frankly, lickspittle governments kissing the dust from Henry Kissinger's soiled shoes. What we require is a definite principle of political order in the affairs of the world as a whole.

We require this ordering of political affairs within and among nations, to state this from a relative negative standpoint, simply because without such an ordering of the affairs of others our nation and our posterity can not be secure. From a higher moral vantage-point, that of St. Augustine, of the heirs of Cardinal Nicholas of Cusa, and the philosophical outlook of the circles of international conspirators associated with the leadership of Benjamin Franklin, our nation exists in this world to a higher purpose. We must be the flagship of the republican cause; we must extend John Quincy Adams's intent for the 1823 Monroe Doctrine, to all of the existing and aspiring republics of the world. We require neither empire nor lickspittle client-nations. We require simply, but absolutely that the republican world-order shall prevail.

We must not only defend, but advance that republican cause within and without our nation's borders. The ordering of our affairs reflected as well as partly explicit in the great, useful compromise which was our 1787 draft of our Federal Constitution, commits us to this purpose. The names for any other notions of our law and national purpose find their place within a range of terms ranging from mere "Folly" to outright "Treason."

We can not serve that purpose adequately unless our statesmen and other principal policy-influences, in the majority, are adequately informed of the content of Judeo-Christian republicanism, as we have rigorously defined that here. We must know such republicanism and its mortal adversary. Everything we adopt as task must be defined according to the purpose of defeating that oligarchical adversary's forces and influence within and without our nation's borders.

We must situate the paradoxical Russian Question of today within that higher order of our ancient and continuing conflict with our mortal adversary, oligarchism.

We must rid our minds of that poisonous driveling which assorts the gradations of political faction among *right*, *center*, and *left*. A right-winger is an Apollonian; a leftist is a Dionysian; and the center is composed of circles which have not yet firmly resolved which of the two political sexes to adopt and practice. We require statesmen and policy-influencers which are neither right, nor left nor center. We require democratic-republicans.

It is the writer's direction of purpose in this particular matter, either that our nation become ruled by a single party which is a democratic-republican party in the Judeo-Christian republican tradition or that a bipartisan combination of the two major parties may develop establishing that result in effect through the competitive electoral interplay of the two major parties: That accomplishment that Franklin's circles hoped to achieve with single-party government through the instrument of the Federalist Party, and what our American Whigs sought to bring into being by various tactics employed during the first half of the 19th century. Such things must occur through a lawfully ordered political process of development, and can not be wished into being any more than we might merely by rightly resolving to do so, to resolve at the onset of the 1960s, to land a man on the Moon. This will tend to emerge lawfully in due course if those Republicans and Democrats adequately informed by the Whig lesson begin to work together in a bipartisan approach to essential issues, freeing our minds of the right-center-left delusion.

We should apply such a resolution to development of our foreign policy concerning the Soviet Paradox.

The problem of communism begins as communism in that comi-tragic event of July 14th which the chiefly ill-informed French nation celebrates as the equivalent of its "Fourth of July," the degraded, evil spectacle of the Duke of Orleans' hiring a mob to besiege and sack the Bastille. It is out of the pathetic myth respecting the French Revolution that communism emerged, and out of the accidents of seating-arrangements in the French National Assembly of that period that the minds of nations and their peoples have been enslaved by the political cult-dogma of "right, center, and left" since. This most influential myth requires brief scrutiny of its essential features, as the myth out of which communism was born.

First, as to the matter of the Bastille itself, and then to the Jacobin phenomenon which Thomas Jefferson attempted to implant in our nation during the 1790s.

At the point of the celebrated event, the Bastille in Paris housed a grand total of seven prisoners. These included a convicted sex-offender: the evil Marquis do Sade had been released a short time earlier. These seven included two babbling lunatics, who certified their mental condition atop the shoulders of their triumphant rescuers all the way those rescuers carried them appropriately to another place of confinement for the insane. The remainder of the seven was a collection of convicted felons whose principal political distinction was that they had avoided that capital punishment which was the common fate of such offenders during those times. There can be no doubt, the mob's passions were exercised by righteous zeal to crush out a great political injustice.

The Duke of Orleans, cousin of the King, assembled, paid and armed this mob from the petty parasites and hoodlums of Paris. In the tradition of the crowning of the beggar-king annually in old Paris, on that glorious day of July 14th, the Pimp ruled triumphant.

The captain of the Bastille's tiny garrison foolishly surrendered under a condition of truce, and was promptly killed and beheaded, together with all of his small party. The victims' heads hoisted as grisly banners of victory on the mob's pikes, the seven national heroes just rescued borne on shoulders of the mobsters, the body moved in glory from the scene of its bloody marauding. Lest the purpose of this enterprise not be clearly understood, at the head of the procession the train displayed proudly the carved bust of the Swiss swindler who has just previously accomplished the national bankruptcy of France, the father of the notorious Madame de Staël, Jacques Necker.

This act of mob-rule achieved the political purpose for which it had been deployed; the ally of the Duke of Orleans, Jacques Necker, became first minister of France.

This Orleans later enhanced his own future political prospects with aid of another, larger mob of the same empyreal moral passions, seizing the person of his cousin, the King, and the Royal Family, in a butchery conducted by night at Versailles. In due course, the King and Marie Antoinette were later decapitated, as Orleans' sans-culottes had decapitated the tiny garrison of the Bastille. After years of impatient delay, the British made this Orleans the King of France, his fare from London to Paris for that coronation generously advanced from the personal pocket of Nathan Rothschild. Truly, a man of great nobility, this Orleans.

Benjamin Franklin would not have been astonished by Orleans' performance. Orleans had been Britain's ally and Franklin's chief immediate adversary in Paris, as the two had fought for leadership over the Paris freemasonic lodges.

These Jacobins, described to Washington by Lafayette as a "jesuitical" concoction (Portugal, Spain's Charles III, and the Pope, had successively expelled and suppressed the Jesuit order for proven, evil practices of meddling in political affairs during that general period), were principally a joint-operation of the British and of Swiss Protestant banking circles including the oligarchical families of Schlumberger, de Neuflize, and Mallet, and were coordinated largely out of the salons of Jacques

Necker and his daughter, the notorious de Staël. This Swiss-centered network promoted especially the neurotic, oligarchical drivelings of Jean-Jacques Rousseau; this was pushed as Jacobinism in politics and as the doctrinal basis for the Romantic movement led by de Staël herself in art. Robespierre led among those persons directly under the patronage of the Necker salon. The most famous among the leaders of the Jacobin Terror, after Robespierre himself, Danton and Marat, were London-trained and London-directed British agents.

Danton and Marat were agents of the circle around Lord Shelburne. Shelburne, who reacted to the victory of the United States by proposing a new approach to destroying the United States and its European republican allies, beginning with France, had entered into an agreement with King George III. The agreement was on behalf of Shelburne's backer, the Venetian-Genoese interest in Britain, the British East India Company. Baring's bank, the political force behind Aaron Burr's Bank of Manhattan (slightly later), was the British East India Company bank of that period. With Baring's money, Shelburne and the King bought up the British parliament, according to well-established customs in such matters of "British parliamentary democracy," and foisted upon Britain and the injured world the long reign of Prime Minister William Pitt the Younger. Otherwise, the two other high-ranking figures of Shelburne's immediate circle were, in order of importance, Jeremy Bentham and James Mill. More detail on this point is not required here. Danton and Marat were protégés of Shelburne, Pitt and Bentham, trained in London over an extended period, and dispatched from Shelburne safe-houses in London to their assigned duties at head of the Jacobin Terror in France.

The object of the operation is one which prefigures the same oligarchical circles' creation of and deployment of Adolf Hitler later. The objective was, immediately to decapitate the friends of the United States' cause in France, to crush the renaissance of organized republicanism which the conspiracy of 1766-1783 under Franklin's leadership had set into world-wide motion. The listing of leading French friends of the United States who had died or were murdered during the 1783-1794 period helps to afford the reader some appreciation of Washington's and Hamilton's misguided views, in particular, during the years just preceding the great President's death.

The central figure of 19th-century radical movements was the notorious Giuseppe Mazzini, the leader of a Venetian-created organization called "Young Italy"--the republican Cavour's adversary.

This was an operation based logistically in Switzerland, with strong support from the same circles overlapping Schlumberger, de Neuflize and Mallet, which had collaborated with Britain in creating and directing the Jacobin Terror. Lord Palmerston is the key British official of importance in this operation, which came to be coordinated in part through a librarian at the British Museum, (Library), David Urquhart, the latter's written accounts on this subject an indispensable part of the scholarly materials available for internal mapping of the far-flung radical conspiracy. This was the same Urquhart who functioned as a controller of Karl Marx for a significant period of the 1850s and into the 1860s.

Out of the kernel of "Young Italy" and its French complement, Venice and Palmerston placed Mazzini in the position of titular head of a far-flung organization named "Young Europe," with a matching, Edinburgh-controlled U.S.A. section called variously "Young America" or the "Concord Transcendentalists" around such figures as the Rousseauvian Thoreau, Longfellow, Emerson, and so forth. The U.S. counterintelligence operative, Edgar Allan Poe, was among those assigned to expose and to attempt to neutralize that latter, Edinburgh-directed British operation against the United States.

Meanwhile, Washington's closest collaborator, and co-leader of the Society of Cincinnatus, Lafayette, was in exile and endungeoned in the Austro-Hungarian prison at Olmuetz. Washington, D.C. was cut off from efficient contact with Lazare Carnot and his circle of republican conspirators until Jefferson was already elected. As the Austrian government informed the U.S. ambassador and special emissaries intervening on Lafayette's behalf at the time, their hands were tied; the orders for endungeoning (and killing) Lafayette had come from the William Pitt featured in Beethoven's operatic account of this matter, *Fidelio*, as Pizarro. ("Florestan," the hero of Robert Schumann's later republican circle of Davidsbundler," was Gilbert Marquis de Lafayette, and Fidelio herself, "Leonore," is a true-to-life dramatic rendering of the courageous efforts of Lafayette's wife to save her husband from the assassination ordered by Pitt. She and the couple's children, in real life, actually entered the dungeon voluntarily, a decision she made as the last means of which she could think to deter Pitt from murdering her husband.)

It was the model of Rousseau and Bentham, magnified in detail by the rantings of the monstrous St. Just and Babeuf, which served as the radical dogma of reference for the radical movements brought into being during the 1830s and 1840s.

One of the operations spawned out of "Young Europe" was the *Communist League*. This was initially established in Switzerland. The Swiss objected. They were quite eager to assist in destroying civilization throughout the rest of continental Europe, but were not disposed to have their little patch participate in the kinds of bloody festivities they exported to others. The Communist League was shipped out of Switzerland, downriver, and arrived in Brussels, where Karl Marx and Friedrich Engels intersected it during the middle 1840s.

Karl Marx, and his father Heinrich before him, are exemplary of the effects of oligarchical methods in wholly or partially corrupting and destroying republican forces in Germany.

During the 1790s, Trier, also the birthplace of the present writer's wife, and the oldest city of Germany, was one of a network of republican hotbeds along the Rhine and its tributaries. The network of "Reading Societies"

(*Lesergesellschaft*) established to collect and distribute news of the 1776-1783 war against Britain and later developments in the United States included Trier's Casino as one of its notable bases of operations. The head of Marx's Gymnasium, the great republican scholar Johann Hugo Wyttenbach, had been elected to that post during the 1790s as the local scholar best equipped to represent the conceptions of "Franklin and Kant" in that capacity.

A matriculation-essay, on the assigned title of choosing a profession in life, written by Marx in 1835 for Wyttenbach's class, affords us a remarkable point of political epistemological reference for tracing the transformations of Marx's mind effected under the influence of Friedrich Engels, Urquhart, and others after his departure from Trier. Already, however, Marx had acquired the first poisonous taint of oligarchism; the writings of Rousseau were not merely standing in the library of his father, the celebrated local attorney Heinrich Marx; the family culture was being poisoned by this taint.

Yet, although the oligarchical corruption of Marx's thought is painfully clear, it did not succeed entirely. The British noted this during the late 1850s and 1860s, as Marx actively took, if critically, the side of the American Whigs against Britain. During the 1869-1872 period, the British and their oligarchical friends destroyed Marx as a living political factor, in his own right. Later, they experienced what they viewed as a similar sort of problem in the case of V. I. Lenin. Neither Marx nor Lenin were republicans in the sense we define republicanism, not philosophically; but, the influence of republicanism upon both of them aggregated to be a decisive influence in affording us the Soviet Paradox today.

The Karl Marx of 1835, departed for Bonn University, and later Berlin, essentially a republican in the philosophical sense (despite the Rousseauvian taint), to become swept up in various nests of oligarchical flavors of students' social life in both centers, associating himself with the so-called "Left Hegelian" followers of Ludwig Feuerbach around Berlin. He was part of the "Young Europe" movement, although by no means fully radicalized. He was still predominantly part of the republican political current of Heinrich Heine, Friedrich List, and Robert Schumann among others, but leaning toward the Apollonian-Dionysian political differentiation within that current, the philosophical tradition of the Stoics and Epicureans. His writings on classical Greek philosophical questions efficiently exhibit the drift away from the philosophical and political republicanism of Wyttenbach.

The break came in two steps. The first was Marx's beating out the republican Friedrich List for the editorship of a leading Rhineland republican newspaper. That was only the first scratch. Later, under the direct influence of Engels, Marx wrote a fraudulent diatribe against List. After that, Marx could never write an honest word concerning List for the rest of his life. Engels had made Marx's break with republican causes almost final--until Marx's attempted collaboration with American Whigs pulled him toward

Carey, but even then, even though most of his knowledge of the U.S. economy was cribbed directly from Carey's writings into his own, Marx's correspondence with Engels shows that Marx had lost a crucial element of his own intellectual integrity with the lying libel against List earlier.

A vestige of Marx's youthful republican education persisted off and on throughout his life. The so-called Paris Manuscript of 1844 is clinically interesting to the epistemologist on this point. More important are the opening pages of his 1845 contributions to a joint-manuscript co-authored with Engels, the so-called *The German Ideology*, and its opening section on the subject of "Feuerbach," which was later described as "settling our consciences" on matters of earlier attachments and ideas. The same point of method from those pages of *The German Ideology* crops up in compacted form in the last section of *Capital III*, and is occasionally echoed in some notable fashion or other in various parts of Marx's writings.

That identifies the etiology of the Soviet Paradox as it manifests itself within the case of Marx. Now, we examine the way in which that Paradox is expressed in the overall character of Marx's writings and activities.

Under the conditions of controlled psychological environment, effected partially under the watchful eye of Urquhart, at the British Library in London, Marx developed a doctrine based significantly on a sweeping falsification of history. On every point at issue in historiography, political-economy most prominently, but also philosophy, the internal history of science, and the ordering of major factional developments and wars, Marx's doctrine embraced and embraces the fraudulent assumptions commonplace to British 18th-century and early-19th-century teaching. The interpretation of history, backwards and forwards from the reference-point of "the reasons the Jacobins failed to develop as a proletarian leadership qualified to establish socialism," is the central characteristic of this undertaking, with nothing significantly contradictory to the prevailing British range of permitted assumptions as to "fact" in that account.

Nonetheless, if that had been the only feature of Marx's activity, the Soviet Union would never have existed to attract the attention of our foreign-policy concerns. Imprisoned within the bars and walls of these defects of knowledge, a strong, insistent eruption of his developed adolescent conscience rebelled, against the variety of radical doctrines which the same false assumptions as to "fact" led most among Marx's radical contemporaries. Marx's contempt for Malthus and Charles Darwin is the most readily accessed point of reference for adducing this in his work.

Marx accepted the British myth, to the effect that the British economic development and British model of political-economy were the highest achievement of civilization to that point. He accepted, conditionally, the "authority" of the Physiocrats, Smith, and Ricardo, to that degree. Yet, working within those fraudulent assumptions, Marx disliked very much the adducible consequences of such a wondrous production of history. His republican commitment to technological and scientific-intellectual progress remained with him, accompanied by an associated, interdependent cultural optimism.

At first, it amused the British to observe Marx drudging away, producing that medley of brilliant, partial insights and monstrous nonsense called the *Grundrisse* of the 1850s. "Let this industrious fool promise a scientific-technological utopia of progress at some apocalyptic, future date. As long as he helps to further the bringing into being of the apocalypse, tolerate the poor fool's dreams of such a socialist paradise." With the gradual shift away from this *Grundrisse*, into *Capital*, matters grew more serious. As a work of economic science, *Capital* as a whole is fatally flawed. Yet, it contains two features which horrified the British (and others) as soon as the first volume was published.

Marx did not discover the notion of "labor-power." It was defined by Leibniz from the vantage point of the heat-powered machine and associated conceptions of *work, power* and *technology,* about a century-and-a-half before Marx was born, and was the conception widespread throughout the 18th and early 19th centuries. The conception is properly stated as U.S. economic policy in Hamilton's 1791 *Report to the Congress On The Subject of Manufactures*, where the American System of political-economy was first defined by name and in substance, as a sweeping refutation of Adam Smith's *Wealth of Nations*, as well as of the Physiocrats. It was the central conception of the Henry C. Carey whose work, published long before

Marx met Engels, Marx libeled incompetently, maliciously, as "amateurish." It was the central conception of the titanic List whom Marx had libelled, and which Marx must have noted, if he actually read any of List's most-widely-circulated writings in the course of preparing that libel.

Marx had no systematic understanding of the process by which the investment of profit in improved technologies determines deflationary processes of economic growth--without thus incurring any necessary reasons for economic cycles. Marx assumed that the British system, based principally on ground-rent and "ground-rent" from usurious loan of money, was the "natural" ordering of a capitalist economy.

What Marx did accomplish, working within the limits of otherwise false assumptions as to fact, was to counterpose the real production and circulation of goods to the monetary aspect of the processes of circulation. Since he refused to recognize that the British monetary system was an unnatural form for a capitalist economy, he trapped himself into the axiomatic delusion that there must be some "natural" interdependency between these monetary processes and social-productive relations in production and distribution. So, because of that fallacy, he obliged himself to adduce two conclusions, one false, and the other substantially correct.

He demonstrated that there exists, within a society modeled on the British system, an ultimately irreconcilable conflict between the accumulation of money-capital and the progressive (technological) expansion and development of the processes of production and circulation of goods. The growth of the former, the accumulation of money-capital in a British system, does in fact lead necessarily to boom-bust cycles and an implicit ultimate collapse: as the source of the means of payment of income to money-capital investment contracts greatly, so the production of real profit by production is contracted relative to the expansion of accumulation of money-capital.

Perhaps in no empirical category of evidence is the fallacy of the oligarchical (anarchist) misconception of "freedom" more readily demonstrated than in this economic connection. That was Mathew Carey's point, in proving that the submission to Adam Smith's free-trade dogma had been the direct and immediate cause for the process of ruin of the U.S. economy under Jefferson and Madison, leading into the disastrous circumstances of the depression which followed the War of 1812. Hence, we Whigs learned never to tolerate removal of the constitutional powers and responsibilities of the federal government for regulating the creation of credit, banking, and tariffs: to ensure that our producers, farmers and industrialists had access to adequate supplies of low-priced credits for productive investment, and that tariffs and regulation ensured that neither foreign dumping of goods, nor lunatic degrees of anarchic competition in markets, impelled producers to lower the prices of goods below the costs of their production.

Marx was a passionate defender of "free trade" for capitalist economy--lest the absence of "free trade" hinder the "lawful" self-destruction of capitalism.

This was not a discovery original to Marx. The causes were understood by Hamilton, the Careys and List. Hamilton's successors pointed out the true reason for this discrepancy: that the British system represented the attempt to superimpose a "feudalistic" order of ground-rent and usury upon a capitalist mode of production, a mixed, feudalist-capitalist form of economy. Marx refused to accept the proposition that the British economy was oligarchical (i.e, "feudalistic"), and insisted therefore that this contradiction was intrinsic to "pure" capitalist economy as such.

Since Marx rejected the true cause for business cycles, he was obliged to seek and adopt a false one: capitalist "anarchic" forms of ownership of the means of production. This part the British oligarchs liked very much, although they much disliked Marx's "apocalyptic theory of business cycles."

It is true that the anarchy of production, especially in agriculture based on owner-operated farms, does mediate disastrous falls in agricultural prices in each case the capitalist system as understood by Hamilton, the Careys and List is not efficiently present. It is state regulation of credit, banking and tariffs, which shapes a capitalist monetary system to the effect such anarchy does not become anarchy; in which case, there is no business cycle.

After *Capital*, they moved to dump him. An old crony of the composer Richard Wagner, the Mazzinian (Venetian) agent Bakunin, was hauled out of his other sordid preoccupations of the moment, to serve as the central figure for an instantly-created Mazzinian organization, the anarchist international. Marx was administered the standard Mutt-and-Jeff treatment: assailed by (principally) the anarchists on the one side, and drawn into the Paris Commune on the other. That finished Marx off as a significant political figure throughout Europe: he began to die, politically, emotionally and physically. He attempted to intervene into the 1875 founding of the Social Democracy at Gotha, but with help of Friedrich Engels, Marx was kept entirely out of that business, as Engels admitted the substance of his role in the matter later, during the period of a shift of Social Democratic assignments following the forced retirement of Bismarck.

The oligarchists had underestimated *Capital*'s potential influence, as we shall come to that point shortly.

Marx's ever-frustrated attempts to intervene significantly into Germany pitted him against two sources of socialist opposition, the British and the Jesuits. The key British agent (as a British publication has rather recently published a partial but conclusive bit of documentation) was August Bebel. The key Jesuits' agent was Ferdinand Lassalle. The two currents were brought together, the Lassalleans and the Eisenachers, in the 1875 unification conference at Gotha, Germany, at which the German (and international) Social Democracy were both founded (in point of fact, as distinct from mere formalities of the matter). Lassalle was funded principally through his Jesuit mentor at Mainz, Germany, von Ketteler, the putative founder of a dogma known as *solidarism.* Solidarism, whether in socialist guises, or fascist guises such as the Russian NTS, is the radical doctrine preferred by the oligarchists to the present date. The fusion of the Social Democratic forces at Gotha established solidarism, or approximations of it, as more or less hegemonic in the Socialist International to the present date.

At least, solidarism has *tended* to be hegemonic. More exactly, to get into the critical matters of detail, a pro-Marxian current has repeatedly threatened to challenge solidarism, sometimes with a degree of success. Lenin exemplifies the case of the occasional success.

Solidarism is essentially a purely oligarchical form of social and political-economic doctrine: there must be no profits of production, except ground-rent and usury. All income of production, except that taken for ground-rent and usury, must be fully distributed as wages. Lassalle is explicit on this purpose in his published correspondence with Bismarck. He proposed what would be interpreted in the literary conventions of the time as an alliance of feudalist and radical proletarian forces against the common adversary, industrial capitalism. The times were not right for such full-fledged solidarist undertakings, the Eisenachers protested angrily. Bismarck was certainly in no position to take on both German industry and the Prussian military officer-corps as a whole in such a matter. Otherwise, Lassalle's commitment to solidarism was consistent and indubitably sincere.

To illustrate the point a bit dramatically, but without exaggeration, attention may be focused again upon the fact that the writer's associates publish a semi-weekly newspaper called *New Solidarity*. The title is a relic of our attempted political penetration of radical circles more than a decade ago, after which period the name had become sufficiently well-established it became counter-productive to consider altering it. The reasons for the selection for that title efficiently demonstrate the importance of solidarism in the radical currents of the United States and elsewhere today.

During the 19th century, Lassalleans from Germany penetrated the United States to significant effect, brawling with Marx's friends here, but also to effects of more general and enduring significance for us since. These Lassalleans and anarchists following them were a significant part of the British effort to undermine and destroy us, complementing those who descended from such foreign precincts as the Hudson Bay Company auspices in Canada to buy out our best cattle-lands and our Rocky Mountains' spine's vast mineral rights at the rock-bottom prices provided by the conditions brought about under the 1876-1879 Specie Resumption Act; this, in turn, complemented the magnificent work the British and their U.S. financier allies accomplished in looting our railroads, our railway companies' real estate holdings, and our farmers, by aid of the same general conditions of our economy placed at the mercies of the London gold-exchange system.

Naturally, the looting of our currency, our credit, our industries and our farmers, fostered a significant eruption of discontent among our people.

A network of Jesuits working through top-down control of the Knights of Labor organization and sundry anarchists and industriously minded other political eccentrics about our landscapes, organized a great social tumult throughout this nation from 1877 through 1886. The war cry, "Profit is theft!" shook the air and ground around restive large assemblies of the ruined many, as well as in the clandestine educational sessions in which the cadre of organizers was developed and redirected to new options under altered conditions.

The anarchists streaming in from Europe into the midst of this creation of our combined folly and British guile brought with them the war-cry of "Solidarity!"--by which they meant *solidarism*.

To the angry, frightened, abused fellow-citizens our foolish Congress of 1876-1879 had thrown into such straits, the popular cry "Solidarity!" or "Solidarity Forever!" meant nothing more nor less than unity of the many to force an improvement in conditions. For this, those former fellow-citizens of ours are in no way to be blamed, but rather admired chiefly for their nobilities of courage and loyalty to one another, under monstrous conditions of betrayal by corrupted federal governments.

Even a poor Hamlet was not so poor that he could not say:

"Yet I,

A dull and muddy-mettled rascal, peak,

Like John-a-dreams, unpregnant of my cause,

And can say nothing: no, not for a king

Upon whose property and most dear life

A damn'd defeat was made. Am I coward?

Who calls me villain? breaks my pate across?

Plucks off my beard and blows it in my face?

Tweaks me by the nose? Gives me the lie i' the throat,

As deep as to the lungs? who does me thus, ha?

'Swounds, I should take it: for it cannot be

But that I am pigeon-liver'd, and lack gall

To make oppression bitter; or ere this

I should have fatted all the region kites

With this slave's offal:--bloody, bawdy villain!

Remorseless, treacherous, lecherous, kindless villain!

Oh, vengeance! . . ."

Who can reflect upon the true circumstances of the 1877-1886 period, and is so unmanly that would not curse so the treasonous Congress which passed the 1876 Specie Resumption Act, and who would not curse so those ignorant, arrogant smug, Anglophile fools, of the Coolidge and Hoover periods, who, for the sake of a mere passion for a foolish ideology, leave our people and nation needlessly in ruin! Who can endure the criminality of what is done to our nation and its people by the Carter administration's unleashing of the Volcker measures of today! Whom with their silly ideological conceits, would needlessly put the people of this nation once again into the paws of oligarchical agents, the anarchists, the solidarists of all assorted varieties?

The passion of those angry masses of people, during the strife of 1877-1886, was misguided, was exploited by anarchist agents of the oligarchy to ruin us. How much can we blame the many drawn so into such manipulated enterprises for that? The writer and his associates have done, do much and will do much more, relative to their means, to attempt to protect this nation from those radical, Dionysiac outbursts of folly; however, gentlemen, that is most difficult work as long as you insist upon continuing to nourish our nation's adversaries' work with your persisting, blind ideologies, your smug, thoughtless follies! The British and Swiss give to you a tailored lie, a tailored ideology, hoping that you will be credulous enough to call it your own belief, and thus assist your own ruin as well as that of our nation, by acting upon such belief. There is the crux of the matter for you.

The relationship of aroused rage and fear to obsessive psychosis is key to the point to be made in this connection. It was a treasonously corrupted Congress which created the causes for desperate fear and rage during the 1877-1886 period. On such account, to that degree, a Congress can blame nothing but its own corruption, its cowardice, for such tumultuous consequences. For that you can not blame the anarchists or the solidarists, but merely yourselves.

If a frightened, desperate people finds itself united as, in its own eyes, a credible political force, those ideas which come to be associated with such association will be seized upon as the ideas of fear, and can not be directly dislodged while obsessive rage defends such ideas. An oligarch, in full regalia, with all the great orders of nobility and title embellishing him, with his liveried attendants streaming behind and about him, is not a likely image to attract the sympathy of people impassioned with the effects of economic collapse. However, that aristocrat's anarchist can and does. Oligarchism, to serve its own purpose, must disguise itself. *Solidarity!* mixed with *Profit is theft!*, directed against *Greedy Industrialists!, Greedy, Rich Farmers!*, and against the technological progress associated with industrial capitalism, transforms too many honest citizens into lunatic solidarists.

These solidarist ideas have been deeply embedded in our population. Although the public promotion of such political changes may be limited usually to a few radicals, or the old speeches of the late Walter Reuther, immediately a profound economic crisis breaks out, since 1877-1886, as people become radicalized, it is these pernicious, solidarist conceptions which erupt once again. Once again, allegedly greedy farmers and the profits of industry become the scape-goat, "If we can only eliminate the power of the farm-lobby and industrialist profits, all will be well."

It will be recalled that during the 1966-1968 period, such anarchist conceptions, solidarist in content, were rampant around Tom Hayden's SDS and the complex networks coordinated by the Institute for Policy Studies. The writer and his associates, then a bare handful of persons, elected to intervene into this ferment and, to employ a popular image, to "judo" it. Since the characteristic of the "New Left" was predominantly an antirationalist and anti-labor disposition, as Hayden and his wife have exhibited and publicly stated recently in California, the key, in our view, was to exploit two weak flanks of the New Left organizers: they were recruiting from campuses, and thus professing anti-rationalism to a section of the youth then largely and proudly self-identified with intellectual accomplishment, and they were representing themselves as neo-Marxist and anti-labor at the same time. So, in the course of attempting to neutralize the influence of the forces then funded, on behalf of the Institute for Policy Studies, by McGeorge Bundy's Ford Foundation, we more or less organically found ourselves playing the contradiction between old solidarist ideology and the neo-solidarism of Hayden, Mark Rudd, et al.

We did what any competent force must do in attempting a counter-operation against the targetting of good people being radicalized, as was the case during the spread of SDS during that period. We were not remarkably unsuccessful either, considering our efforts were unfunded volunteer efforts and so few of us to conduct it. We failed to stop the forces around Hayden, but we did create a situation in which they were forced to break up SDS during spring 1969. Although persons of rank much higher than McGeorge Bundy have adopted us their target of hatred since, to this day the crowd around Hayden and Rudd from 1966-1968 are still obsessed with the near-miss we deployed in the effort to disrupt and destroy their evil movement back then. One must attempt to present to frightened people being radicalized a correct conception for practice, posing an alternative to the evil scheme the enemy, the oligarchy's, radicals are otherwise successfully introducing. When good ordinary sorts of people are being driven into fear and rage, there is usually a cause. It is urgent to address one's efforts to correcting the cause, if it is possible to do so. One must "judo" the enemy's work whenever that is possible, just as one must struggle to develop a literate language out of the rubbish-heap of a brutish local dialect in use by a population.

You have now been informed how the radicalization process operates, in essentials, by an expert in the matter. You have been given indication of the extent and dangerousness of this oligarchical evil called solidarism. The positive conception with which to fight solidarist radicalism is reason, as exemplified by Henry C. Carey's "harmony of interests": that the industrialists, farmers, and working people of our nation have a higher, common interest in developing the economy and security of this nation.

At its best, Marxism has attempted to combat solidarism in an analogous fashion, at least with respect to the economic issues per se, and those conditions of individual life which are directly linked to economic matters in the most obvious way. The flaw in the Marxist variant of Carey's "harmony of interests" is that it addresses the material interests of the society, without defining the deeper and higher purpose served by advancement of those material conditions of life. Marx's attack on Carey's form for the "harmony of interests" bears, in significant part, on this distinction.

To be certain that the profundity of the evil represented by solidarism is adequately understood, we refer the reader's attention to the earlier portions of this report, in which we compared negentropic and entropic functions in social processes. Solidarism is intrinsically Malthusianism.

Briefly, in a capitalist economy (for example), the *energy of the system* is the sum of the paid-out costs for production and circulation of goods, including those services to production, to government, and to the well-being of the population, which pertain to that production and circulation. This aggregates as the sum of incomes (in goods-terms) of the households supplying industrial and agricultural operatives, consumption of production's output as replacement capital for production, plus administrative and services expenses (society's "overhead burden"). The portion of total production in excess of those combined costs and expenses is the net operating profit of the society as a whole. It is principally the investment of that profit in a manner which increases the productivity of production and distribution of goods, which enables a society to maintain and improve its potential relative population-density. What happens, then, if we decrease combined agricultural and industrial profit to zero? The society must collapse, ultimately with famine, epidemic, pestilence and homicidal squabbling over scarce crusts of food--the Four Horsemen of the Apocalypse--the consequence. In the guise of solidarism. the oligarchs attack in practice the two fundamental features of our Judeo-Christian culture: the exercise of the divine potential of our creative powers in fulfilling the injunction to be “Fruitful and multiply, and to fill the earth and subdue it.”

This is evil; this is oligarchism; this is solidarism. This, in fact is the variety of fascism associated with the fascist NTS and its allies of the “conservative revolution” 's Nazi International (e.g. “Malmö” International”) today, of the “universal fascists” which Haig’s advisor Michael Ledeen admired in print so shamelessly.

It is on this account that prominent circles of the leadership of the Socialist International today are so dangerously evil, and why the parties of the Socialist International, to the extent good and decent people and currents exist among them, are so paradoxical. This is reflective of the differences between the predominantly solidarist current of the Socialist International (e.g.. Willy Brandt), and the so-called conservative, “normal,” pro-industrial factions of Social Democratic parties.

By Sealed Train To Russia

Parvus negotiated with the German intelligence's command through diplomatic channels. Stopping in Vienna, paying funds due to his agent G. Riazanov, he arrived in Berlin to deliver the document known as the "Parvus Plan." For this he was paid a reported 1 million Reichsmarks. It was a plan, based on the model of the 1905 Russian Revolution, for the internal destruction of Russia. The year, according to the documentation, was 1916.

Parvus, taken into employment by German intelligence, set up shop in Denmark and Sweden (chiefly), operating in cooperation with the leading resident British intelligence agent in the vicinity, Sweden's leading Social Democrat, Hjalmar Branting. Radek and Bukharin were among those recruited to Parvus's payroll, but Lenin insisted they withdraw from Parvus's employment, or else. They went through the motions of appearing to withdraw. Lenin's writings from that period, 1914-1917, are crucial for insight into the transformation in strategic estimations developing within his mind. Parvus either missed the writings, or underestimated their significance.

As soon as the February 1917 Russian Revolution had been effected, Parvus proceeded to pour in radical reenforcements intended to deepen the crisis to the point that Russia collapsed. Through oligarchical channels into New York City, Parvus's friends contrived to advise the

British to release Parvus's old protégé, Trotsky, from internment in Halifax, Nova Scotia. Parvus pressed to have Lenin added to the collection. Lenin, Parvus, was certain, had the special quality of toughness needed to make a real mess of the situation.

So, the proverbial kit-and-kaboodle of German intelligence types appeared in Switzerland, with Branting hovering in the vicinity. Lenin agreed to the sealed-train arrangement. Parvus slipped a reported three millions Reichsmarks' worth of money into Radek's pocket, and, with Branting's and British cooperation, Lenin was off to Petrograd.

Lenin, to make short of the matter, outmaneuvered everyone, including both the nervous and the tainted figures of his own party, drawn into an October Revolution which they would either never have thought of undertaking themselves, or whose sequelae were not exactly what they had in mind for a socialist state in Russia. It must be assumed on the basis of a powerful mass of circumstantial evidence, that Lenin knew more or less the extent of what he must have considered a "pack of scoundrels" in and around the Bolshevik leadership. They being part of the troops under his command, as Alexander the Great had had many among his father's generals, Lenin pursued his own policy as a capable general would under the circumstances.

He conducted his policy over the following months and years similarly, retreating, conceding, advancing, to consolidate forces for battles to come. If one examines his policies only in terms of small intervals, as if in isolation, the whole thing might appear to make no sense. Taken in the larger span, the pattern is clear. In both the period from April 1917 into October, and in statecraft thereafter, the image of the working of Lenin's mind is that of orchestrating history, as the variety of conductor who produces reproduction of a musical idea from the succession of notes in the movement of a symphony, first, and then out of the succession of movements as a whole. That is the way history is effectively orchestrated by any able statesman, or a group of statesmen over successive generations.

For the oligarchy, the crucial decision about Lenin was made immediately after Rapallo. Lenin had entrusted Chicherin, Lenin's own foreign minister, to negotiate a treaty of economic cooperation with Germany at Genoa. Chicherin, at a special meeting at Rapallo during that conference, drew Lloyd George of Britain, as well as numerous others, into the agreement, providing political cover for what Lenin clearly desired most, economic development cooperation with *capitalist* Germany. Lenin had turned out to become, in the eyes of the horrified oligarchs, a "Red" version of Sergei Count Witte, a new heir of Czar Peter the Great. The oligarchs' Organization Consul, the assassination-bureau for the same Thule Society which created Hitler and the Nazis of Bavaria, assassinated Walter Rathenau. Shortly, every Western signator to the Rapallo Treaty but Britain's Lloyd George, was dead in one fashion or another.

Go back to the period from 1890 into 1905. Look at the

actual and threatened developments of that period which fearfully occupied the attention of Lord Alfred Milner and his kindergarden--the future Round Table faction. Centered around Gabriel Hanotaux in France, Sergei Count Witte in Russia, and the Meiji Restoration's "American System" in Japan, there was a determination to free the world from the domination of the City of London and British Empire. Britain's agents of influence were to be destroyed in China by the "New China" movement. Otherwise, with cooperation of German industrialist circles, an accelerated economic development of Russia was to create a powerful force, united by an active common economic interest on the continent. Britain and its oligarchical allies on the continent struck out desperately, to attempt to destroy every force which might bring this into being immediately or in the future.

The orchestration of the Dreyfus affair in France, the treaty-agreements involving Korea, by which the pro-British faction was put into power in Japan, and the ensuing Russo-Japan war, the series of maneuvers and destabilizations in Russia, culminating in the 1905 Revolution, and the assassination of President McKinley in the United States, were taken variously as direct measures or as supplementary precautionary measures. (McKinley was shot by a Swiss anarchist assassin, deployed by way of a British safehouse in New York City, Emma Goldman's Henry Street Settlement House.)

The "geopolitical" scheme through which the British and Venice orchestrated the events leading into World War I was the further action taken to remove the potential of such a threat in the future. Carve Russia up into a set of petty, helpless states, while bleeding Germany into impotence in the war.

Lenin's course of action, beginning the October Revolution itself, with all oligarchical fears corroborated by the import of Lenin's initiation of the Rapallo agreement, forced the oligarchy to abandon its plans for early destruction of the institutions of the nation-state throughout the world. Another world war, a second version of the World War I geopolitical scenario, must be fought, this time to remove Russia surely.

There are two features of Lenin's personality and outlook which are implicitly reflected by their presence or absence in Soviet policy-making today. Understanding these implications is key to the necessary close assessment of the Soviet state and leadership which must be made as an integral part of shaping the conduct of U.S. foreign policy in that quarter.

The key to Lenin's imprint on the Soviet state is found chiefly in two of his writings of the early years of this century, his famous *What Is To Be Done?* and his *Two Tactics*. The first is crucial for understanding Lenin's mind, and so to see the presence or absence of those same qualities of mind among Soviet leaders today. The second is key to Lenin's long-range policies, and for understanding how those policies, either directly or in chain-reaction fashion over time, affect the character and responses of the Soviet Union today.

The reader is cautioned against an excessively scholastic, literal interpretation of any part of these writings; one must look at these writings as a musician might attempt to adduce the musical idea of the study of the score as a whole; the thing on which to focus is the exhibition of the characteristic manner in which Lenin's mental processes attack a conception, and to avoid what many Sovietologists foolishly do, attempt to construct a Leninist "ideological" edifice piece-by- piece. The key to understanding Lenin's actions and their consequence for the Soviet Union during and following his lifetime, is to focus on what might be termed best "Lenin's method for *changing his mind*," without losing his connection to his essential objectives.

The first thing to notice in Lenin's *What Is To Be Done?* is the choice of title. This is a borrowing of the title of the most famous publication of Cherneshevsky, perhaps a more significant influence, or at least a deeper point of agreement with the inner core of Lenin's mind than even Karl Marx. The leading Russian Social Democrats bitterly complained after 1917: "We wuz robbed." Lenin had not adhered to what they regarded as "Marxist objective laws of history;" he had "cheated" by employing the "voluntarism" of Cherneshevsky. They should have been forewarned by noting the title of his *What Is To Be Done?;* had they any doubts on that point, they might have read the content.

Anarchosyndicalists, L. Trotsky among them in unchangeable practical disposition, complained on the same point in different terms of reference. They alleged that Lenin proposed, and employed "elitist methods," Lenin rejecting thus the populist principle that valid ideas are an organically developing epiphenomenon of people, and that different classes, according to their experience of life, secrete the ideas reflecting their interests and conditions. It is the anti-"voluntarist" argument of the Social Democrats, stated differently.

This was old stuff in 19th and early 20th century Russian culture. Just as it is the culture assimilated into one's youth that chiefly determines one's philosophical tendencies, even before university-age years, so the persons entering the Social Democratic and anarchist movements of Russia during the later 19th century and the decade immediately following, reflected in political activities those philosophical outlooks they had acquired from (chiefly) Russian culture prior to adulthood. Granted, people can change as adults, but this occurs only through an activated, efficient, and motivated preconsciousness, which occurs in the form of a large-scale social phenomenon only under special sorts of environmental circumstances of change, or through aid of a deliberate mobilization in cultural developments, such as the 15th-century Golden Renaissance or the effect of the Weimar Classic cultural revolution upon Germany. For young Russians of this indicated period, Cherneshevsky and Herzen are among the exemplary, pairable polarities of cultural-philosophical outlook. In the case of Lenin, it is not Marx who defines his "mental map," but Cherneshevsky.

As we noted earlier, the defeat of the efforts of Ivan Grozny and Boris Goudonov, and the impact of events correlated with the 1618-1648 Thirty Years War in Central Europe, made the emergence of the Romanov dynasty, and most emphatically the role of Peter the Great, a renaissance in Russia, a revival from a previous period of decline. Under the policy-influence of chiefly Leibniz's design for economic development, Peter and his immediate successors had maintained a policy into the period of Potemkin, under which Russia became the leading economic power in Europe after France as an industrial nation, outstripping Britain.

Under Venetian intervention, exemplified by Venice's appointment of its citizen Capodistria as Russia's foreign minister during the Napoleonic wars, Russia subsided into relative backwardness. Pushkin typified the voices of republicanism speaking as if in a wilderness of drift into the bestial Great Mother cultism which the figure of the evil Tolstoy exemplifies for that period.

Then came the Crimean War. The Geneva gang of Schlumberger, de Neuflize and Mallet had a significant hand in this atrocity, as during the Jacobin events in France earlier. Czar Alexander II reacted to this war, seeking to introduce the American System of political-economy of Hamilton, the Careys and List into Russia, to the point that his alliance with President Lincoln, his sending a newly-developed and powerful Russian fleet to New York and San Francisco as Lincoln's ally, and his threats to Paris, and to Palmerston and Russell in London, saved the United States from being destroyed by aid of an Anglo-French expeditionary force in 1863. Alexander unleashed an economic, scientific and moral-cultural renaissance in Russia, which Sergei Count Witte attempted to continue and further. Cherneshevsky exemplified the awakening of Russia's cultural life from Tolstoyian bestiality.

One epitome of the oligarchical opposition to Cherneshevsky was Alexander Herzen, in his time an important British conduit of such functions as funding of Bakunin's anarchist movement. It being believed that the Czar had been provoked to the point of ordering forfeiture of the scalawag's estate, London protected Herzen's estate by purchasing it. Herzen employed some of the income from the sale to purposes interesting to the Russian policy laid down by Palmerston.

Herzen was by no means the source of such doctrines of Hegelian stoicism as Plekhanov's. Herzen typifies something, rather than causes it. Was Herzen an Apollonian, as some admirers have painted him; or. did his funding of Bakunin's efforts reveal him as covertly a Dionysian? Was he, then, merely a natural son of the evil Tolstoy, a product of that Great Mother cult spread by the Eastern Rite: "Mother Russia" with her Slavic "soul," and that "soul's" attributes of affinities for pan-Slavic "blood" and pan-Slavic "soil?"

Ladies and Gentlemen of the policy-influencing community of the United States! To what have we pointed here? Is this the dark bowel of 19th-century Russia and only that? Or, does something flash by the comer of the mind's eye from contemporary Soviet life? What flickered so at the corner of your attention: did it not frighten you a little?

There are those among you who gloat as you nod agreement with the allusion just made. It is said in certain circles that Rage will arise bloodily in Eastern Europe, and, risen, will march eastward, as Hitler did, into the Ukraine, will resurrect ancient pagan warriors' souls in the Caucasus, and continue to arouse in Soviet Central Asia the sleeping pestilences of al-Ghazali and that green-eyed Mongol, Temuchin. *We see you nodding, gloating.* So, you believe, there is another force, alternative to the hazards of thermonuclear warfare, by which the Soviet Empire may be ruined from within.

This alternative Bertrand Russell prophesized to Lord Alfred Milner's Coefficients in 1902. When those gentlemen rejected Russell's proposal--in favor of preparing to fight World War I--the petulant Russell, that peevish priest of Dionysus, made the infantile exhibition of himself he deemed appropriate to the circumstance, and walked out. Modern war was Apollo and Russell's alternative was Dionysus. Tavistock, Henry Kissinger's spiritual mother, is also a priest of Dionysus. Dr. Teller has helped to spoil the fun of another devastating world war, so now you gentlemen would unleash the Dionysiac beasts of psychological warfare.

Gloating gentlemen, you are mad fools! You do not know what a beast you arouse when you prod so the Russian soul, and spill Slavic blood on Slavic soil. In a moment of despair, it is alleged, Josef Stalin went into St. Basil's and made a pact with Satan against Hitler, to unleash "Mother Russia" against the invader. Do you wish to unleash the Great Mother, that she might throw H-bombs? Your alternative to actually fighting thermonuclear warfare is to provoke thermonuclear warfare: it is your detour from Samarra which brings you to Samarra.

You mad gentlemen gloat at the rising attendance in churches of the Soviet Eastern Rite, the churches of Mother Russia. Your little philistine minds, gloating over what a silly RAND Corporation computer, or the mad friends of the mad Zbigniew Brzezinski assure you will be the scenario, are like a savage finding a spill of gasoline in a cellar, lighting a match to see better whence the source of the strange aroma. If you transform men into beasts equipped with the conscious capacities of modern man, then you have armed the beast with H-bombs.

You catch our argument in a contradiction? You do not fear that beast, Great Mother, since you yourselves are the worshippers of the Age of Aquarius, Dionysus-Satan's age? Great Mother is your God? *Then, you also have the Emperor Nero for your loyal friend.* The name of Great Mother, that Whore of Babylon, is Entropy. She is insane. She is the ultimate existentialist, whose ultimate source of passion for her jaded appetites is suicide, Götterdämerung.

As to presumption of pre-historical fact, a part of what is interpolated next, here and now, is admittedly supposition. It is a license of the classical dramatist, to invent a fact or two to make the stage a more efficient medium for the communication of unshakeable truth. The principle we employ here, as we have learned this from the best classical dramatists, is the employment of the principled fact of fiction, that the audience knows that it is fiction, to impart more forcefully the essence of the truth. The mind of the sane audience, knowing that the facts of the drama are fiction, looks for truth not in the fictional facts, but rather in the ordering of fictional facts by the mind, as we have earlier stressed the principles involved. We return to focus again on the Atlas Epic's topical area, to develop two critical points bearing upon NATO Soviet policy today and also on a deeper appreciation of the circumstances which produced Lenin and the Soviet state.

Who Overthrew The Uranus Civilization?

What kind of explosives are being played with by those attempting to unleash Great Mother from within the Soviet Empire? If we knew certain details of the Atlas Epic which appear not to be recorded, we could answer that question from the pages of history. The lack of such historical records does not leave us helplessly ignorant. The writer knows what Great Mother is as her nature bears on the underscored feature of current NATO Soviet policy. The problem is one of communication of that knowledge by means of something less than six months to a year of intensive classroom work by the readers. To circumvent that labor, we resort to the indicated method of dramatic devices. We project to you an image of our conception, by means of a highly informed supposition bearing upon the character of the Olympians, the putative founders of astrology, of oligarchism.

The Atlanteans' oral tradition as reported by Diodorus Siculus reports two purported details of their own pre-history bearing directly and crucially on this question: Who were the Olympians?

The first of these two crucial facts is the Atlanteans' report that Uranus, the great astronomer and ruler of a city, reached out to people living in the mode of existence of man-beasts in that vicinity. Uranus drew these enmiserated people toward the culture of the city, and uplifted them by introducing agriculture. The situation of such a pre-historic occurrence in the indicated region of modern Morocco and its adjacent areas below sea-level today is most interesting in respect to the known potentials of that area under better water-resources than exist today. The philological evidence in the Greek, referencing agricultural products to his region, is also interesting.

The second of the facts is crucial if there is a direct connection between this and the first cited fact. Chronos is reported by the Atlanteans to have had one wife, whose children were named Titans after her maiden-name, and four concubines, whose children were the Olympians. The obvious question posed by this report is: Were the concubines women from the people which Uranus had been civilizing? Why did the Atlantean tradition account the mothers of the Olympians as having such a distinctly inferior social status to the mother of the Titans? We do not propose to draw here a working-hypothesis respecting the mother of the Titans. We employ this point merely to jog our consciousness toward the kind of problem implied.

At some time during the 11th millennium B.C., several ships of an astronomical-age culture might have arrived in the vicinity of the straits of Gibraltar. If they were of the numbers and disposition typical of Peoples of the Sea later on, and disposed and able to establish a settlement there, they would have constructed an urban settlement, with fortifications facing inland. Within this urban site, they would have early attended to the business of constructing an astronomical observatory consistent with the center of practice of an astronomical-age maritime culture. They would have attended, throughout this process, to securing their food-supplies.

Let us presume that the chieftain of this small colony was named Uranus, a person speaking a trans-Atlantic language which might have included at that point the characteristic "atla" whose philological remains are distributed rather widely on both sides of the Atlantic, as reflected by "Atlas," "Atlantic," "Thalassa," and so forth, if not also "Etruscan (Atlascan)," as well as among Atlan indians and among the Aztecs and their Lipan cousins, including the association of the "atl" with the sea-serpent who slithered on both sides of the Atlantic in the later astrological degeneration of maritime cultures.

The Atlanteans' oral tradition says this happened, at least by implication. The sophisticated ancient astronomical-age calendar was not invented in a lifetime, nor was agriculture developed in a lifetime. It would seem so, however, to a superstitious group of savages at first conscious encounter with such a maritime culture. Astronomy and agriculture had been previously developed elsewhere. If the Atlanteans' oral tradition had been recorded in their own language, by aid of the obvious phonetical principles during the 1st century B.C., instead of the form Diodorus Siculus reported what he had received, we would have much, much more to work on today. However, if there is historical truth within the account of Uranus and his immediate descendants, and the overwhelming weight of evidence supports that conclusion, then it happened more or less as we have indicated: Uranus headed a sea-faring party of colonists, who brought seeds and an astronomical-age culture to that region.

Now, let us consider the kind of people these colonists attempted to civilize. We can summon broad, but adequate estimates of the demographic characteristics of such a population.

Their potential population-density would not have been better than one person for each fifteen square kilometers of average habitability of land for a hunting-and-gathering culture. The life-expectancy for surviving infants would be in the general vicinity of not better than sixteen to twenty years of age. The characteristic population-profile would center on young children, below the age of ten, constituting much more than half the population, if the population were viable over successive generations. The dominant feature of the culture demographically would be those mothers who survived to the exceptional age of thirty years or more. The mother-dependency of the under-ten-years-of-age child would have been the dominant feature of mental life of the population as a whole. *The fabled matriarchy.*

We must reject more or less completely, all of the so-called standard categories of the anthropologists in this matter. As the case of pre-Columbian populations of the Western Hemisphere illustrates this point, the cultural condition of folk classed as "primitive tribes" is, as in the relatively extreme instance of the so-called "digger indians," a degenerated relic of an earlier, higher state of culture. In the case of the Melanesians and Polynesian cultures distributed among the islands of the Pacific basin, we know that a higher level of trans-Pacific culture dominated that region thousands of years ago. We can adduce certain things from the demographics of various sub-literate forms of cultures encountered, but we can not assume, except in the rarest of exceptional cases, that the culture encountered is part of such a statistical series that they represent data to be plotted in such a manner as to map the lawfully ordered ascent of mankind from a state of primeval-hordedness. The case of the "tla" among tribes which ascended to power from a known, preceding, "primitive" condition, warns us with the force of a unique experiment against overlooking the point that the Aztec-Lipan culture's putatively primitive condition was the consequence of a catastrophic degeneration of a group of people from a more advanced cultural condition earlier.

We must not overlook the danger of confusing the way in which a degenerating culture adapts to a descent into a depopulated, baser condition of society, with the kind of culture developed in an upward ascent to a comparable economic level.

The case of the Vedic and Avestic literature emphasizes most dramatically that it is not the experience of a few generations which shapes the mental life of an immediately following generation, but, rather, the culture transmitted over a relatively enormous span of generations. To develop a culture in a backward condition is monstrously difficult. The mere addition of modern artifacts does not suffice to reorder the processes of judgment to the degree of rationality a scientific age requires. We must always introduce the advanced culture as a culture.

This does not mean that the peoples sharing a common Bantu language-origin must necessarily throw that language itself overboard, and learn only English, French or German. It does mean that the only alternative to such language-substitution is an upward revision of Bantu-language culture, aided by philological approaches to reconstruction of its form in a relatively more advanced, earlier form of usage, and to employ comprehension of that more advanced, earlier stock of language-culture as an informed basis for developing a Bantu-language's culture containing what is provably essential (as distinct form idiosyncratic) in scientific language-cultures.

In thinking of the backward culture encounterd by the party of colonists accompanying Uranus, we must think of a people who had lived in such a matriarchal form of demography over hundreds of years or longer, in which almost the entirety of the cultural development (and transmission) was mediated through the natural or foster-mother. The most awesome conception in such a culture must necessarily be "Great Mother."

If marriage or concubinage between the colonists and the indigenous people produced a population in the city itself which was composed significantly of children encultured by mothers from a savage culture of the variety outlined, we have in this exactly the social pre-conditions for the variety of social-cultural catastrophe reported in the Atlantean and coinciding accounts.

This would "explain" much, as the British with their Aristoteleans' view that science is merely "plausible explanation," might wish to put the point. Scientists must despise all such plausible explanation, as do all competent classical dramatists as well. We must focus upon evidence with the force of unique-experimental qualifications.

The fictive account we have constructed from the cited, crucial fragments of evidence, leads to a picture of mental processes' ordering identical with a well-documented historical phenomenon: the Phrygian Cult of Dionysus, the Biblical Satan.

The Dionysus cult is a Great Mother cult. The children of the city are recruited to orgiastic-practices prefiguring the most extreme degeneracy encountered in contemporary "jet-set" and rock-drug-sex youth-counterculture. The political object of such fornication and other practices is to transform these children into terrorists, to go back into the city from whence they came, and to slay their parents. By means of this act, urban civilization is to be destroyed, and humanity to be returned to a bucolic form of existence: the Hesiodic program, the program of the Hapsburg Pan-European Union's Malthusian world-federalist scenario today.

The Uranian sea-serpent, the ships of the maritime culture long before the Vikings put the serpent's-head on the dragon-ship, now becomes apotheosized within the astrological system by the Olympians, the transmission of Satanic cultism by the Olympians wherever they rove and establish their colonies. This is what the Phoenician and cognative Isis-cult myths and paraphernalia insist upon: the marriage between the horns of the bull and the *golden* circle of the serpent. The transmission of knowledge by the serpent-ships becomes the most monstrous evil befallen mankind: oligarchism. The evil of infantile, savage regression, armed with a relatively advanced technology of warfare and logistical basis for conduct of warfare.

On the one side, our quasi-dramatization of the matter presents a conception. On the other side, the conception so articulated, corresponds in every crucial feature to the result we witness as oligarchism during the historical period to date.

The Book of Genesis is a very wise book, the more wondrously wise the more we know of the ordering of the universe and human existence. Its injunction, respecting labor, is scientifically sound, lacking only the notion of the divine potential in mankind as the instrument to inform labor. Eve and the serpent providing knowledge, is the evil which in fact befell many Adams, which seized in Adam upon that infantilism which is the condition of evil to which each new-born child is born. Adam's infantile hedonism was already the problem, conflicting with his divine potential, long before the 11th millennium B.C. The catastrophe reported by Plato and the Atlanteans, and pointed to by Manetho, did occur in some form not distant from the oral tradition as to characteristic features bequeathed to later millennia. It was a worse setback for humanity, a setback toward man's originally evil, primitive, infantile, matriarchal condition, than even the U.S. Congress's treasonous enactment of the 1876-79 Specie Resumption Act. The Olympian Satan, Dionysus, that son of the Great Mother, was indeed a fallen creature, sunk into debasement from the condition he foully betrayed, his betrayal of the divine.

This persisting problem of evil, of infantilist, matriarchical tendencies, is that we must combat, above all else.

The French peasant, of the time of the Salian emperors, came into the urban center, at the center of which assembly of marketplaces, entertainments, and other buildings, rose a great cathedral, designed by the builders of Chartres according to the Platonic harmonic principles of design specified by St. Augustine. The harmonic proportioning of light and shaping of space within that cathedral's interior transformed something inside the peasant's awestruck mind. Then, the priest spoke, and the acoustical characteristics of the interior, determined by that harmonic ordering of design, filled the interior in a manner the peasant had heard in no other place. Then, there was singing, filling that space according to the same wonderful design. The peasant's powers of consciousness, in respect to both sight and hearing, were wonderfully inspired by this address to his creative potentials of mind. When came the music, he was lifted to a higher state of mental being by this wonderful unity of both vision and hearing in such a wonderful place. So, we republicans build culture, build civilization.

Meanwhile, In Russia

Gentlemen, put from your minds for a moment whether you are amused by or hate the result which Lenin shaped. People are killed rather easily, but historical facts can not be so easily eradicated, and the lawful principles underlying the ordering of historical processes is a more powerful force than any armed force of humanity could ever aspire to challenge without crushing nothing but itself in such a foolish undertaking. To submit to the infantile whim, to deny something as if one could wish it away, or crush to the same effect by an exertion of brute force, is the mark of a childish, bungling fool. You must, to a certain degree, get into the inside of Lenin's mind; the point of such inquiry is not so much to know what Lenin thought, but rather to see his mental processes from a higher vantage-point than--and of this we may be certain--even he knew his mental processes.

The most powerful of the driving forces of nation-builders (and others of the same quality in other aspects of the matter), is never primarily an impulse to alter merely the material conditions of life of a people. If a person has aroused within him that which corresponds to the divine, creative potential, what drives him forward is a deep hatred against both philistinism in others and his passion to eradicate the overflow of such moral sewage into the cluttering of his own mental processes with such banality, such prejudices. To understand the power associated with Karl Marx's influence, and the extraordinary power to orchestrate history displayed by V. I. Lenin, one must distinguish among their prejudices, the outcome of their efforts, and that creative passion which drove them forward in their principal enterprises.

Only once that first step of approximation has been accomplished can we judge competently how prejudices misshaped the direction of their efforts, and how, in this and other ways, a defective result was produced. In those cases in which an idea is spread in the face of ferocious efforts to suppress it, discredit it, and so forth, rather than by means of public-relations favor by the leading institutions of society, we must account for that feature of the content of the idea as idea which locates this remarkable kind of power to influence. That power is either the attractions of hedonistic degeneration to the infantile impulse within persons, or, otherwise, is the impact of efficient reflections of creative processes of mind which are recognized, although usually only unconsciously, by other minds. It is chiefly these two, opposing considerations which determine how ideas, as ideas, find sympathetic response among those populations to which their communication is addressed.

On this account, it is not only of direct relevance to focus upon the total opposition between the political course of Lenin and that of his terrorist older brother. The curious fact, that Lenin reported his reading of Cherneshevsky occurred in the course of bringing himself to browse through his executed brother's library, emphasizes for our attention the opposite character of philosophical world-outlook which the two brothers each brought to their reading of even the same sources. L. Trotsky, for whom Lenin was only the last in a series of adopted fathers, was much closer to Lenin's terrorist brother than Lenin himself; the issue is the combat of reason against populist irrationality.

For the irrationalist, popular opinion is axiomatic. Populism, as Max Weber justifies the populist (*völkisch*) policy by which Weber made Nazism possible in Germany, says there must be numerous public opinions, each an ideology reflecting an arbitrarily, irrationalistic choice of adopted self-interests and goals, and social processes are to be treated as rational only as they bear on one group of opinion's efforts to impose its arbitrary beliefs more or less completely upon society as a whole: the *Triumph of the Populist Will*, as the Nazis understood and practiced it, exactly.

Like Max Weber, the consistent populist rejects with deep-going hatred all efforts to impose upon society, upon the populist's environment of behavior, the "tyranny of reason." Consequently, populist (liberal) politics first seeks to impose its capricious demands upon society by confidence-games. and when society resists acceding at the rate the liberal desires, the Apollonian liberal unbuttons his trousers and becomes a Nazi, seizing government, and avowing that the force of government is the principle which sweeps away all considerations of constitutional law, the same potentially fascist, irrationalist doctrine introduced subversively into U.S. law by Justice Oliver Wendell Holmes, the Fabian convert of the Holmes-Laski correspondence.

So, a populist liberal, a Stoic, is merely a criminal mind temporarily holding itself in check. When Weberian Germany lost its temper, to the point of desperation, it became a Nazi, with Hjalmar Schacht's liberals providing the crucial part in bringing down the Müller coalition-government, introducing Volcker-like austerity-measures, and then sliding Hitler liberally into power. (Gentlemen liberals, see what little monster may be squirming inside, and expel the rascal before he does you and this nation more damage.)

The populist, persuaded by experience that the masses are not responding to his whims at a sufficiently rapid pace, seeks to "awaken" them. He assumes that prevailing, institutionalized ideas are "repressing" the "people's" natural ideas and passions. Therefore, the populist must demonstrate to the people that real institutions can be physically destroyed, and so the people may learn from this

Dionysiacal example, that the reflection of these same varieties of institutions within their own minds can be similarly destroyed. The person of reason knows that it is the people's ideas which are themselves in some degree at fault.

The person of reason seeks to uplift his or her people from a debased state of mind by seeking to inform their minds, and, more urgent than merely informing those minds of facts, to inform those minds to the point of arousing the creative powers within those minds.

The "world-map" of the mental processes of the populist and the person of reason is, respectively, irreconcilable for practice with the other. The one approach is creative and "elitist" in that specific sense; the other is liberal-Jacobin. The one takes the determination of popular opinion as given, the populist; the process by which popular opinion changes may be explained, and one may attempt to follow the unfolding of such a process, however, the populist or the Plekhanov, forbids attempting to interfere with the workings of those "laws" themselves. In brief, the preconscious must be kept unconscious, not awakened to the "painfulness" of being made conscious. Reason demands that the laws of development of public opinion be changed upward, and employs the same principles as classical tragedy to inform the minds of people to this purpose.

What drives the populist, is the urge to "come closer" to what he persuades himself is the deep "feelings" of the people. He is determined to succeed in gaining access to those popular feelings, even if this requires attempting to dynamite his way in. The irrationalist does not say, "Mrs. Jones, what do you *think* about . . . the irrationalist asks, "Mrs. Jones, how do you *feel* about . . . ."

What drives the person of reason, his abhorrence of the philistinism, the banality which inundates him from the expressed opinions and behavior of the people.

For Karl Marx, this hatred of philistinism was summed up in his praising capitalist development for freeing humanity from "the idiocy of rural life" (serfdom). For Lenin, the code-term typical of him, was "Philistine!" For Lenin, the image of what he hated in the Russian people generally was that of *Oblomov. That must be changed!* That is the key to his identification with Cherneshevsky in his *What Is To Be Done!*

We shall come, in due course, to the matter of the Russian Orthodox Church, which is negatively and otherwise the secret of the absence of any direct comprehension of the Judeo-Christian republican tradition in October 1917 or Soviet culture since. *This is impolitic to say? Gentlemen policy-influencers, on the day that one is forbidden to include in policy-shaping accounts, those topics which are unpleasant to say publicly, but bearing importantly on the subject addressed, then from that moment on, any policy you concoct will be to that degree a bungling farce. Without dealing openly, analytically, with the mediation of the Mother-Russia cultism through the Russian Orthodox Church, you understand absolutely nothing crucial about either the Russian Revolution or the*

Soviet Union today. Be assured, however, we are in no instance of this attacking any part of the Christian clergy, but only frocked "Magicians."

Primarily, there is no evidence that Lenin cared much one way or the other for any a priori sort of predisposition as to what sort of revolutionary transformation would accomplish his purpose. Any approach which appeared to be most efficient to get the stink of philistinism and Oblomovism out of the Russian people would probably have been acceptable to him. He was not a doctrinaire, nor an opportunist--at least not in the usual connotations of such characterizations. To adduce his socialist doctrine of practice one must adduce that which, aggregately, impelled him to more or less eliminate any other choice of efficient service to his purpose but what he adopted, as an evolving notion of what appears to foolish scholars from the outside as an evolving body of socialist doctrine as such.

If Lenin appears as a very sly fellow, and at times he confessed to deliberate slyness appropriate to clandestine life, the principal cause for this appearance is not so much his deliberate deception, as the simple fact that his primary conception of purpose was not doctrinaire: to the effect that his purpose must necessarily elude the notice of observers who measure the behavior of others by the standard of reference of their own doctrinaire notion of purpose and goals. Lenin's adducible purpose, as What Is To Be Done? reflects this with exemplary efficiency and immediacy, is to move in a more or less definite direction, a direction essentially away from the Russian population's saturation with those degrading banalities typified by philistinism and Oblomovism. From that standpoint of reference, Lenin's conduct is not difficult to follow. From the standpoint of any assumed political-doctrinaire "belief-system," Lenin's most crucial course of action might appear either inexplicable, or an utterly incompetent interpretation must result.

To see the implications of *What Is To Be Done?* and the complementing thesis of *Two Tactics*, one must situate these against the background of the broad sweep of the 19th and early 20th century inside and outside Russia. One must put to himself the question, given Lenin's kernel-motivation--the motivation which made Cherneshevsky's *What Is To Be Done?* so agreeable to him, what was the intellectual-social environment which shaped his prejudices and choices?

Broadly, the calamity which struck the United States during the 1870s, exemplified by the treasonous Specie Resumption Act, correlated with and contributed a broad cultural decline in Western civilization which has continued into the present point of rotted overripeness for collapse of that civilization. The most advanced achievements of mankind up into that point, the capitalist industrial and scientific development erupting out of the 15th-century Golden Renaissance's launching of the sovereign nation-state, appeared to have "run out of steam." They appeared to be still the dominant form of society's ordering, but their credibility had been severely called into doubt.

The pessimism which pervaded society increasingly from the 1870s onward struck the intellectual strata of society in various direct and indirect ways. The original sources of this pessimism were two. First, the oligarchical faction, as typified by the work centered in the Pre-Raphaelite Brotherhood and rise of the Fabian Society in Britain, was determined to bring down civilization as rapidly as might be accomplished; they spread irrationalism and cultural pessimism willfully. Second, the irrationalist and pessimistic cynicism, being spread by these oligarchical currents, seemed to find supporting evidence in the objective developments and cultural developments in the society on which the cultural pessimists commented. The cynicism generated by the confluence of these two original sources became a miasma of peer-group opinion spreading throughout society.

This affected the internal development of the socialist movements and those movements' impact upon the society around them. First, the oligarchists fostered socialist movements. The British oligarchy's fostering of Ruskin-Morris, British socialism is exemplary. The Anglophile "families" sponsorship of the Socialist Party of America, especially that party's orbit of pragmatist, Anglophile intellectuals, such as John Dewey and Walter Lippmann, is also exemplary. Second, the abrupt decline emerging over the 1870s made the ideas of Karl Marx seem plausible among socialists. Marx, at least, had a worked-out analysis--and forecast--of such a collapse of capitalist culture. The oligarchs variously attempted to exploit Marx's reputation (especially now that Marx himself was safely dead), and yet busied themselves to check unwanted by-products of such spread of Marx's writings. They used the putative Marxist, Eduard Bernstein, to promote a revised version of Marx coincident with Fabian policy, they also toyed with various apocalyptic versions, as the case of Parvus in Germany during the 1890s--Bernstein's nominal adversary--illustrates in part.

From the 1890s (e.g.. Karl Kautsky), through Rosa Luxemburg and Lenin's *Imperialism* and associated writings, the Marxist faction of the Social Democracy vacillated between the influence of Lassalle's solidarism and Marx, in attempting to construct a theory describing the form of capitalist society emerging out of the collapse of capitalist progress during the 1870s; capitalism (at least, nominally *capitalist*) was continuing--into 1914--to increase in manifest power, even though the character of capitalist society and its development had been radically transformed. What was this new form of capitalism? The name *imperialism* emerged as the preferred description of the new state of post-1870s affairs. The Treaty of Berlin (1878) appeared to define the watershed for the new order in world affairs, and so the name of imperialism stuck.

In Russia itself, the development, from the Crimean War until his assassination in 1881, defined the reign of Czar Alexander II as a golden age. Although the industrialization of Russia continued through the 1890s, especially under the leadership of Witte, the defeat of the conspiracy centered around France's Hanotaux and Witte brought forward impetus in Europe virtually to an end;

what might have become a new golden age, had Hanotaux and Witte held power, was aborted. The destruction of the impetus for Russian industry, especially the Baku oil fields, by the Anglo-Venetian 1905 Revolution and the humiliation and retreat of the Russo-Japan war, was followed by a rapid overall degeneration and demoralization, intersecting the world-wide monetary and economic crises of the 1905-1907 period. Everything good occurring after the 1870s seemed only an ephemeral exception to an overall downslide of civilization as a whole.

This was complicated by the position of the legal and semi-legal Marxist activities around industrialists of Russia proper and the Jewish center around Vilna. Marxism had been to some degree a "kept" plaything of certain capitalist circles. To the Russian Social Democrats, and it might be said that Plekhanov more or less typifies this, the question was, "Would the capitalists of Russia succeed, with Social Democratic support, in reversing the ebb in the progress of capitalist development?" The Bernstein-Kautsky and Bernstein-Luxemburg debates in Germany spilled over into the Russian Social Democratic ranks, especially in exile centers.

To interpret the division developed around this question in "right" versus "left" terms of reference is an absurd approach to the case of Lenin. For Lenin, every issue of importance was a "concrete question." Whether his judgment was seen as relatively "right" or "left" by others seemed to amuse him, and provide them with occasion for much chattering debate; but, except as he might pick up something of "concrete" usefulness to his purpose from such debates, he was merely amused by such attempted interpretations. For Lenin, the question was not "Will the Russian capitalists carry out the needed actions with Social Democratic support?", but "Concretely, will they?" His assessment was, "Concretely they will not *lead* such an endeavor." He posed a different question: "Concretely, if the Social Democrats lead the charge and control the capitalist government, will the Russian capitalists efficiently support such an activity?" That, concretely, is a fair approximation of his *Two Tactics*.

Lenin's method, the subject of his reflections on Hegel in the years of exile proximate to a Swiss library, was that processes determine history, and always determine the breaking-points of choices in history in terms of a concrete issue, a concrete task posed.

This method has impact upon the character of the institutions of the Soviet Union and its leadership, but it is not presently their method except in the sense of parody. The manifest method of the Soviet leadership, as examined in terms of their reaction to crucial features of the global situation outside Russia, and as reflected in their own press's observations on the issue of method, is a mixture chiefly of Plekhanov and pragmatism, with frequent references to the dangers of "voluntarism." Under well-defined conditions, they could become "voluntaristic," but during the recent decades to date, they have shown little comprehension of what Lenin himself would regard as the distinction between "voluntarism" and "adventurism;" from the pages of the Soviet press, comment of leading circles asserts that the two are more or less the same thing.

That fairly describes the political-strategic picture as it presented itself to Russian Social Democrats on the inside. We shift the point of reference to what Lenin (in particular) did not comprehend, the reality of the problem confronting him. To accomplish this most effectively, we shift our attention briefly from Russia to contemporary Italy.

The Catho-Communists

It is the standard myth of our national opinion that Communists are ipso facto "atheistic communists." Hearing an American expostulating on this such a presumedly self-evident truth, any informed figure of Italy or some other nations of this world would make a show of politeness by merely thinking, rather than saying out loud, "You American ass!" Not only is the Communist Party of Italy the political habitat of a large number of fully persuaded Catholics, but that party is the battlefield of hard-fought battle between the Catholic and Venetian factions, the principal constituents of the largest Communist Party in the world outside Communist nations.

This phenomenon, generally unknown to U.S. public or official opinion, is endemic among a number of Spanish-speaking nations as well as Italy; the usual term of reference is "Catho-Communists."

As a further point of reference to our foreign policy on this and related matters, the former, terrorist-assassinated

Prime Minister of Italy, Aldo Moro, was the spokesman for a policy called the "Historical Compromise," a policy of political coalition between the Christian-Democratic and Communist parties of Italy. It was a stroke of genius, actually. The problem inside the Christian-Democratic Party is the powerful faction of black oligarchs; the problem in the Communist Party, the other mass-based party of Italy, is a current most conveniently identified as linked to that one time supporter of Benito Mussolini's fascist coup, Benedetto Croce. If, however, the DC and PCI are en bloc, the result is that the non-oligarchical Catholics of the DC and the Catho-Communists of the PCI effectively dominate the government of Italy.

Henry Kissinger, among others, has objected violently to this proposal. Kissinger is a heathen: he is not morally Jewish, not Christian, and we are persuaded by our Arab friends that he is certainly no Muslim. We would add, he is no Brahmin. Kissinger is, by profession, an oligarchist, and we must assume that that is also his religious preference. Therefore, Kissinger may be assumed to have oligarchical varieties of heathen religious objections to Aldo Moro's proposal, and the other prominent objectors around Washington must be assumed either to share Mr. Kissinger's curious beliefs, or to act in the matter out of either ignorance or merely opportunistic adaptation to prevailing winds of ignorant opinion on the water around our nation's capital. It should be stressed, moreover, that persons of Kissinger's general persuasions on policy-matters around Washington, D.C., and Manhattan, are on collaborative terms with the Communist factional opponents of the Catho-Communists, and also with the most heathen elements of the Socialist Party, as well as the oligarchical currents of the Christian Democracy.

This point of comparative reference is introduced now to situate our further exploration of the case of Lenin and the Soviet state. There are visible no "Catho-Bolsheviks" or anything equivalent. For this, the Russian Orthodox Church is chiefly to blame. This ostensibly impolitic, but true and crucial fact, is the key to understanding our most essential problem in dealing with the Soviet question; it is key to the Soviet Paradox.

It should be viewed, especially in light of what has been developed earlier in this report, as paradoxical that the same Lenin whose characteristic method is most distinguished by implicit reliance on creative mental processes, should have been weak to the point of being negative on the point of classical culture. The issue is underlined by his consistent and sincere support for and endorsement of the work of the behaviorist dog-torturer. I. P. Pavlov, the forerunner of the Harvard pigeon-teaser, B. F. Skinner. This fallacy of Lenin's world-outlook, as reflected in the case of Pavlov, is exemplary of everything which flaws essentially the best achievements of himself and the Soviet state. It is the immediate and persisting issue for all among us who view the matter properly, as we shudder at the thought of Communist ideology's dominating the world at some future point in the future.

We must understand our vital interests on this point, and the Soviet leadership must understand us in the same connection.

All among us who share in common the protestant or Catholic heritage of St. Augustine's defense of Christianity, are so defined by the issue of the *Filioque*, as we treated the *secular* relevance of that earlier in this report. As we also emphasized, there is no methodological quarrel between Christian culture and the exposition of Judaism by Philo of Alexandria on the point of culture and statecraft involved. Now, we must reference our earlier treatment of Judeo-Christian republican culture to the problem presented to Lenin, for example, by the impact of a contrary culture. This was the culture mediated through the oligarchical composition of the Russian Orthodox Church during his lifetime, the mediation under putatively Christian auspices of the "blood and soil" characteristics of the Great Mother cult in the guise of the Mother-Russia cult.

As we indicated earlier, for Augustinian Christianity--which is a defense of Apostolic Christianity mounted in the West, the issue of Christian belief can not be separated from *Christian practice*, as is also the case for Judaism. To each soul is assigned implicitly a potential talent and an implicit mortal task. This work, situated in respect to the cited injunction of the Book of Genesis, requires us to act negentropically, which is to develop and employ that creative potential of our mental processes for discovering more perfectly, and governing ourselves more perfectly by the lawful composition of the universe, the reflected Logos for our knowledge.

We have acquired the prudence in our republic to separate church from state, to the effect that in no matter of statecraft do we mark a man or woman lesser or greater on matter of church. This separation of church from state has however acquired an unfortunate and radical misinterpretation: the separation of church from state has been radically misconstrued to the point of ignoring what our forefathers did not separate from state in this matter. We enquire in political life into no man's or woman's church, but *we do rightly demand a coherence with Judeo-Christian republican standards of personal and public practice.* That latter requirement is unignorably implicit in our Constitution, and we aim ourselves toward the gates of an earthly Hell whenever we may persist in ignoring that implication.

We hold a man or woman, and also a religious persuasion accountable for their *practice*. If an association should call itself church and practice cannibalism, or Aztec heart-gouging ceremonies, as part of its ritual, it is an abomination whose members as persons and an association are accountable to our appropriate criminal code. If it employs dangerous drugs for its religious rituals, the same rule of law applies to such persons as persons and as a *secular* association. The essence of the matter is simple to permit no establishment of a church as a state church, and to permit nothing which constitutes a foot-in-the-door in the direction of such a development. It is not intended to be a license to any sort of abomination which chooses to cloak itself in the fiction of "religious association." All men and women are accountable for their policies of practice according to Judeo-Christian republican standards for acceptable practice. These standards are not set by any religious denomination; they are, in matter law, entirely secular matters. Yet, we derive them from, chiefly, the defense of Christianity by St. Augustine, and we judge these matters in point of law and other public policy according to our knowledge of that origin and what that point of reference implies.

We defend society against oligarchism; that is the meaningful distinction of the term *republic* for us.

In the battles within the Eastern Rite, and between the Eastern opponents of the *Filioque* and Western Christianity, there developed in various currents and sects of the east, doctrines converging on the lunacy of Asharism in Islam. This tendency was characterized by an effort to separate the spiritual domain hermetically from the domain of secular practice, with hideous consequences for secular practice as well as monstrous, Chaldean-like concoctions in theology. In connection with secular practice, these theological aberrations tended to work to the effect of licensing ground-rent and usury.

In Western European civilization, we have experienced horrors in the name of both particular churches and Christianity generally. Yet, acknowledging all the disagreeable impedimenta which doctrine and so forth of sundry denominations and times may have bequeathed to churchly practice and schismatic this-and-that, the kernel of the Apostolic tradition has been preserved. Once man discovers that within him there is the potential divine, and that Christ assures that connection, this precious assurance will not be let go so easily. That saved us, and carried us through thus far when we might had been otherwise destroyed. That is the essence of the secular implications of *Filioque*, and the essence of the reciprocal connection between Judeo-Christian secular practice and Judeo-Christian belief as such.

When that connection to practice is lost, Christianity is readily perverted by oligarchism into becoming a parody of itself, absorbing and reflecting the syncretic intrusions of Phoenician and kindred cults. For, the fact that creative practice can be demonstrated proves the efficient existence of that which is the divine potential. A personal-social experience of the divine is in that sense and in that way *empirically provable.* Without that mooring in practice, how could a man or woman prove which emotionally cathexized aspects of their mental behavior were in correspondence with a universal Good?

For those of Lenin's generation, religion and religious institutions in Russia had become an abomination. The judgment was, broadly speaking, well-founded; as we have indicated. For Russia, there was no deeply embedded connection in culture to some expression of the *Filioque.* In face of monophysite superstition, degenerating into a parodied Phoenician cult-like influence, to escape this lunacy, the intellectuals tended to flee to what they believed to be science, which for many of them became British and French *materialism*, the standpoint of the discrete manifold of Descartes's specifications, or, worse, Newton's.

No doubt, there were within the Russian Church authentic currents, but this was not the image projected by the oligarchy-controlled Church hierarchy as a whole, a bestialized section of the Russian aristocracy with nothing in common with Peter the Great or with Alexander II; indeed, the same breed of oligarch who had assassinated Pushkin. This was of the breed of the evil Tolstoy, the breed of boyar which Ivan Grozny had rightly desired to crush.

It was against that evil church hierarchy, most of all, that Lenin's anger was either directly or implicitly focused within Russia itself.

The degeneration of the monarchy, the evil of the church hierarchy, and the lecherous parasitism spreading in a demoralized aristocracy generally, were compounded by the apostasy of Russia's capitalists. On this point, Parvus and Trotsky were to a certain degree, perversely correct.

Russia had become virtually a colony over the period since the fall of Witte. We are reminded of the debt-ridden condition of eminently viable developing-nation economies, including those of Ibero-America today. The London-centered monetary system sucked the debt-service of a pyramided debt out of the country, looted the nation's grain-exports. The rural landowner and the urban industrialist or merchant, became in effect merely, in Biblical usages, a publican, a usury-collector for foreign rentier-financier forces.

To reverse the trend inside Russia, it was indispensable either to fundamentally reform the international monetary order, or to break Russia out of the existing monetary order. The only viable policy for Russia depended upon, in Lenin's methodological terms of reference, a concrete political force of national leadership to lead Russia to solve one of these two problem-tasks. So the problem became defined with emerging, greater clarity of thought on the point during the period from the outbreak of war in 1914 into spring 1917. The shocking news of the German Social Democracy's voting for war-credits abruptly tottered Lenin's last remaining illusions respecting the Socialist International. This awakening intersected the course of his watchful appreciation of the Russian Social Democratic factions and the Russian capitalist circles and associated political intelligentsia. His estimation became, that all established institutions had reached a point of virtual irreversibility in the degeneration of their moral and intellectual character. A new institution created from ashes of the self-accomplished mutual collapsing of the old institutions, appeared to him the only remedy. Others reached parallel assessments during that general period; the difference was that Lenin thought and acted concretely and hubristically.

Reform of the international monetary order on capitalist terms was not something Lenin was intellectually qualified or disposed to think through with any competence. His *Imperialism*, which served then and after as the principal reference-point for the 1914-1917 shaping of his own and his associates' policy of revolutionary transformation, is pathetic on the subject of economic science. Lenin broadly accepted Marx's insistence that political-economy must be adduced from the relatively pure British early 19th-century "model." Whatever he thought of Hobson or the Vienna-educated, pedantic muddler, Rudolf Hilferding, on other accounts, he was disposed to accept their accounts as to "fact." The fact that what Lenin called "imperialism," was, in its most objectionable feature and consequences, a "feudalist" rentier-financier monetary order, superimposed upon a capitalist mode of production of goods, was something he neither believed, nor was he prepared to challenge Marx et al. on this point.

To the point, like Marx, Lenin evaded all fundamental issues bearing on this same Marxian fallacy, by relegating the solution, the alternative, to a post-capitalist, socialist-directed ordering of affairs. Essentially, Lenin shared the general drift of Marxist peer-group opinion, that only a socialist-led reform could remedy any devastating problems apparently intrinsic to the capitalist order's international or national expressions.

The behavior of the Russian Social Democrats, the Russian entrepreneurs and the salons of the intelligentsia, consolidated Lenin's tendency to view those strata as become, in any adducibly concrete circumstance of the period, irreparably decadent. He became objectively pessimistic, but from the point of reference of an enhanced methodological optimism. If one has studied Lenin's writings from the indicated period, and if one takes into the same account the pattern represented only by the incontestable aspect of reports of his actions during the period into the October Revolution, the characterization of "objectively pessimistic while methodologically optimistic" is the only admissible one.

To those familiar with this writer, it might appear to be the case that this writer is projecting his own "mental map" upon the facts respecting Lenin. In this specific aspect of the matter, this narrow aspect of the matter, that allegation would be a valid one, on condition that it is also acknowledged by the critic that such a projection is the only valid judgment of Lenin's state of mind. It should also be well-known that the writer's "mental map" in this respect is more like Charles de Gaulle's than Lenin's among figures of this century.

It must not be forgotten that this writer is producing the most devastating criticism of Lenin ever produced to date: only from the vantage-point of a personality of the mental disposition of a LaRouche or a de Gaulle, can a competently devastating, accurate criticism of Lenin be produced. One must know the inside of the tragic figure, in this case, Lenin, to account for the tragic outcome of what most would view as Lenin's undebatable success.

Since the writer's own "mental map" is employed by him as a "measuring-rod" for gauging the Soviet Union as a developed process, and most immediately Lenin's part in that process as the key point of reference, a handful of remarks concerning the "measuring-rod" being used must be interpolated here.

The writer's relative congruence with de Gaulle on this account indicated, can be broadly explained as a common reference-point in Judeo-Christian republicanism in the youthful determination of our respective personalities. The agreement between this writer and de Gaulle, on this account and also in a not-accidental similarity of statecraft and strategic outlook, may appear to be greater than it is in fact, because there are so few known public figures of this general mental-map disposition during the present century to date. For reasons related to this, a LaRouche or a de Gaulle is axiomatically attracted to a personality such as that of General Douglas MacArthur. One does not therefore necessarily agree with a MacArthur in detail: it is a matter of affinities within a sub-species of behavioral types. MacArthur is also clearly a representative of the republican tradition, which defines a close affinity of this sort.

It is a matter of fact that MacArthur's most visible adversary during and following World War II from within the U.S. policy establishment was W. Averell Harriman. Harriman otherwise reflected a broader circle of our Eastern Establishment oligarchical "families," allied to MacArthur's most visible adversary in Britain, Prime Minister Winston Churchill. Churchill, as the documentary proof has been assembled and presented by a scholar associated with this writer, plotted to have a long war--island-to-island--between the United States and Japan, extending into approximately 1955. MacArthur averted that hideous bleeding-destruction of our nation, and defeated the military incompetents around Churchill in

Britain--with "complicity" of support for MacArthur by President Roosevelt--by executing a strategic course in the Pacific War of which no merely British military mind could conceive. Churchill's oligarchical-family allies within the United States have never forgiven MacArthur or his memory for that.

Stripping away the libelous falsehoods directed against MacArthur's image by press-orchestration and other means, it is clear that we would have been fortunate to have him President of the United States beginning 1949. He would have served to become, if perhaps only by "instinct," an American "President de Gaulle." The world as a whole would have been freer for all. and consistently more prosperous, and de Gaulle would have come to power again in France much earlier than he did.

The difficulty presented to most readers here, is that while the comparison made is plausible in form, the reader has an obvious source of difficulty in assuring his or her own mind that such comparisons can be justified by any knowable approach to empirical verification. The purpose of introducing those comparisons into this interpolation, is to aid the reader in grasping that specifically tragic aspect of Lenin's work and outcome which set into motion the Soviet Paradox. Only from that vantage-point, as we are amid the elaboration of that vantage-point here, can that Soviet Paradox be understood in the terms of reference indispensable for U.S. foreign policy today. With aid of resort to precisely the comparison we have identified, we are enabled to direct the reader's attention to the needed approach to empirical verification. With aid of that, those inner workings of Lenin's mind, as they bear on the crucial points of his "voluntaristic method," are accessed as a subject of scientific knowledge.

The type of personality cited can be developed in only one general mode, in a manner which must become a matter of consciousness for such a personality no later than childhood. The trigger for the personality's consciousness of a certain "difference" within himself or herself, is the awakening of a tragic sensibility: a sense of a need to cure the "philistinism" of those one deeply loves. This is most readily enhanced within a certain sort of Christian family and associated culture; the child so preoccupied associates early the power to change his or her own mind in a direction leading away from philistinism, and readily, with what Christianity identifies as the "Holy Spirit." This sense of efficient self-consciousness becomes the objective reference for Christian belief, associated with the efficient means not only to improve oneself, but to improve oneself by directing that efficient self-consciousness to the uplifting of those one loves.

Nonetheless, the same divine potential may be awakened as a determining force for shaping the sense of identity under non-Christian circumstances, as in the case of a Lenin raised in Russian culture.

In the indicated circumstances of Christian culture, it would be the writer's judgment that his own experience is not dissimilar to that of a de Gaulle, et al. One is not only self-conscious of his distinguishing point of emphasis in one's own character-identity, but that awareness is the driving force of motivation--*especially under stress*. Our sort thrives amid stress.

For us, notions such as Georg Cantor's elaboration of the *transfinite* are most agreeable, since the fruits of Cantor's work on this matter over the 1871-1883 period define, as they did for this writer during 1952, a recognition of the connection between the objectivity of the higher self-consciousness in oneself, and the ordering of physical processes in the universe generally. From that vantage-point, the point of view for mathematical physics of a Bernhard Riemann has a quality of immediate accessibility it must lack for those who study that matter from a different starting-point of reference. For us, once we have captured for our own consciousness this beautiful comprehensibility of a coherent ordering of man in the universe as a whole, it becomes clear to us that we must dedicate our lives to the principled longer-term purpose of fostering the future development of more persons qualified as we are qualified in such matters. We look back to our own childhood, to the experience of our first recollections of the awakening of these powers as conscious powers, and we avow that all children, if this can be made possible, will have the circumstances fostering the awakening and nurture of such capacities, to become better so than we have become. Without the *lovingness* which directs and energizes that sort of development, and without a complementary ruthlessness against that which destroys such a prospect for future generations, this quality in oneself can not be realized.

In precisely that setting, Lenin's quality as a tragic historic figure is rigorously definable. *He lacked a developed instinct for consciousness of the divine.*

The very character of his response to stress, an eruption, a self-mobilization of intrepidity, a tragic sense of the situation combined with exuberant optimism as to method, is as recognizable as reflection of his mental map as a hunter's recognition of the species upon whose spoor he has struck. If one examines Lenin's writings and actions in the knowable circumstances those occurred, as we have broadly defined that historical setting here so far, the case becomes conclusive: more spoor. Now, with what we have said on this immediate point, any capable historian can adduce and prove a case one way or the other without necessarily sharing the mental map of this writer's outlook. We have translated the fact of the matter from the writer's language into a language in more general usage.

In form, the tragedy of Lenin is a commonplace experience. Why, having succeeded beyond all odds, as he did, did he not build something better?

There are, in the experience of those among us who are in their fifties or older, numerous cases of "Dorian Greys." As we knew them in youth or adulthood, as peers, they exuded a nobility of moral sense, and a driving sense to put that moral sense to work in an effective way. "We must accomplish something to make this a better world," so many among us said, returning from service overseas at the close of the last world war. What became of us, almost the lot of us? Most among those who became "successful," encountered today, are bitter, cynical, personalities of the sort they would have abhorred in their own youth and young manhood or womanhood. What became of us? "You learn, as you grow older," the philistine explains his transformation; "Excuse me. I've just retired, and I have a lot of sun and fishing to catch up with."

Lenin was more consistent, at least; he may not have arrived at some definite goal, but he was riding the train of his choice in direction at the time he died. Yet, although so better than most among our poor "idealists-turned-successful-philistines" on that account, his direction itself was a tragic choice. He was wrong, tragically wrong, not in any of the simplistic terms of anti-Communist reference currently and recently popular; his direction was tragic in a more profound, historic sense. He would have stubbornly resisted this writer's view of the matter, but he would have done so flatly and also with a resolution to reflect on the way he were going to compose a rebuttal later.

He would have reacted reflectively, and polemically to our criticism, looking in himself for intellectual resources of polemical composition, resources of a variety he had not considered exploring earlier. He would have found the accusation profoundly interesting, and concrete.

Lenin's morality intersected a French Enlightenment species of secular humanism, the French materialists who were adversary to Lazare Carnot, as they were adversary to the standpoint of Leibniz, Kepler, Leonardo, Cusa, and St. Augustine. For such a viewpoint, man is a higher form of animal life, and must adopt for himself a rational morality centered upon compassion for the condition of a fellow-human. Within that, Lenin situated himself as a rationalist in the extreme, a very Hegelian sort of rationalist--a crucial epistemological point, if one knows the pivot-point of evil as it is embedded in Hegel's *Phenomenology of Mind.* Lenin rejected empiricist "ethics," as that term is employed in the Aristotelian or British sense, as a substitute for morality in the outward forms of normative behavior. He believed in a rationally-determined morality, a morality of the individual focused within the concrete, rationally-moral tasks of nation and civilization at large.

In short, he was moral, consistently moral, but his morality wanted a concrete sense of the divine.

This same point is concretely provable by focusing upon Lenin's approach to subjects he would have insisted upon distinguishing as "science" and "culture," a distinction made on premises and in terms of reference this writer would not and will not tolerate. This is exhibited in his book-length attack on the intrusion of the influence of Ernst Mach as a factional current extended into Bolshevik ranks. He is correct against Mach, and ingeniously so, but from the wrong positive standpoint, the French materialist standpoint. Despite his affinity for Cherneshevsky's compact imitation of *Don Quixote*, his *What Is To Be Done?*, as to so-called "cultural matters" generally, Lenin was purblind toward the divine, toward the poetical principle of composition.

In other words, his hostility to the divine was not simply an *anti-religions* posture derived from an anti-church posture.

His anti-church posture was purely and simply that he regarded the church hierarchies as a collection of hypocrites, frauds and bamboozlers, whose impact upon society was otherwise simply that of parasites, or not-infrequently conduits for enemy intelligence-operations ranging up, provably in some instances, to insurrectionary activities.

His writings show no comprehension of even the principle of the divine. Although his own creative powers reflected a divine potentiality within himself, he saw no objective reference-point for this quality in himself outside his own skin, except as the results of such thinking were expressed as informing policies of political practice in a concrete way. Except for the fact that some people observably exhibited more creative potentialities than others, a principle of creativity was for Lenin "not a concrete question." For him, the matter simply did not exist, or, if someone were to present such a proposition, he would tire of the subject quickly: "Another of these idealists!"

Curiously, Stalin was much more positive on the matter of cultural development than Lenin. There is no indication Stalin actually understood any principle underlying art, in the sense Plato, St. Augustine, Dante, Leonardo, et al. understood the Socratic method underlying the classical poetical principle of composition universal to poetry, drama, music, painting, sculpture, and architecture. He is not to be entirely blamed for the sheer philistine awfulness of "socialist realism"; Stalin's policy of a cultural uplifting of the nation in depth is a matter worth appropriate study under other auspices.

Lenin's haste to afford extra rations for Pavlov under circumstances of cruel austerity in Russia generally, and his own and others' praise for Pavlov as the Bolshevik approach to psychology, are the best clue to the tragic feature of his own successes and to the essence of the Soviet Paradox today. Of Pavlov's work, one must say, "This is evil, wickedly incompetent stuff, " as one must say with regret, rather than ferocity of misdirections superimposed (with aid of British influences) on the actually interesting work of the brilliant biochemist, A. Oparin.

The ups and downs in the Soviet career of the "father of Soviet atom-projects," Vernadsky, is an interesting, correlated topic of inquiry. We summarize the point here, to the purpose of indicating the way in which a lack of the sense for the "concreteness" of the divine affects Soviet life broadly, in a manner consistent with the general character of the Soviet Paradox today.

Vernadsky was of first rank among the world's scientists of this century. Clearly shaped by the influence of the heritage of Leibniz maintained in Czarist Russia's Petrograd science-center, Vernadsky had the good fortune to travel to work with one of the leading science-centers in the world, the only really valid, outgrowth of Carnot's Ecole Polytechnique surviving the destruction of French science led by Augustin Cauchy, the circle of Louis Pasteur.

He returned to the Soviet Union, and became a leading proponent of focus on radioactive fission as the basis for a potential Soviet leapfrogging of the world in respect to energy-production. This was already a heated topic of policy-deliberation in the Soviet leadership during the mid-1920s. Vernadsky was also the leader of the "Atom Project" assembled by Stalin in 1940, and was identified by the RAND Corporation, during the late 1940s, as the most dangerous man in Russia, in its estimation.

It is the methodological distinctions of Vernadsky which were, at once, the source of his power of accomplishment, and also the source of recurring ebbs in his career-fortunes, during his lifetime, and in respect to his reputation after his death. Vernadsky was the leading proponent of the work of Bernhard Riemann in the Soviet Union, and thus crucial to Soviet success in developing a deployable form of H-bomb. Soviet papers in the public domain reflect this fact, tracing the connection between the determination of thermonuclear-fusion ignition and Riemann's 1859 paper predicting a unique-experimental method for determination of accoustical shockwaves ("plane air waves of finite amplitude").

Vernadsky insisted that Riemannian physics determines not only galactic and microphysical domains' orderings, but also is the mathematical-physics standpoint of reference for study of living processes. This is a direct, and correct assault against the central, and evil fallacy of the Hegelian system.

Our study of the work of Vernadsky has struck upon certain aspects of the ebb and flow in his career and reputation within Soviet circles, but this writer is not of the opinion that he is equipped to explain adequately exactly what issues immediately determined the ebb or flow at each turningpoint. Nor is such a specific question of much adducible usefulness for speculation here. The interesting issue is that of how a correct appreciation of the implications of Riemann's work necessarily conflicts with a Hegelian system and certain Marxian and Soviet outgrowths of Hegel's influence.

When Alexander von Humboldt and an exiled Lazare Carnot, the latter then working chiefly in Berlin, recruited, beginning 1815-1823, the core of the work of the Ecole Polytechnique to Berlin University (Humboldt University), the leading opponent of this effort within the University was G. W. F. Hegel. The archives have demonstrated Hegel to have been a witting and vigorous Metternichian agent, and an ally, politically and philosophically, of the Augustin Cauchy dispatched from Italy to destroy science in France. With help of the Prussian General Staff's military school, Humboldt circumvented the opposition of Hegel, Savigny, et al., who were very efficiently determined to prevent the greatest scientists of Europe from securing professorships at Berlin University. Humboldt circumvented this opposition with such means as having the professors first habilitated at the Prussian military school, and built up the nucleus of Germany's 19th-century world-hegemony in science through the auspices of the university's philology department. So, the Leibnizian current of Karl Gauss at Göttingen was connected with Lazare Carnot's Leibnizian current in exile from France, to produce nearly every fundamental advance in science from 1815 into World War I.

However, the British agent and hoaxster, Helmholtz and that evil Mutt-and-Jeff act, Leopold Kronecker and Richard Dedekind, teamed up to destroy Weierstrass and Cantor, and others, from the 1860s onward. Philosophically, these were the allies of Cauchy and Hegel, leaning then toward the emerging neo-Kantian mysticism.

So, the impact of factional currents within science from Cauchy-rotted France, from evil factions in German science, from Viennese lunacy, and British influences, converged upon Russian science before and after the October Revolution.

Contrary to popularized myths, factional affrays within scientist-circles are predominantly "political" in the most literal sense of that term, and have been occasionally downright homicidal. There is more than competition for posts and publication in these donnybrooks; the seizing of professorships and control of editorial boards is usually regulated by considerations of long-term grand strategy, *political* strategy, among various factions among scientists, and the non-scientific political factions which sponsor such factions among scientists. It is a war to determine how the scientific policy of nations shall be directed, and usually involves a directly related fight over the economic policies of nations, as promoting certain directions of scientific work and opinion, or anti science currents within scientific circles, does very efficiently determine what a nation's potential economic policy will and can become.

On that account, we would not propose to explain the ebbs and flows of Vernadsky's status merely in terms of any simple sort of direct conflict between Vernadsky and the political-per-se neo-Hegelians. We merely emphasize that in the proverbial last analysis the implicit political issues must tend to be determining.

Riemannian physics, as we have shown earlier, implicitly defines an ordering principle subsuming all phase-states and processes within phase-states, for the universe as a whole. This ordering-principle is congruent with the empirically provable reflection of the Logos, and, as we have also shown this to be the case, the ordering-principle respecting those aspects of mental life corresponding to creative mentation. We noted that Riemann's antinomical critique of Herbart's work asserts, that his method is consciously directed to those results we have listed.

It is the consistent, central feature of the Hegelian system that it insists that no such principle exists. Hegel was fully conscious of deliberate fraud in his attempts to prove this case, including a fraudulent account of epistemology in his lectures on the history of philosophy. The fragments, such as those of Sixtus Empiricus, of Heraclitus' writings, have a correct view' of the matter methodologically, where Hegel's approach is willfully, a wickedly motivated willfulness, absurd. Leibniz had resolved the problem, as had Kepler and his late 15th-

century predecessors, as we have already demonstrated the crucial points in this report.

Hegel purports to explain the creation of physical and organic space by his dialectical processes, but this is for him merely a plausible explanation of a slow-combustion form of detonation of an Aristotelian "Big Bang." The principle of mind, almost-monophysite Hegel argues, is a principle which is "no longer actively determining" in inorganic or organic processes apart from human behavior. Hence, Hegel is classed as an idealist--the better term were "a delphic variety of monophysite."

"Dialectical materialism," as the words of Marx put the point, turns Hegel on his head. Mind is denied except as an epiphenomenon of the dialectical unfolding of the inorganic. The "dialectical principle" becomes an "observably embedded," but otherwise unseen superimposition upon Cartesian physical space: dangerous mysticism.

The case to be compared with Vernadsky's, is that of long resistance against the somewhat reduced approximation of a Riemannian universe projected from the work of A. Einstein. It is not to be asserted that Soviet circles of influence actually understand "how this works."

There are two features of Riemann's physics which demolish the Cartesian or derived (Hegelian, dialectical materialist) construct.

First, the proof that the discrete manifold is bounded by a continuous, higher manifold: self-evident objects, such as elementary particles, or purely imagined objects, such as quarks, vanish from our picture of ontological reality, to become merely projected reflections of real actions occurring in the continuous manifold. Cartesian space vanishes instantly, as Kepler already conclusively proved such a notion of physical space to be absurd.

Second, the principle of the unique experiment, such as the illustrative case for plane waves of finite amplitude, makes the ordering principle of the continuous manifold empirically verifiable beyond doubt from the vantage-point of evidence demonstrated in terms of experimental treatment of a discrete manifold. This principle is shown thus to be necessarily the common principle underlying both ordered changes in phase-states and ordering within phase-states for all phenomena in the universe.

This, as we have repeatedly underscored here, proves the principle of the divine; moreover, it requires the creative aspect to be made a conscious object for itself.

For reasons we have adequately demonstrated and developed in this report thus far, it should be clear that society can not be secured against subversion by oligarchism, without a development of the society and the individual which focuses the work of society both on increasing the potential relative population-density of the society, and a correlated emphasis on the true purpose of society: to order society to perfect consciousness of the divine potential, as an active potential, within the individual, and within the ordering of the internal affairs of the society.

The examples we have just cited, in connection with the Vernadsky case, merely illustrate one of the more crucial ways in which the absence of the emphasis upon the divine efficiently impacts every aspect of practical life, an impact which can be conclusively adduced from examination of the appropriate selection of characteristic evidence, from observation of aspects of a society's day-to-day practical life.

Insofar as Lenin established a Soviet state with the chief outward features of a republic as to economics and related matters, the positive achievements effected in technological progress and so forth are not to be underestimated. However, the kind of human individual determined by such a social process is in large degree a "hollow man," a variety of Apollonian, normatively rational mankind. Unless this fault is corrected, that very oligarchism which Lenin "betrayed," by turning his coopted outgrowth of 19th-century radicalism a most deadly enemy to the oligarchy in the short term, overtakes Lenin's creation. *The vacuum within the "Soviet man" will be filled by something.*

During the last world war, it is alleged, Stalin went into St. Basil's, to make a pact with Satan against Hitler. Mother Russia was awakened in Dionysiac fury against the Nazi beast. So, the Russian people, in the large, were mobilized by a cultural principle--not Leninism.

Can Bolshevism be blamed for the cultural condition of so much of the Soviet population then? Let us be fair. The condition of the people prior to 1917, the period of the civil wars, and so forth, are not exactly the circumstances conducive to a gradual enrichment of the human spirit. Soviet Russia was not then exactly such a paradise as to secrete nothing but "beautiful souls."

It is now thirty-seven years since the close of the last world war in Europe.

Again, let us be fair. The losses in people, especially in fathers and potential fathers, was monstrous, with demographic effects and related economic problems, to the present time. Nor, can we imagine that the living nightmare of that time--such as the deaths and circumstances of death in besieged Leningrad alone, do not arise as active memories to shape the making of Soviet policy in not only every Soviet official who fought during that war, or among those who experienced that war as children, but among those who, born immediately after the war received transmission of the physical consequences of the war in the physical circumstances of the nation, and in discovering how long the list of immediate family who had died in that war and in what manner by what hand. This central emotion of the post-war period has been sustained by the crisis-atmosphere of threatened preventive nuclear warfare, of crisis perpetuated as "mutually assured thermonuclear destruction," and by rage escalated by vanishing of a brief period of détente, for a second time, with the Watergating of President Richard Nixon. A certain tendency for rage to become irrational is to be expected.

However, the Soviet Union is not today essentially a garrison-state. It spends more than double what we do of its nominal GNP on military and immediately related costs.

This does directly and indirectly keep pressures of a garrison-state type on the economy, and thus on the social life of the members of the society as a whole. Rather, Soviet society is rotted only to a lesser degree than our own by an emergence of youth-counterculture. This is not a nation of bright-eyed, idealist Bolshevik nationalists. It is a nation of people who are even for themselves chiefly paradoxical. They are attached to the society in an ordinary nationalist way no different that we would assume for the members of any modern form of sovereign nation-state.

Broadly, the form of the paradox of the Soviet Union is that it has the outward forms of a sovereign nation-state republic, eroding in a way which appears to converge upon our own worst aspects of cultural and moral decay within. Like growing numbers of our youth and others, a similar process appears to be in progress there. We are becoming too much like one another, in a manner looming catastrophic to us both.

The difference is this. Despicable as we have become, we retain among our people and our abused traditions an adherence to the notion of the divine as the proper ultimate end of policy and practice. They do not.

One hears a gentleman speaking now among us. "Who are you, sir?" we enquire.

"That's not important. Let us say that I have some very well-informed friends, who I am certain know a lot more about what's happening inside the East bloc than you do. What you say is pure garbage! You don't know, for example, how many Russians are returning to the churches."

"You are wrong on all points, sir," we must rebut this silly, smirking fool among us. "I do know of the return to the churches, and speaking from a Christian standpoint, that should terrify you, if you and your so-called well-informed friends had any sense in your heads. You may know what goes into those churches, but your friends clearly have no appreciation of what comes out of those churches." It is "Mother Russia," Slavic blood and Slavic soil. It is Great Mother. "You fool! Do you imagine that that is a rise of Christianity!"

"If the Soviet Union is driven into a state of rage with such a growth of the Great Mother-cult's influence on the rise, do you know what that portends for civilization?"

That is the kernel of the tragedy of Lenin's success.

The Soviet Paradox Today

The objection will be either stated or merely registered in unspoken consciousness, that it is presently nearly sixty years since Lenin's death: "What about modern Russia? We have an immediate situation to deal with." It is a useful objection, in the sense that a very crucial point is to be made by showing why the objection is profoundly wrong.

In social processes, as in the universe more broadly, a change from one physical state of a process to another implies an ordered series of such changes, which series ranges between well-defined limits. Those latter limits involve changes in physical state in a higher sense.

The simplest variety of example of the first-order of successive physical states is the series associated with the melting of ice and the vaporization of water. This is, however, only a small segment of the states of matter through which that material may be passed. At the lower end on the caloric scale, there are critical values of the sort we associate with cryogenic superconductive phenomena of an ordinary sort. At the higher ranges of the caloric scale, we have thermal ionization, and so forth and so on. In other words, within the range of ice, water, and vapor as we ordinarily experience such states of water, the structure of the process is characterized by a common principle we associate with molecular behavior. At the extremes, such as those we have indicated to exist, this ordinary sort of molecular behavior vanishes from the experimental domain. We still have what we call substance in the most rigorous sense of our notion of what "substance" ought to signify, but the sub-structure common to the states of ice, liquid water and vapor has vanished. So, the transition from a non-molecular to a molecular state, and vice versa, obliges to distinguish the phase-changes of ice, water and vapor as of a lower class as to generality, than the phase-changes we encounter at the points molecular behavior vanishes. Then, in the plasma state of highly-energized substance, we have before us a (presently undetermined) range of phase-states, or different regimes which merit the distinction of phase-states. Enough, then, of that illustration.

We emphasize that a similar principle is characteristic of society's transformations.

For example, in broad terms of reference, the establishment of our federal constitutional republic with the 1789 inauguration of our first President was a phase-change of a relatively higher order. This persisted up to the assassination of President Lincoln. The shifts in policy and institutions occurring over that interval of our national life often greatly stressed, but did not qualitatively alter our national character. Even the most brutal stress of that interval, the war between the Union and Confederacy, was prosecuted by Lincoln to effect changes in certain institutions, such as that of chattel slavery, but that was not the essential purpose of Lincoln's policy, as all moderately informed citizens as well as historians know without further qualification of that point here. Lincoln's policy was to affirm the Constitution, and preserve the constitutional ordering.

Witness, President Lincoln's last public address, of April 11, 1865. We excerpt a crucial passage from that address.

> "We all agree that the seceded States, so called, are out of their proper practical relation with the Union; and that the sole object of the government, civil and military, in regard to those States is to again get them into that proper practical relation. I believe it is not only possible, but in fact, easier, to do this, without deciding, or even considering, whether those states have even been out of the Union, than with it. Finding themselves safely at home, it would be utterly immaterial whether they had

> ever been abroad. Let us all join in doing the acts necessary to restoring the proper practical relations between these states and the Union; and each forever after, innocently indulge his own opinion whether, in doing the acts, he brought the States from without, into the Union, or only gave them proper assistance, they never having been out of it."

To which we add our recollection of that famous passage from the Second Inaugural of March 4, 1865:

> "With malice toward none; with charity for all; with firmness in the right, as God gives us to see the right . . ."

With such words, that national character which defined us as a nation since Washington's first inauguration, spoke for the last times in public. Lincoln was murdered by a British assassin, Booth, sent from London and Canada: Under Lincoln's successor, Andrew Johnson, there was unleashed the disaster of carpet-bagging by that unwholesome New York crowd, which changed our national morals and principles of public practice for very much the worse.

A phase-change was unleashed by that assassination and that carpet-bagging policy, to the effect that the Specie Resumption Act, by 1879, had repudiated in practice the constitutional requirement of the Congress to exert sovereignty over our nation's credit, banking and commerce in our national interest.

The failure to repudiate that surrender of our national sovereignty, in any subsequent ordering of our credit and central-banking legislation and practice, rendered a condition admittedly episodic during the pre-1865 period an unlawful and implicitly pervasive amendment of the essential character of our Constitution. The mythology, which asserts the alleged "independence of the Federal Reserve System" to willfully destroy our credit, our currency and our economy, is a reflection of that phase-change which has been dominating our nation's character since 1879. (From his own, monetarist vantage-point, Professor Milton Friedman has emphatically agreed with that estimation of the significance of the Specie Resumption Act for effecting what became in practice a sweeping revision of our Constitution.)

In the case of Britain, the constitutional arrangements which might be adduced from the Stuart Restoration were never fundamentally modified, to the present day. There was an attempted shift in emphasis, under James II, toward a thoroughly Hobbesian experiment in capricious tyranny. There was the Glorious Revolution conducted by William of Orange, in fact a parliamentary arrangement better named the "glorious swindle," from which the British subjects (they have no citizens) have not since contrived to become *unLocked.* There was Shelburne's revolution of sorts, and shifts during the middle 19th century. The 1689 decision, that it were more prudent to rule the foolish British subjects by encouraging parliamentary forms of political masturbation to distract them into submissiveness, rather than iron bars, was really no essential change in the character of ruling monarchical-oligarchical institutions, except to increase the power of the oligarchy in respect to the monarchy. Since 1689, no changes in outward forms of composition of British government have been more than a very low order of phase-shift.

With a nation-state, as a person, the constitution, physical and mental, which a people and nation acquire in that nation's manner of birth and into early childhood, determines the characteristic behavior. The behavior may improve or decay, or may oscillate between ups and downs. The constitutionally-determined character does not change, but tends to be adapted to changing circumstances. This underlying character of its disposition for response persists until some critical change in its implicit constitution occurs.

This does not mean to encourage the ultra-orthodoxist Sovietologist's insistence that Brezhnev, perhaps two days ago, during an exchange with a security guard assisting him into his vehicle, savagely violated some crucial comma inserted into the protocol of a 1919 Soviet leadership meeting. One is not speaking merely of the remote corners of the Trotskyist tribes; but also of poor Sovietologists who can not order a simple hamburger or cup of coffee without enquiring whether the short-order cook's grandmother was a Bolshevik sympathizer. Sovietologist literature, generally speaking, is as tiresome as attempting speech-therapy with a dedicated schizophrenic. Unfortunately, some of the authors of utter garbage appear to enjoy favor as experts in some policy-influencing circles.

It is not difficult, if one views the matter from a practical rather than doctrinaire vantage-point, to adduce which features of the young Soviet state were efficient, and which others ephemeral fads of the moment. The only important changes were the long process of disengagement of the soviet state from the Communist International's dictates, and, more profound, the ebbing of voluntarism up to the death of Stalin; the phase-change occurring during the Khrushchev period, and the post voluntarist phase of the recent decades.

One must view the Soviet Union as the state which Lenin established, to the point that all developments contrary to that original design of essential characteristics must be defined as some degree of "un-Leninism", if one wishes to situate the significance of this facet of developments within anything efficiently approximating a coherent assessment of the Soviet Union as a whole.

Apart from the emergence of the Orthodox Church's influence upon the Soviet population, there are two features of the past two decades' Soviet internal developments which require special treatment, and one final consideration, beyond those two, to be taken prominently into account.

The first is the increase in pragmatism, which need be merely noted as a category, since the Soviet literature available abundantly demonstrates the scope of this.

The second is the introduction of what is called "applied systems analysis." Insofar as this technique, more narrowly typified by the worthless technique of "econometrics," pertains to its stated points of application as an administrative method, I would not wish so ruinous a concoction to be adopted even by Britain. Charity toward the British population should not be as quick and uncomplicated as Lincoln's toward the states of the Confederacy, but most among them are, after all, redeemable human beings. It is the ideological implications of this which are of more prominent concern here.

Both pragmatism and applied systems analysis are products of 19th-century British philosophical radicalism. As we elaborated something of this connection earlier in the report, that means essentially intensifying the radical assumptions already embedded in David Hume's description of "human understanding" and "human nature," by means of stripping away to a greater or lesser degree the normative inhibitions which substitute for the place of morality in Hume's system. In other words, as we have elaborated this connection as well, a shift from the center-position of the normative Apollonian outlook toward the Dionysian outlook of Bentham et al.

The moral-psychoanalytical significance of radicalism of that systematic definition is an increased emphasis on the infantile in morality and world-mapping features of the mind as to scientific and other judgments. The essential feature of both pragmatism and applied systems analysis is an axiomatic repudiation of knowable higher lawfulness in the universe; this is consistent with Hume, of course. Both, however, are distinct from normative forms of Humean empiricism in the respect that the characteristic action of sustained application of pragmatism or applied systems analysis is a moral-psychoanalytical self-degradation of the practitioner, and a correlated degradation of capacity for rigorous forms of systematic analysis.

These must be the effects of such influences in practice upon the Soviet mind, and must also reflect a previous degradation of outlook and judgment, through means of which such British practices were introduced. This, as a climate of official posture, must also effect the Soviet population generally in the way correlating with increased attraction toward infantilism, and thus to resurrecting to a more active role latent tendencies for pan-Slavic and related manifestation of Great Mother-cultish world-outlooks for social and individual practice.

Systems analysis itself is the putative offspring of the late John von Neumann, who proposed the initial approach on the basis of three axiomatic assumptions. Two of the three assumptions he set forth explicitly; the third was so axiomatic for him that he did not trouble himself to state the fact that the two assumptions advanced depend upon this third as a precondition. First, without stating this, he rejected any ontologically-efficient form of higher lawfulness in the universe, most emphatically in matters bearing upon human behavior. Second, he asserted that human behavior could be mapped adequately by arrays of statements of linear inequalities, which is absurd except to the extent certain modes of psychotic mental behavior do behave in a manner resembling linear systems. Third, he asserted that all human behavior is ordered as to values entirely by the hedonistic principle intrinsic to his theory of games, the hedonistic principle of Bentham's which J.S. Mill adopted explicitly as the centerpiece of his entire utilitarian dogma, and which Mill, Jevons, and Marshall made the axiomatic basis for their attempt to explain economic process entirely from an monetarist basis.

For related reasons, applied systems analysis has devastating incompetence in this application to economic analysis or any cognate form of administrative procedures. It has had an erosive influence in Soviet policy-making, not entirely unlike the effect of the systems-analysis approaches introduced to the Pentagon's planning by Robert S. McNamara, or the Wharton School/Brookings Institution approach to this dogma's implementation in effects on federal government budgetary and related practices of the OMB.

It is probable, however, that both pragmatism and, most emphatically, applied systems analysis, will be downgraded in Soviet policy-making during the period immediately ahead. The manifest incompetence of applied systems analysis is only a contributing aspect of this. More important is the role of systems analysis in the interface between the Comecon and Western economies and financial institutions; the weakening of the role of the kind of loose interface existing earlier, under influence of détente, undermines the basis for spread of applied systems analysis. The shocks recently administrated to détente-centered economic and financial relationships, will downgrade applied systems analysis within the Comecon, and most emphatically the Soviet Union. Finally, even were some of the attempted containment measures recently pressed to be reversed, the recently demonstrated unreliability of East-West agreements and the potential implications of this unreliability, will impel Moscow, for a range of interrelated reasons, toward what many would prefer to describe as a "neo-Stalinist" variety of increased emphasis on autarkical capabilities and dirigism. What the Soviet language may wish to describe as increased emphasis upon objectively determined priorities in goals, and direct application of resources to goals, will require approaches to planning and administration which are most inhospitable to systems-analysis applications, and are counter-pragmatic in tendency.

The intensification of the war-danger, as Moscow sees that danger, will increase the task-orientation in the Soviet leadership to the point that this dominates in a more immediate manner all aspects of Soviet administration and related policy-making. The fact that this task-orientation pivots on a military mode of strategic thinking will produce a climate favorable to eruption of something outwardly approximating "voluntarism" in Soviet leadership behavior.

For example, a comparison of the prices and relative performances of MIGs and either U.S.A. F-15's and F-16's, or of T-72's and newer model main-line battle-tanks with U.S. and NATO first-line equipment, poses problems, to both sides, of how best to exploit these incongruities, and how to situate that assessment for practice within the overall incongruity in best application of capabilities. This problem, posed to both the Soviet military command and the Politburo, poses the kind of problem begging for a creative approach, in the sense we have rigorously defined creative in this report.

In first approximation, what we seem to be implying immediately here is that the constitutional ordering of the Soviet state over the decades has been preserved to such a degree that what appear to be lapsed behavioral characteristics of earlier periods could readily reappear under the kinds of patterns of development now emerging. To a certain degree, and with some rather large qualifications to be added to that, that is the general direction in which we are pointing.

There have been changes in the Soviet character which are unchangeable, irreversible without the equivalent of a phase-shift degree of shock-impulsion. These changes in the character of the Soviet state and so forth are much less pronounced than the radical, seemingly irreversible shifts in our institutions and national character, especially since approximately 1966-1967. They are qualitatively more traditionalist than we are, in approaches to problem-solving, in military policy, and so forth.

The writer and his associates have resurrected recently the neglected practice, formerly a rigorously enforced principle for students under Professor Felix Klein at Göttingen University, that no theoretical construct purporting to define the characteristics of a process, can be accepted unless an appropriate construction by means of synthetical-geometrical methods of construction, be employed to prove the coherence and closure of that construction in such a geometrical model. If we were to oblige ourselves to construct an image of Soviet developments over the past periods, we would project to you a strange-looking sort of spiral on a construction having obviously some distant, hereditary connection to a cone. Precisely back to a previous state of potential, no culture can ever return. However,we can speak of returning to a rate of change of function analogous to some earlier performance, a possibility which inheres in the general way in which the geometry of the cultural-historic space has evolved since that earlier point. It is in only that sense of things that we would wish to even imply a possible Soviet return to a likeness to earlier policy-making tendencies in Soviet leadership behavior.

Putting to one side those problematical features of U.S. foreign policy in this quarter which we identified form the early portions of this report, we are stressing here the absurdity, the utter lunacy, of continuing to project estimations by aid of what might be most concisely identified as “Palo Alto Methods.”

Insofar as such methods are being employed for behavioral forecasting of the Soviet leadership and nation as a whole, have such silly results led to the edification and amusement of one or another of those night-club audiences which admires being described as a “sophisticated set,” but which are really a poor, jaded lot in need of something new in the way of scripts to be read by their favorite comedians. Or, better, perhaps they could be sold to Soviet night-club administrators, for use as script-material by Soviet comedians.

Finally, on the possible shifts in characteristics of behavior of the Soviet leadership: there has emerged more or less a qualitative shift in Soviet strategic capabilities to their relative advantage. This fact, and the more readily adduced causes for this continuing shift, are pushing the Soviet leadership into a kind of tragic optimism, with certain formal, which is to say outward, resemblances to Lenin of 1917.

We catalogue the most relevant general reasons for this pattern of shift to which we have just referred.

First, following the 1962 missiles crisis, we have all observed a secular trend of Soviet build up toward military parity with the NATO forces. Prior to 1974, the most significant feature of this build-up was a mid-1960s' acceleration of technological education of Soviet youth, through improved public-school and other education, to the effect that the Soviets are now approximately double our capability in numbers of professionals with advanced technical and related degrees employed in their appropriate profession. This occurred at the point we accelerated an earlier erosion in our educational system--beginning approximately the introduction of the "new math"--with radical movements in the direction of reducing our technological-employment opportunities, and outright de-schooling thrusts, beginning the 1966-1968 period.

There was a marked, post-Vietnam take-down of our in-depth strategic capabilities, aggravated by the efforts associated publicly with James R. Schlesinger's pushing of a forward-based theater-limited nuclear-war posture in Europe. We increased our posture of provocative aggressiveness as we tore down our in-depth capabilities. The net effect of this, combined with the Watergating of Nixon, was to accelerate Soviet military efforts.

We accelerated Soviet military efforts to a higher notch with the performance of Secretary of State Cyrus Vance in 1977. First, Vance carried a childishly insolent posture into his first meeting with Foreign Minister Andrei Gromyko, and then "welshed" on the later 1977 "Geneva" memorandum almost as soon as the signatures had dried. A certain grimness around Soviet jaws, and practice to match, followed that 1977 experience. Meanwhile, Carter administration policies savagely gutted our economy, and thus the logistical and political resources for our defense posture. The nastier we posed ourselves, the more we destroyed the capability of backing up such threatening displays.

The Volcker measures--which Volcker himself avowed to be intended to cause "controlled disintegration" of national economy, and--in the policy-papers from which he took that particular choice of phrase--West Germany's and Japan's economies as well, have almost ruined us.

In Moscow's eyes, we appear determined to insist upon bringing the entire Western World into the depths of a new general depression worse than that of the 1930s. We mobilize ourselves for fighting "population and raw-materials" wars against the nations and peoples of those nations of Africa, Asia, and Latin America we used to regard as precious, friendly assets of our general strategic posture.

Moscow says, in effect, to the United States: "We are ahead of you in the margin of strategic balance, and we will not permit you to attempt to overtake us in that matter."

Generally, Moscow believes that the world is verging toward the edge of thermonuclear war-fighting, and has most recently tightened their finger on the "hair-trigger" of total war. This is their sense of tragedy, of pessimism, their sense of the danger of thermonuclear holocaust, their fear that it is near to unavoidable. On this point, if the present drift in NATO and U.S.A. policies persist, they are correctly estimating the situation.

At the same time, they can not refrain from a growing tendency even to gloat at the witness of our obsessive compulsion to destroy ourselves, to commit every blunder, almost at every turn, a nation-state adversary of ours might most devoutly hope might occur.

Their growing sense of this pattern of shifts in relative strength affords them a source of long-term strategic self-confidence. If they can ruthlessly negotiate their way through the immediate high-probability of thermonuclear war, there will be soon only one superpower in the world, and that will be the Soviet Union. We speak merely of a few years of "window of vulnerability"; with our present policies, gentlemen, such talk is wishful lunacy. There is presently no basis in U.S. policy, or in the parameters of U.S. policy-making and policy-making institutions, which would project the kind of economic-boom-conditions during 1982-1983 on which such a recovery of military parity might be estimated, outside the precincts of astrological charts and gypsy tea-rooms.

Gentleman policy-makers, you have been permitting yourselves to be made fools of by our monetarist doctrinaires and such friendly sources of wise counsel as our ever-loving British ally.

It is much worse than that, and on this point the Soviet leadership is as blindly miscalculating as we have been. Washington and Moscow refuse to face the essential reality thus far that they are but two gladiators in that global Nero's arena administered by the oligarchical families.

5.

A Benjamin Franklin Foreign Policy: The "American Century"

There are two, and only two sovereign nation-states which are or could become in the foreseeable future, global superpowers. We of the United States are locked in a thirty-five-year adversary relationship with the other superpower, the Soviet Union. We are becoming weaker--but through our own persisting, fifteen years of folly, the Soviet power is becoming materially stronger.

We two superpowers, flanked by the second-and third-rate military powers we respectively call our allies, are locked in shuffling postures of imminent mortal combat in a world which has become for us, in point of fact, a Nero's arena, with the spectators, gloating oligarchical families, manipulating the environment of combat and provocation within the arena itself. Those spectators are resolved to enjoy the process by which we nation-state combatants both die.

Why do we not leave the arena, to slay this Nero? Each gladiator fears, perhaps, that the adversary in the arena will plunge his weapon to our midriff if we turn our flank to move? Rather, foolish United State, foolish Soviet Union, play to the oligarchical gods as two wretched gladiators in Nero's arena, hoping that Nero will tip the balance in our favor in this matter of arena-combat. If we continue so, we have degraded ourselves to a point of want of moral fitness to survive, and we shall not survive.

Are we so obsessed with the fantasy-life of "winning at sports," that we have lost the mental capacity to recognize this game for what it is: a game that only fools play to their death? Are we ourselves so corrupted by hedonistic irrationalism of our ostensible masters, the immensely wealthy oligarchical families, that we would rather another moment's pleasure permitted us by those degraded spawn of Hell, these oligarchs, than defend that which lends some expression of higher than bestial purpose to these mortal lives of ours?

For the Soviet Union, such comprehension is perhaps not possible. For us, if we could but capture again the world-outlook of that Franklin-led conspiracy which created our republic, we have the potential moral qualities to match our largely-idled physical potentialities. We of the United States have the potential to change the world, to crush the satanic power of the oligarchy, to so embrace the vision of St. Augustine in our practice.

Our best statesmen, including our beloved former President, Franklin D. Roosevelt, and the justly admired military commander, MacArthur, had a patriotic vision for this republic not so many years ago. In the circles of President Roosevelt, this patriotic and noble vision was called the "American Century." Only this approach, as a practical approach to our foreign policy, can rescue us from what this report has painted or clearly implied to be the case.

Let us combine our unilateral adoption of this "American Century" policy for today, with a proposal to the Soviet Union that we reaffirm the old Yalta agreement in a new way, with new dimensions of meaning. We propose that the interpretation of the Yalta agreement, and humane adjustments in the terms of that agreement respecting third nations, be based on extermination of the last vestige of oligarchical rentier-financier insolence in the ordering of the relations among nations.

Let us compact with ourselves, and offer to compact with other nations, including the Soviet Union, the following structural-policy features of a new world economic order consistent with the principles of the great encyclical, *Populorum Progressio*, of the late Pope Paul VI.

Let us compact with ourselves, and propose to compact with other nations, to establish a new world economic order modeled as to principle on the specifications of that policy of the administration of President George Washington, admired subsequently by nations throughout the world by the name of the American System of political-economy. Let us employ the proven advantages of the American System, moral as well as economic advantages, to create from henceforth a new. happier century in world affairs, and let us call this among ourselves the American Century.

The proposed terms of the American Century are these.

1. Henceforth, no government compacting to establish the American System of new world economic order, shall permit any other form of creation of credit in excess of

deposited savings by financial institutions, excepting the issuance of gold-reserve-denominated currency-notes of sovereign nation-states. All other creation of credit by financial institutions shall be treated as unlawful and immoral usury.

2. The gold-backing of currency-notes shall secure only payments against imbalances in payments among nations, payments in gold to be made in international transfers only against payment of lawful currency-notes issued by the nation selling gold in payment for these notes.

3. The price of monetary gold shall be a fair market price, a parity price, based on allowing a fair margin of average profit to miners, in excess of the average costs of production of a volume of gold-production adequate for the monetary requirements of all participating nations. On the basis of agreements, a pegged stable parity price shall be established, probably at approximately $500 an ounce for gold.

4. The compacting governments shall each establish a national bank fully accountable to its head of state for administration, and to its legislature as to its lawful authorities in respect to policy. This national bank shall coordinate a well-regulated national banking-system in each participating nation. The national bank shall be the channel for lending of currency-notes issued by the treasury of the government.

5. It is agreed that such notes shall be loaned through national banks as participation in portions of individual

loan-agreements, subject to restrictions as to category of loan-agreement for which such loan-participation shall occur, and as to the percentile of allowed participation within each designated category.

6. These categories shall be primarily investments in the expansion of the production of agricultural and industrial goods, or for transportation and other basic economic infrastructural improvements bearing upon the immediate environment indispensable to production of goods and their distribution. The additional general restriction shall be that the level of technology of production must be generally raised in terms of physical output per-capita of the population and per-hectare output of not only agricultural, but total goods.

7. The purpose of such lending of currency notes for medium-term and long-term loan-agreements, shall be to employ otherwise idled available goods, productive capacities or idled labor, in such a way as to increase the output of goods per-capita nationally, and to raise the average level of production per member of the totality of the nation's labor-force.

8. The required effect of such lending of currency-notes must be to effect a deflationary form of expansion of scale and per-capita output of production, through improvements in basic infrastructural environment of production and technology employed in production.

This requires, in nations with less relative advancement, emphasis upon rapid technological advancements in agricultural production, and an emphasis upon those varieties of capital-goods-producing industries suitable to the nation's raw-materials potentials, plus either representing a finished-goods export-production or, preferably, goods required for agriculture and the building of basic infrastructure and capital goods of domestic industries.

9. On the assurance that such lending-policies are adopted and executed, interest-rates on loan of currency-notes shall be kept within the range of combined administration and reasonable average risk. We project a 2-4% prime-rate range for such lending.

10. It is desired that the performance worthiness of the borrower be judged by private banks, wherever this is feasible, and that the local bank participate with loan of deposit, and administer the total loan, being allowed a small margin for this function of service to the national bank's portion of the loan-agreement.

11. It is agreed that these methods shall be used for lending among nations of the compact.

12. It is agreed that "American methods" in the sense the import of "American methods" was understood internationally during 1941-1945, shall be the style for defining large-scale projects, and for economic activities of nation-building in international transactions within the compact.

13. That the members of the compact establish a common bank to assist their respective national banks in

fostering international investments, loans, and purchases within the compact.

14. That each and all of the members of the compact shall defend one another and the compact as a whole against any and all practices which threaten to undermine the compact through action of financial agencies and other agencies and powers outside the compact.

By aid of such a compact, it becomes possible to conduct the variety of financial reorganization of outstanding international indebtedness, which must be quickly accomplished now, to prevent general collapse into chaos of international monetary institutions.

The gist of the matter is to create a low-yield, but otherwise highest-grade set of series of bond-issues, which are fully discountable for application of funds to approved categories of new loan-issues within the compact. These bonds are used to purchase outstanding, currently or imminently non-performing aggregations of debts from creditor-institutions. The multiple effect of this, properly executed is: (1) Reschedule the debt-overhang of nations in a way which makes those nations creditworthy for large volumes of capital-imports through new loans: (2) place an umbrella of gold-reserve security around the presently-jeopardized holdings of essential financial institutions active in international lending; (3) put those latter institutions back immediately into the international lending-business, but to shape their lending-policies into medium-term and long-term lending to the variety stipulated by the compact.

The debts to be purchased with bond-issues of this type, are purchased by the debtor at the aggregated balance of principal and interest-payments due at a cut-off date. The contract so purchased is thus terminated at that cut-off date.

The shaping of the payments-schedule on the bonds newly issued for this purpose shall be governed by principles of: (1) Nominal coupon, consistent with prime-rate standards specified by the compact, (2) A distribution of maturities of payments on bonds consistent with sound principles of financial planning, as applicable to the case of putting a viable corporation on a future profitable basis, through creating margins for borrowings of improved productive capitalization; (3) Deferred-payment arrangements built into the scheduling of bond-issues, as financial planning warrants this.

Then, as we bring the leftover financial mess created by the decay of an old monetary order into manageable form, we instruct our farms, industries and bankers: "Now, since we have brought your follies of the past under control, forget the past, and get yourselves to new business!"

There is much more to be said on this subject, both as to its implications for the domestic economy and in respect to the kinds of priorities which must be developed in shaping long-term capital-flows throughout the portion of the world's economy corresponding to such a compact. In principle, however, all those additional matters are already more or less implicit in what has been written just above, or in earlier portions of this report.

We now turn to the most obvious varieties of broad objections, as to international law and international agreements, bearing upon what we have proposed, excepting those aspects of the matter bearing upon our relations with the Soviet Union. Next, after that, we turn to the matter of relationships to and with the Soviet Union.

Law & International Law

One of the principal, recurring sources of confusion in the making, interpretation and execution of our law, and in the matter of actual and implied international agreements, is that we have broadly lost all conscious connection to that distinct body of moral law within which the design of our Constitution and of our institutions of self-government was situated. If any man, any nation, or any foreign agency of another category should imagine that we are implicitly subject to any ordering as to law contrary to the law of our Constitution's design, let that party beware. If we become angered, and if we then choose to exert our material and other power to defend the original meaning of our law, the consequences may then become most unpleasant for any party which mistakes our recent and present torpor in this matter for assurance of future compliance.

The kernel of our argument to this general point is historically irrefutable; the facts are writ plain and large in the blood of our patriots, from Concord to Yorktown, and in the occasion to which Francis Scott Key dedicated his composition of the stanzas which became our national anthem. Briefly, then, the issue of law itself, and then the relevance of this to the execution of our foreign policy.

At the time our republic was constituted, European culture knew two, bitterly contending bodies of doctrine of law. The one, to which our British adversary adhered, was explicitly modeled on Roman Law. We rejected this, and adopted instead the Christian, Augustinian tradition's adoption of Greek republican law. The one, the British, was intrinsically oligarchical, our choice was anti-oligarchical.

In respect to the culture of the republican English-speaking colonies from which our republic was assembled, our English heritage was immediately the English Commonwealth Party, in regard to which we preferred John Milton to Oliver Cromwell and the Presbyterians. Insofar as Protestant religious denominations informed our notions of republican public policy, we rejected emphatically the Anglican, and eyed with suspicion our Commonwealth Party allies, the Presbyterians--a latter suspicion much informed by Scottish betrayal of Britain to the Stuart Restoration of 1660. Otherwise, the kernel of our literary culture was a version of the Bible, written in an English more beautiful and powerful than popular usage has recognized in the past hundred years of our national cultural decay. This noble translation, compiled under the Tudors, and wrought by dedicated and informed souls working in the tradition of Erasmus, honored the poor wretch who inherited the honor of publishing it; it was called the King James Version, and is much to be preferred to the silly, significantly falsified "improved" translations rendered since. Otherwise, our preferred literary works were the compositions of our beloved John Milton.

Such matters greatly shaped our disposition respecting what varieties of available formal law from which to choose.

Our formal law featured large the name of Grotius, and more indirectly the great Prussian law-commentator of the late 17th century, Pufendorf. As to the heart of the law, its rational principle, it was the direct and indirect influence of Gottfried Leibniz which informed our more profound reflections. Immediately beyond Grotius loomed the most gigantic figure of modern times, the great 15th-century canon, Cardinal Nicholas of Cusa, beginning with his powerful and comprehensive earliest major work, the *Concordantia Catholica.*

It could not be otherwise.

How rightly our ancient republican forebears cursed those Tudors. They were all half-insane or more, from Henry VII on.

We had selected them, as expediency advised us at the time: we, of the circle allied with Erasmus of Rotterdam and his friend, Sir Thomas More. Dante Alighieri and his design had reached us during the 14th century, from such radiating points as Petrarch spinning the webs of a future renaissance from Avignon. We had our Chaucer, for example, who had attempted to build a literate language of the shattered, brutish English dialects of the time. Out of the ruinous Wars of the Roses, we picked a compromise candidate, we thought a compromise adapted to our intent. France, under Louis XI, had become the first modern nation-state, but we would be second. Then, that foolish Henry VIII, that scandalous, mad creature, sold church estates for title to those who had sold their souls to the Genoese, and so came the Cecils, the Portlands, the Russells and the rest of that unwholesome tribe, who later proved our undoing.

Broadly, Dante and Cusa, like Charlemagne and Alcuin long before them, undertook to build a republic of Christendom (then, chiefly as a bastion against the twin pestilences of Byzantium and the Ummayads) against the heathen hordes Byzantium orchestrated against civilization in the West. The flaw in Charlemagne's design was the attempt to maintain a Latin-speaking administration, to the effect of perpetuating brutish local dialects in daily life, a people poorly reached even by the Christian transformation of Roman Latin into a Greek-like language of some elegance for transmitting conceptions. The use of brutish local dialects perpetuated a brutish culture, and divided peoples to become the easier prey for the divide-and-conquer tricks of the employers of the "Persian model." To destroy the brutishness, the tribalistic fragmentation, a people must be united by a literate form of language. This defined the need for a system of sovereign republics, each based on a commonality of literate form of language. Yet, sovereign and distinct, these nations must be united by a common law of Christendom, so realizing Charlemagne's design as to purpose, but with such an alteration in internal political composition.

Civilization has a purpose for its existence. The nation has a higher purpose, situated within its contribution to the cause of civilization as a whole. The individual has a purpose, which is on behalf of civilization's purpose as a whole, but mediated through the governing purpose of the nation within civilization.

This conception of purpose is the Judeo-Christian republicanism we have elaborated in this report, centered around the cited injunction from the Book of Genesis, and the implications of the *Filioque*. The divine potentiality of the individual must be perfected for its expression in social practice, and civilization and the nation must be ordered to foster such forms of individual social practice, and to nullify that which threatens the fruitfulness of such practice for the benefit of present and posterity. Law within nations and among nations must be ordered to this effect.

The essence of the law is that we are implicitly accountable to our posterity for what our present policies of practice bequeath unto countless generations after us. What increased power over nature do our policies of practice and our institutions bequeath, what enhancement of the divine potential, as we have defined that in this report, do our policies of practice, our design of institutions, bequeath? That, that, and the sacredness, under law's protection, of the divine potential of the living person, is the kernel of the law, the never-failing test to which the law must repeatedly return, to examine itself accordingly.

That variety of law is the distinction of a republic.

The nation does not belong to the episodic majorities among the living. The republic belongs at once to the past, present, and future generations. We, the living, are but trustees of our republic, and our will is foul, however, numerous its supporters, unless that will is efficiently bounded, and self-bounded, by a compact with past and future according to the terms of the kernel of the law.

The elaboration of the doctrines of laws is not better than it serves those principles, as to the internal affairs of nations, and as to the ordering of affairs among nations.

In our relations among the nations, not all nations are morally nor lawfully equal for us. Those nations whose efficient principles of law coincide with republican principles are equal in respect of their sovereignty, since they represent a *concordantia*, a community of principle, of which we are a part. Those who have an opposed form of efficient law are not part of this community of principle, and are inferior and immoral nations.

Although the root of the matter is Charlemagne's attempt to establish a republic of Christendom on the principle of the *Filioque*, Cusa stipulated what was implicitly in germ in Charlemagne's pact with Caliph Haroun al-Rashid, against the evil Ummayads and, implicitly, against the evil of Byzantium. In *De Pace Fidei*, Cusa elaborated, by aid of Socratic dialogue, the basis for ecumenical affinity among Christian, Jew and Muslim. We define community of principle not by church, but according to an ecumenical affinity among all nations whose law is bound by principles in common with the law adduced from Christianity's direction to Greek-republican methods of science and statecraft.

Other, morally inferior nations, outside of that community of principle, we seek to uplift to the condition of reason, with charity on account of the divine potentials within the people of those inferior nations.

We will not have, nor will we tolerate, a Hobbesian ordering among nations, nor, as Franklin angrily rejected his naively favorable perception of John Locke, will we tolerate a Lockean ordering of affairs among nations.

The United Nations, for example. It is like a public latrine along a busy street. We may have compelling reasons, including regard for decency and public health, to employ its facilities occasionally, but would we therefore make it the home in which we receive our guests for dinner? It was an ill-conceived design, which, characteristic of its nature, has never accomplished anything of notable effectiveness in preventing war when the impulse for war had reached a certain level. There is in that body no efficient principle of law with which the law of our republic's founding has any quality of community. We may resort to the temporary advantage of its facilities, but we must not tolerate any impulse to make that poorly conceived, immoral thing in any degree an institution of world-federalist government. The Constitution of our republic forbids the submission of the United States to any governmental-like action by the United Nations, the

International Monetary Fund, the Bank for International Settlements, and so forth and so on.

A treaty effected according to our law with a sovereign nation-state is a different matter. A treaty establishing common institutions within a community of principle as to law, is also permissible under our proper notions of our law. But, we can not lawfully surrender by assignment any of those authorities of self-government of any body which attempts to act as a supranational government, most emphatically a body which is not in a community of principle as to law with the environment of Cusa-Grotius natural, international law, in which the design of our Constitution is situated.

Nor, can any treaty be lawfully construed to afford any other government veto-powers over our internal ordering of affairs of government or relations with other nations. What we agree to lawfully as a stipulation of treaty-agreement is law; but it is an unlawful abomination if that treaty is misconstrued to allow foreign nations to exercise functions of government over our affairs.

All secret agreements, most emphatically unwritten agreements, are null and void except as they are implementation of a specific authority which is itself lawful. If a U.S. official shall subordinate the interests of the United States because of a secret agreement which is not lawful, that action is probable cause of indictment for high crimes or misdemeanors.

As to our monetary and economic affairs, we can not

alienate that power lawfully to any foreign or private agency. These are the explicit powers of the Congress, which may be delegated by Act to the President, but to no one else. If any agreement exists which violates that principle, such agreement is axiomatically null and void.

The constitutional sovereignty of the United States must be enforced, and enforced according to our Constitution, as that Constitution is rightly understood in the setting of the view of the law prevailing at that time. For exemplification we properly refer to the model of Chief Justice John Marshall, whose practice is that extended practice of constitutional law most proximate to the comprehension of the framers of the Constitution.

Within a community of principle, the sovereignty of our treaty-partners is implicitly as precious to us as we, in our moments of nobler passions, zealously guard the sovereignty of our republic. Toward the sovereignty of other varieties of nations, not fit to be a member of such community of principle, we are as prudent and charitable as circumstances and considerations of our law permit us to be.

With those points and what they imply in view, there is no proper impediment as to law in implementing the range of measures recommended here.

How We Stand Properly With Respect to the Soviet Union

It has been the commonplace prejudice often informing

our policy, that our principled objection to the form of government of the Soviet Union is its hostility toward private ownership of the means of production. It has been the burden of this report, that our objections to the Soviet Union are of a different nature. We object, most energetically, to the prospect of being destroyed by Soviet military forces, or of seeing our friends subjected to such force. There may be a few strange fellows about who are differently persuaded on that point, but there is prevailing agreement on this specific issue. Otherwise, our objection lies properly not with the Soviet Union's internal composition of its political-economic affairs, but with the extension of the objectionable features of its ideology to shape the world within or around our nation.

Does Soviet political-economic doctrine, as applied only to its own orbit represent, in itself, any form of injury to us? Generally, our exporters appear to think otherwise. If we were truly concerned, with such passion as some prejudice might imply, to protect our capitalist enterprises from being crushed by a power like that of our government, we would have conducted war against Paul Volcker's Federal Reserve System more than a year ago.

Put the adversary situation aside for a moment. Let us examine critically what we should not, and should find objectionable in the institutions of the Soviet Union--*as a foreign nation*, a neat and most significant distinction.

Insofar as a socialist state, as a form of society, promotes technological progress efficiently, to the effect of increasing the productive powers of its people generally, if by means of state ownership, do we properly object to that? Is that state not, rather, meeting at least the requirement of the much-cited injunction from the Book of Genesis? On this account, that particular socialist state has lately conducted itself in a more Christian fashion that the governments which lately reduced Britain to a rotting pile of formerly industrialized refuse.

Is it not, then, the case, that our proper objections to the Soviet Union reduce to two? It is our adversary, and on that account undesirably successful? That, in a way augmented in importance by Soviet power, it embodies an absence of efficient emphasis on promoting the divine as such, and the potentiality this feature of Soviet ideology might spread further throughout the world? Reducing matters to their barest essentials, is there any other valid issue? Was ever a question more deeply explored, and set before the policy-making table, in our national history, than we have probed this matter in our present report. To all practical purposes, we have exhausted the subject.

Shall we destroy the Soviet Union, then? Wishful delusions about the imminent "internal crumbling of the Soviet Empire" must be discounted as tripping over the threshold of an in-depth H-bomb launch. It is full-scale intercontinental warfare, or the Soviet Union will probably stand as "the other super-power." In any case, for the past sixteen years, we have concentrated so effectively upon destroying ourselves, that we have only a deterrent, not a war-winning capability. Any opinion to the contrary is wishful babbling.

Could we change our policies to the effect of acquiring a wide margin of potential war-winning capability? Were I President, and faced such a proposition, as Lenin would put it, concretely, I can imagine at present what direction I would take. Abstractly, as one might infer from between the lines of this report, there is a workable direction in which we have potentially a conceptual-scientific advantage, on condition we acquire a correlated dislike for British ideology.

Abstractly, the answer is "Yes." Abstract questions aside, let us consider a more likely approach to the problem. Is there an effective war-avoidance approach to the matter, an approach which in no way violates our proper principles?

The essential problem is that the Soviet Union, because of its embedded ideology, as we have defined that problem of ideology, *could not generate from within itself an acceptable ordering of world affairs.*

On the surface of our governmental institutions' projection of ideology, and the present projection of ideology from the leaderships of the major parties in the Congress (in particular), the United States would have to be judged as as morally unsuited to ordering the world's affairs as the Soviet Union. A nation which tolerates a policy for practice a hundred times more murderous than Hitler's, that genocidal *Global 2000* and *Global Futures* policy, is not to be viewed as exactly a "beacon of hope" for humanity in respect of its manifest morality of practice.

The difference is that we have the potential to become again a moral nation, to project a moral government if we can arouse the morality in three-quarters of our adult citizenry, to break free of its presently shrinking "littleness," and to become a foundation constituency for a proper resumption of a proper national purpose for this nation.

The initiative for this can not come from our belittled moral citizenry. Their capacity to break free of their present imprisonment in littleness must be awakened by actions of leading national institutions. Our citizens do not need an anarchist's sort of "electrifying action." Rather, precisely because their capacity for shaping national policy is limited to their allegiance to powerful institutions, they can not act now except in the form of aroused expressions of support for initiatives by powerful institutions to which they have given their allegiance.

The issue of Volcker is exemplary. There was a mood to hang Volcker developing already during the spring of 1981. Institutions, including Democratic Party Chairman Manatt and others moved in to pressure local constituency leaders to capitulate to Volcker's policies. The leadership of the Congress acted similarly, the administration acted similarly, and so forth and so on. Now, they will not act until they have either themselves broken in rage with the institutions which have temporarily intimidated them against their own best judgment, or until one of those established leading institutions of political power elects to mobilize an anti-Volcker motion in support of its anti-Volcker actions.

Gentlemen, there is no assurance that you or any other leading institution of government is capable of acting effectively in time to prevent catastrophe. Your own estimates of the likelihood of enactment of the measures indicated here is a good point of reference on this point. The reasons you yourselves might estimate that these measures--which we know to be sound and urgent--are not “politically practicable at this time,” are precisely that reflection of our national inability to act in time to which we refer. That inability has, because of the crisis-circumstances developing into an advanced, explosive phase, now become a measure of our nation’s moral lack of qualifications to take those forms of timely action, those abrupt reversals of almost axiomatic directions in policy, by which we could assure our survival. Perhaps, in that specific sense, we have become the new Belshazzar. Perhaps we are already doomed, if you are correct in judging these proposals “politically impracticable.”

However, if we are still fit to survive, and can reawaken memory of the time this nation was still a “beacon of hope”rather than the object of fear and contempt it has become abroad, and among its own citizens, then the direction of measures outlined here will quickly reverse the present situation.

If we can adopt the course indicated by the “compact tactic,” the community of principle we so establish, we afford to us a new’ source of recovery to prosperity through export of capital goods, and prosperity among those to whom we export, through the employment of those capital goods. This would mean the rapid emergence of a new dimension of political as well as economic power, and an ensuing emergence of a kind of global intellectual and moral hegemony not seen before.

This aching world may not understand the nature of its oligarchical adversary, that literally satanic force of families, but it does wish this terrible nightmare of growing chaos and despair to end. Who proves efficient in reversing the present downward spiral, who brings order as a weapon against the forces of chaos and growing cultural pessimism, will be the rallying-point for the world.

If we teach the Soviet Union such a lesson in grand cultural strategy against oligarchism, it is perhaps by that means alone that the scope and impact of such an "objective result" might prompt them to reexamine their ideology, to recognize that no culture deserves to endure unless it places the divine as the motivation and goal of its constitution of practice. That, gentlemen, is perhaps our only real hope in this gruesome moment of history.

Made in the USA
Columbia, SC
16 September 2020

20763372R00186